TRUTH IN PERSON

⊕

I am the way, the truth, and the life
John 14:6

Luke Bell, OSB

TRUTH IN PERSON

⊕

Angelico Press

For information, address:
Angelico Press
169 Monitor St.
Brooklyn, NY 11222

angelicopress.com

pb: 979-8-89280-114-0
cloth: 979-8-89280-115-7
ebook: 979-8-89280-116-4

Cover Image: Christ before Pilate (c. 1520)
© The National Gallery, London

Cover design: Michael Schrauzer

In homage to
Fyodor Dostoevsky

CONTENTS

Chapter F: Friendship & Fraternity

Chapter G: Grace & Glory

Epilogue

Acknowledgments

Introduction

Forgotten Truth

Truth is eternal. I cannot grasp it, but I want to be open to it.

The son of the famous French film director and I were, as I remember it, walking in the hot North African sun in the courtyard of the former barracks which formed the building of the university where we worked. "You will find the truth, Nick," he said, "because you are looking for it." I doubt I was aware that words from Saint Luke's gospel, "Seek and ye shall find,"[1] underpinned this comment; certainly I had no idea that one day I would change my name to honor the author of this gospel. It was, even in retrospect, a surprising thing to hear, for my life at that time was better characterized as that of one of Tennyson's heedless and forgetful lotus-eaters who sing:

> Let us alone. Time driveth onward fast,
> And in a little while our lips are dumb.
> Let us alone. What is it that will last?
> All things are taken from us, and become
> Portions and parcels of the dreadful past.
> Let us alone. What pleasure can we have
> To war with evil? Is there any peace
> In ever climbing up the climbing wave?
> All things have rest, and ripen toward the grave
> In silence; ripen, fall and cease:
> Give us long rest or death, dark death, or dreamful ease.[2]

I was enjoying "dreamful ease": not thinking of death, but not knowing what made for true life. The adjective "true" did not speak to me for, under the influence of intellectual fashion, I fondly supposed that all things were relative; I did not imagine that there could be any absolute truth. "What is it that will last?" I could have said.

---

1. Luke 11:9. All Bible quotations are from the King James Version.
2. www.poetryfoundation.org/poems/45364/the-lotos-eaters.

I did not know (I was in my twenties and so, not grown up) that there is an answer to this question: "truth." Since then, I have read much on this theme. The influences on me will emerge in the text or the notes, but there is one who (alongside the dedicatee of the book) deserves an explicit mention from the start: Pavel Florensky, a Russian priest, scientist and profound thinker, who was martyred under communism in the last century. His thinking inspires my undertaking of this writing and illuminates its final pages. To him I owe much, including an insight which is the starting-point of my reflections. He observes that the enduring nature of truth is implied by the etymology of the Greek word for truth, *aletheia* (ἀλήθεια): that which does not succumb to Lethe, the river to drink from which is to forget. Truth is that which is eternally remembered, for it is value worthy of eternal remembrance.[3] Truth abides. It characterizes the anointing of the person spoken of in the first letter of Saint John:

> The anointing which ye have received of him abideth in you, and ye need not that any man teach you: but as the same anointing teacheth you of all things, and is truth, and is no lie, and even as it hath taught you, ye shall abide in him.[4]

Truth is the abiding of the person. Love alone abides, so "if there is no love, there is no truth. If there is truth, there is inevitably love."[5] God is love; His Spirit is the Spirit of both love and truth. I came to see that. I remember asking a colleague, in my early thirties, if he believed there was truth. "I believe in God," he answered, implying that there is truth but that it is not at our disposal. I have come to see that the contemporary difficulty with truth (affecting both those who claim it and those who deny its possibility) is that it cannot be possessed. It is not graspable in the sense that it can be defined by limitation, for, as Spinoza famously wrote, *Omnis*

---

3. Cf. Pavel Florensky, *The Pillar and Ground of the Truth* (Princeton, NJ: Princeton University Press, 1997), 17.

4. 1 John 2:27.

5. Florensky, *The Pillar and Ground of the Truth*, 65.

determinatio est negatio.[6] Every definition is a negation, saying what something is not, whereas truth is unlimited. So, although I am now in the decade the psalmist reserves for the strong, I cannot say that I have found the truth, only that I have become less inclined to keep the door locked when I hear the voice of Truth standing at the door of my heart and knocking.[7] As in this last sentence, so throughout this book, I will sometimes refer to truth without a capital letter and sometimes with. In the latter case I am drawing attention to God as Truth.

Truth, in either sense, partakes of unlimited mystery. To define it would be to deny that mystery, so my concern is not to wrap it up but rather to allow it to emerge. I hope that as a seed germinates and a shoot pushes itself through the cultivated soil which has nourished it, so truth will grow in your own person—not because I have told you what it is, but rather because I have picked a few stones out of the earth: the false closure that pretends to knowing, the practical rule of thumb that is mistaken for the absolute, the ideology that excludes deeper thought. So this book is a sharing of my present understanding of what in the contemporary mind-set blocks an openness to truth. In essence it came to me all at once, on the eve of that day in Advent when Wisdom is apostrophized in the antiphon *O Sapientia*, like copper sulphate crystallizing in a super-saturated solution. In more than one sense it is a personal account. It is a sharing of how I have come to understand reverence—the awareness of the holy—as (in accordance with its etymology) a respect for the veridical, for truth; it is an unfolding of how I have come to see that truth as, in Florensky's words, "value worthy and capable of eternal remembrance;"[8] it is the story of how my mind and so my life changed from one forgetful of the true, the eternal, the divine to one that deliberately memorializes it in monastic worship seven times a day. In an important sense all of that began long ago.

---

6. Spinoza to Jarig Jelles, letter of June 2, 1674.
7. Cf. Revelation 3:20.
8. *The Pillar and Ground of the Truth*, 17.

Missing Persons

*The personal touch matters. The abstract and virtual take us
away from truth, which depends on life.*

When I was *very* young, I was frightened and upset by the noise of a
vacuum cleaner. My mother put her arm around it and said, "Nice
Mr Vacuum Cleaner!" It worked! What was random became personal. I was able to relate to it. The person of my mother mediated
sense. The personal touch was all-important in my learning. I
learned from her personally that what surrounded me at that
moment was not threatening. The fiction that the machine was a
person enabled me to see the truth that I need not be afraid.

Nowadays we are surrounded by less maternal claims of personhood: bots impersonate some kind of loving presence that would
solve our problems on the "help" pages on websites. Those who run
businesses realize, of course, that we are happier talking to real people and so they also offer telephone numbers we can ring. But the
people who answer the phone are looking at computer screens, as is
evident from the way they say things like "I've nothing coming up"
or "the system won't let me do that." The person is subordinate to
the machine. Even if a real person is generating content on the
internet, the machine delivers that content in a way that generates
the illusion that the receiver is the personally intended recipient: the
inter-personal becomes the parasocial, preparing disappointment
should there be an actual meeting.

It was not always thus. I can remember a time when there were
people to carry your bags at stations. There is a sort of re-creation
of this era in the steam railway on the island where I live. People,
such as retired clergy, find joy in restoring the old world of personal
service where, for example, you do not have to put your ticket into a
machine but instead deal with a human being. Volunteers defeat the
arithmetic of budget divided by the number of salaried workers that
makes seeking personal service in some shops an option for the
minority who would rather queue than scan their own shopping. I
can remember the time before supermarkets in the United Kingdom, where your groceries were hand-picked by the shopkeeper in
person. I remember living in a foreign country with a traditional

civilization where butter, personally weighed and wrapped for you, was not yet replaced by stacks of standard prepackaged units you had to find for yourself.

Persons are missing from our lives, yet the longing for persons is still with us. Why else would there be so much pretense that persons are present? Why does artificial intelligence use the first person? Why have I received a package on which is printed, "I am made from 100% recyclable corrugated paper... I biodegrade in 3 months: shred, soak & mix with soil"? Why, when I searched the internet for ways to help refugees, were nearly all the results about giving money? Why is charity so often seen as a transfer of funds and so little as a personal encounter? Being more connected than ever is, it seems, concomitant with being lonelier than ever. It is easy to imagine a future in which a real, rather than simulated or mediated, human presence in the desolation of an entirely technical environment has all the wonder of the appearance of an angel. Persons seem to cower behind machines, legitimizing doubt about whether they are there at all. This absence of the personal touch came to a head during the years of the pandemic: hug-hungry hoards were in statutory isolation and such contact as there was followed the pattern described in E.M. Forster's prescient short story (first published in 1909), *The Machine Stops*, in which ideas are exchanged by Zoom *avant la lettre* and it is considered somewhat indecent to actually see a person in the flesh.

But persons were losing their authority long before that. In the heroic age bards, not books were the point of reference. Time was that a person would authenticate a document. Now a document authenticates a person, and if you do not have it, you can be deported where you do not wish to go. There are merciful exceptions, but characteristically, when engaging with a business or a government department you have to go very high up the chain of command to get a decision not based on an algorithm. The prevailing assumption seems to be that an assessment is truthful to the extent it does not involve a person. Scientific papers in particular are coy about personal involvement. Writers prefer the passive voice as in, "Such-and-such was introduced into the test-tube, which was then heated." This paradigm of investigation is so pervasive that one adopts it almost unconsciously: the copy-editor of my last book helpfully suggested I use the passive voice less. The root assumption appears to be that if a person is involved the result will somehow be less truthful because in some way biased, although it is obvious enough that if you are not looking from a particular point of view you won't see anything at all. The pretension of person-free research looks like an aping of the omniscience of God, even a replacing of Him. As in science, so in government: the ideal is for decisions to be unsullied by personal favor. This was strikingly in evidence, when a UK politician had to resign because he had used his position to obtain documents for a particular person with whom he had a connection. This violated the system and could not be tolerated: by contrast, that he had abandoned his wife for another woman was regarded as irrelevant. She was a person, not a system.

Of course, there is a real issue about fairness in this case. Systems have indeed their value in promoting values such as equitable treatment for all, yet there remains the danger that the tool will be mistaken for the truth, the servant for the master. Moral emphasis placed on conforming to an abstract pattern can weigh against the moral importance of friendship and fidelity. One sort of morality can be demanded at the same time as another is ignored. This is the case in academic life. Its requirements for what is supposed to be scientific objectivity and for hyper-specialization are unconcerned with the kind of knowing which contemplates the whole and is at the service of spiritual life. There is an academic system with its protocols and norms, but it tends to keep the person out of knowing. You are expected to be true to the system, but not to throw your whole self headlong and adventurously into the abyss of unknowing. You are not encouraged to have skin in the game. That would put you under suspicion of being biased, though it is a matter of common observation that people are strongly incentivized to get things right when their life depends on it. You are not expected to have more than an academic integrity: whether you are holy is a question not even asked.

I do not mean to imply that academic endeavor is without value, even though I regret the late medieval move from the cloister to the university. An academic training has been valuable to me personally in developing my mental abilities. Rather, I am arguing that the academic paradigm is part of a general trend to abstraction (which I shall consider more fully in the next chapter) and that—this is the whole direction of my book—a move away from the personal is also a move away from the truth. Speech to someone in person is more likely to be true than speech about someone from a distance, which is abstracted, tending to be separated from that person. That is my experience, both as spoken about and as speaker. The facile or caricaturing can be called out from a distance but, in normal human discourse, does not survive personal relations. It is too easy to see only one side of someone's story, and to talk to her in person fills in the picture. We see this dynamic very clearly in virtual communication. Not *actually* facing a person one can post or retweet the derogatory with far less compunction than when speaking to that person face to face. Then there is the way algorithms feed social media with material that flatters the recipient's opinions—so much so that it can be quite a shock to realize that someone has won an election whom one's own (obviously not everybody's) feed of online content showed to be totally unworthy and unelectable. There is a truth deficit. As well as affecting receiving truth, algorithms also impede communicating. You may well share my experience of filling in a form online by way of responding to a survey or applying for something and being offered (from which to select) a limited number of options, none of which is true. The algorithm prohibits proceeding unless one such option is chosen. The only way to be truthful is to abandon the communication. Algorithms can deny people's reality; they can also pretend to have that reality it, as is evidenced by the frequent online injunction, "Prove you're not a robot," which clearly implies that there is many a bot out there programmed to pretend to be a person.

The important difference between the robot and the person is that the latter is alive. The Russian word for (sacred) truth, *istina*, has the Sanskrit root, *as* (linked to the Latin word for "is," *est*) meaning, "breathe." Breathing is synonymous with being alive and its celestial concomitant is the eternal, undying life which the Spirit gives. So, delving into the archeology and chronology of meaning, we find that truth is first of all breathing, then what that signifies (being alive) and only then simple being.[9] Nowadays death is associated with truth, which is linked to the overcoming of nature. If you can pin it down on a dissecting board, so the assumption goes, there you have the truth. William Wordsworth, taking a stand against this trend, sang of "truth breathed by cheerfulness" and observed:

> Sweet is the lore which Nature brings;
> Our meddling intellect
> Mis-shapes the beauteous forms of things:—
> We murder to dissect.[10]

William Blake too witnesses against this forensic approach in his poem *Eternity*:

> He who binds to himself a joy
> Does the winged life destroy
> He who kisses the joy as it flies
> Lives in eternity's sunrise[11]

If truth is linked to eternity as indeed "value worthy and capable of eternal remembrance,"[12] then trying to pin it down is exactly the way to lose it, the insistence that it be static the way to arrest the dynamism of its life. Which indicates that our culture has been barking up a seriously wrong tree: not, that is, the tree of life. It has prioritized defined and deathly distinction over living wholeness in pursuit of a knowledge that could only ever be fragmented and partial, as the devil persuaded Adam and Eve to do.

An Ascending Scale

An outline of the book, which argues that truth transcends reason and is known through the human person. This is evidenced in the Bible and in Christ. Truth emerges in dialogue among all persons. Seeing nature as personal and devotion to a person helps us to see

9. Cf. *The Pillar and Ground of the Truth*, 15.
10. https//www.poetryfoundation.org/poems/45557/the-tables-turned.
11. poets.org/poem/eternity.
12. *The Pillar and Ground of the Truth*, 17.

well. Friendship and fraternal relations cure us of blindness to the truth, which is known fully in sharing the life of the Holy Trinity.

The following chapter (A) considers these two trees: the kind of reason that wants everything cut and dried (i.e. dead) and the paradoxes of growing, flourishing and bearing fruit (i.e. being alive) that orient us to eternal truth. It presents the conclusions of extensive scientific research that can be summarized in the words of Saint Paul, "The letter killeth, but the spirit giveth life."[13] The merely rational is not enough and living by it exclusively, as our age tends to do, is seriously demented. There is so much more to everything than mere reason can grasp: a depth of being that cannot be rationally defined, since it is open to the infinite. The only way our minds can reach towards this infinity is by accepting apparent contradictions that find their transcendent resolution in God. The human person above all embodies this true life that is manifest in contraries and comes from God. It is by looking towards Him that our faces can radiate it.

The book as a whole develops this theme of personal channeling of truth. It argues that God shows us His truth through persons. The Bible, the word of God, presents it this way, for example through the person of "a merciful man, which found favor in the sight of all flesh, even Moses, beloved of God and men, whose memorial is blessed."[14] Moses speaks to God for his people and to his people for God. Through him, his people encounter truth. Chapter B considers him and nine other key Biblical figures as sources of divine truth not just for their contemporaries but also for those who come after them. In the Bible there is repeated reference back to the patriarchs and prophets who embody humanity's encounter with God. The sacred text chronicles the blessings that come through them, whatever their flaws. Above all, and indeed through all, it presents Christ, the sinless and so fully truthful One.

I have taken His saying "I am the way, the truth, and the life"[15] as the epigraph of this book because I believe with Saint Peter that He

13. 2 Corinthians 3:6.
14. Ecclesiasticus 45:1.
15. John 14:6.

is "the Christ, the Son of the living God"[16] and with Saint Paul that He is "the image of the invisible God."[17] In other words, He is the truth in person. Chapter C starts from this truth and explores how to be open to it. There is also the possibility of refusing it. Pilate's archetypal encounter, imaged on the cover of this book, exemplifies this. Truth is naturally symbolized by light, so Christ is "the light of the world."[18] His followers can be such also, radiating Christ's light manifest in His transfiguration. They share that light through communion with Him and also have communion with each other in Him. The divine gift comes through the hands of priests, who personally stand in His place. This happens in the Church which is, in the words which Florensky took from Saint Paul for the title of his *magnum opus*, "the pillar and ground of the truth."[19] As the pillar of cloud led the Israelites through the wilderness to the promised land, so the pillar of the Church leads us to heaven's truth; as the fire in the tabernacle gave light to them, so the fire of the Holy Spirit gives light to those in the Church. This light can come through anyone, so it is important that all are listened to on the common journey. Such is the synodal way, which has its equivalent in *sobornost* in the Russian Orthodox tradition.

It is not to be supposed, however, that it is enough to listen to other Christians, even if they are both western and eastern. The fullness of truth requires that we listen even to the enemies of Christ's truth, for all persons are made in the image of God. We cannot *own* truth simply by virtue of belonging to a particular group. If we limit ourselves with an outlook like that, we cut ourselves off from life and life is shared with all. Truth is alive and is among and between us; we know it as shared life, not as private possession. This is so even on the practical level: if we refuse to be informed by the knowledge of others, there is very little that we can get done. Truth emerges in dialogue, that is the word between us, as the Greek etymology (*logos*/λογος, "word" and *dia*/δια, "between") implies. Even

16. Matthew 16:16.
17. Colossians 1:15.
18. John 8:12.
19. 1 Timothy 3:15.

if the gathering of those in dialogue is not in the name of the truth in person, it remains the case that "all things were made by him; and without him was not anything made that was made"[20] and so the word of dialogue is in some sense, however obscure, the Word. Dostoevsky is the supreme chronicler of such dialogue, fearlessly giving voice to all and refusing to be superior to any. Chapter D, which develops the dialogic theme, therefore pays special attention to his work.

"All things" that were made by God and so in some way express His truth, clearly include not only people but also all of His creation and so it is apt to reflect on the ways in which that can be considered as personal. In his book, *The Discarded Image*, C.S. Lewis questions the nineteenth-century belief that we can by experiment "'know' the ultimate physical reality more or less as, by maps, pictures, and travel-books, a man can 'know' a country he has not visited; and that in both cases the 'truth' would be a sort of mental replica of the thing itself."[21] A map is not a country and does not give us its truth in any complete sense. In the same way, says Lewis at the end of his introduction to the medieval world view, "No Model is a catalogue of ultimate realities, and none is mere fantasy."[22] A "model" in this context is a way of looking at the world, such as seeing it as the work of a personified nature. In Chapter E, I consider how personal models of, or ways of imagining, creation can be truthful in ways that a merely mechanistic, or even legalistic, model cannot. One such way is Biblical: seeing the organizing principle of the creation as Wisdom, who "reacheth from one end to another mightily: and sweetly doth she order all things."[23] This is developed in theology, particularly eastern, as sophiology. In a more direct (and certainly related) sense, the Blessed Virgin Mary contains the truth of creation. She is a true person, bearing the truth in person. Yet one can in a way see the truth of creation simply by

20. John 1:3.
21. C.S. Lewis, *The Discarded Image* (Cambridge: Cambridge University Press, 1964), 216.
22. Ibid., 222.
23. Wisdom 8:1.

being in love: a single person can mean the world and so be the world, for what is existence at root but meaning? There is a correspondence between the beauty of a person or of the earth and the divine beauty. This is an indication of our eternal destiny: if what is furthest from the divine in the sense of being physical or material as opposed to spiritual is what is most beautiful in creation, then it is coherent to believe that all of this is given to us so that we may come home to the perfect beauty of God. The extremities coincide; the outermost is an expression of the innermost, in which it finds its fulfillment.

This raises the question of how we realize that destiny and fulfillment. The answer, as implied by the foregoing and indeed by the whole of the Christian tradition, is in our relations with persons. That is where we receive truth and learn to live truthfully. Yet we cannot do that merely by acquiring the sort of impersonal functionality that a state welfare system has, bestowing algorithmically-determined benevolence on all and sundry, beneficial as this may be on one level. The only way is the royal and difficult road of loving particular people. In this, friendship has a particular place. If another particular person is so important to you that you see things from his or her point of view, then *ipso facto* you are becoming more truthful, for you are no longer seeing things from an entirely partial viewpoint; you are beginning the journey away from myopic self-interest. Yet this alone does not make you holy; there is such a thing as *égoisme à deux*. Finding a second self can be the extending rather than the transcending of the self. For the latter to happen, there has to be good will towards all: each person a brother or a sister. Friendship is the beginning of being a truthful person; its fulfillment comes when all the world and his wife is a sibling because each and every one of them is known as child of our Father in heaven. So Chapter F considers friendship *and* fraternity.

The way the book is heading will be clear to you, dear reader: towards the very summit of personal life. If truth lives among persons, it does so supremely among the persons of the Holy Trinity. Our truthfulness is realized when they dwell in us, when we love Christ indeed and lay claim to His promises, "If a man love me, he will keep my words: and my Father will love him, and we will come unto him, and make our abode with him"[24] and "If ye love me, keep my commandments. And I will pray the Father, and he shall give you another Comforter, that he may abide with you for ever; Even the Spirit of truth ... for he dwelleth with you, and shall be in you."[25] Holiness is truth embodied. It is in our sharing in God's holiness—and so His glory— that we, together with all the saints, receive the ultimate gift of divine Truth. The final chapter, G, reflects therefore on how, through His grace, we can come to share the life of God. It gives examples of people who have done so: the young, such as Saint Carlo Acutis (for whom it took less than sixteen years) and Saint Thérèse (for whom it took less than twenty-five), and the old, such as Saint Benedict. The latter wrote that length of days is given for amendment of life,[26] and so while I cannot say like Saint Thérèse that I have only ever sought the truth, I do not lose hope now that it seems more important than ever. I seek the truth, however much it might change me; I seek your fellowship as I do this. Please feel free to put me right about any errors in what I have written.

This is the direction of the book you are (I hope) about to read. To help you navigate its thought I have put brief summaries of its content after each sub-heading, but do skip over these if you do not need them. And think of the titles of the chapters, arranged alphabetically from A to G, as an ascending musical scale: we begin with the fumblings of human reason towards the truth and progress towards the glory that is the Truth of God. May it be His always.

---

24. John 14:23.
25. John 14:15–17.
26. *Rule of Saint Benedict*, prologue.

A: Abstraction & Antinomy

Dethroning Reason

Abstraction misses the truth of the person, as in abortion. Reason cannot be its own foundation; it depends on an intuition of truth. A thing is never just itself; it exists in relation to the unfathomable depth of being. A person embodies this mystery. Reason with self-will alone destroys it.

There is, I believe, a link between forgotten truth and missing persons. Truth, I shall argue in this book, only reaches us through the life of a person or persons and trying to find it independently of personhood is turning away from life and light.[1] Abstraction from the personal is a departure from reality. It is heartless, and we can only find truth if we give to that search our heart, open to the heart of the other. In his encyclical letter on the Sacred Heart of Jesus, Pope Francis points out that we need the word "heart" to convey "the idea of a personal centre, in which love, in the end, is the one reality that can unify all the others," since "abstract language" can "never acquire the same concrete and integrative meaning," for it can articulate only a single aspect of what it describes. There are "messages that the mind alone cannot communicate." To engage with them, the mind and the will need to be guided by the heart to sense and savor truths, "rather than seeking to master them as the sciences tend to do." The language of abstraction cannot show us who we truly are, whereas the word "'heart' evokes the inmost core of our person." Indeed, "everything finds its unity in the heart" and the "Sacred Heart is the unifying principle of all reality."[2]

The heartlessness of abstraction leads to insensitivity to persons: "He was young, abstract, and consequently cruel," writes Dosto-

---

1. Cf. John 1:4.
2. https://www.vatican.va/content/francesco/en/encyclicals/documents/20241024-enciclica-dilexit-nos.html, Chapter One.

evsky of the murderer Raskolnikov.[3] Abstraction can indeed be deadly. Waging war from a computer screen is much easier and much less demanding of courage than riding into battle. Not seeing the persons being killed lowers the bar for their slaughter. And abstraction takes on its etymological meaning (from the Latin *ab*, "from," and *trahere*, "drag") in deadly earnest when babies are dismembered and dragged from their mothers' wombs in abortion. This has become socially acceptable because the truth of their personhood is denied. Those trained for this work are offered such advice as, "If you say, 'Suck out the baby,' you may easily generate or increase trauma; say instead, 'Empty the uterus,' or, 'We will scrape the lining of the uterus,' but never 'We will scrape away the baby.'"[4] The same draining of personhood from language is evident in the refusal to apply to abortion the word Pope Saint John Paul the Second applied to it: murder.[5] And the personhood of certain categories of people suffers detraction, even if the majority of abortions do not arise from such a particular prejudice. Those with Down's syndrome, for example, can have their personhood impugned because of their lack of facility in reasoning, despite reason's disqualification as ultimate arbiter of truth (of which more below). Having a limited capability for abstraction, they are all the more vulnerable to being abstracted in abortion. That the truth of personhood can be more powerfully evident in love and fidelity than in reasoning is brought out poignantly in an anecdote from the son of a Jewish doctor in Austria:

> On one particular day, two babies had been delivered by one of his colleagues. One was a fine healthy boy with a strong cry. His parents were extremely proud and happy. The other was a little girl, but her parents were extremely sad, for she was a [Down Syndrome] baby. I followed them both for almost fifty years. The girl grew up, living at home, and was finally destined to be the one who nursed her mother through a very long and lingering illness after a

3. Fyodor Dostoevsky, *Crime and Punishment*, trans. Richard Pevear and Larissa Volokhonsky (London: Everyman's Library, 1993), 323.

4. Randy Alcorn, *ProLife Answers to ProChoice Arguments* (Sisters, OR: Multnoham Publishers, Inc., 2000), 70.

5. *Evangelium Vitae* (CTS, 1995), 104.

stroke. I do not remember her name. I do, however, remember the boy's name. He died in a bunker in Berlin. His name was Adolf Hitler.[6]

This points to the truth of a life issuing in service and to the untruth of the murderous lies told about the Jewish people. Refusal of truth is bred in the swamp of refusal of personhood, with murderous consequence. Abstraction is dangerous if its limitations are not understood. Abortion is born (the oxymoron expresses the pain of it) from abstraction and so is pornography, which in its own way draws people from life. Especially in its online manifestation, it abstracts people from reality, from life and love, from respect and parenthood. Separation is of its essence.

Separation is essentially what reason does too. It abstracts elements of reality in order to compute the relation of one such element to another, dividing them up for its analysis. Reason is a well-tried tool when at work in its proper context but a terrible tyrant when mistaken for what is foundational. It is as though somebody has a thermometer which he knows he can rely on to tell him that the sea is warm enough to go for a long swim without danger of hypothermia. Putting total confidence in its assurance of the safety of the sea, he plunges in, willfully ignoring the presence of sharks of which, of course, the thermometer has nothing to say. The thermometer cannot say everything and nor can reason. Reason always has to start with a premise that it does not itself establish. Thinking is inevitably a matter of, in Saint Anselm's celebrated phrase, "faith seeking understanding." That faith does not have to be faith in God: it can be something as simple as the intuition that there are many dangers involved in sea bathing. Of course this premise can be found out by raising in a rational way the question, "What danger is there here?" But that question is itself based on the premise that the swimmer's life is worth preserving from hypothermia, sharks and so on. There is an infinite regress unless at some point the swimmer just knows something. The fallacy that reason can do everything comes from mistaking what is isolated by abstraction for the pur-

6. Randy Alcorn, *ProLife Answers*, 227.

poses of practical assessment for a foundational reality without any hinterland. Yet, in the words of the Russian philosopher S. L. Frank, "Nothing is conceivable as absolutely autonomous except all-embracing total unity itself."[7] Clearly, a thermometer is not independent of all contingency, but nor is that which it measures. We can be reasonably sure whether the sea is hot or cold, but never from this information know the whole of what it holds. In Frank's words again, "Objective being grows, so to speak, out of the womb of *unconditional being* and is only conceivable as rooted in the latter."[8] There is an infinite hinterland for everything, above all for the human person made in the image of the Infinite. To see only what is materially manifested and can be computed is to live in darkness.

This is the darkness in which the ideologues of the French revolution were living when, on November 10, 1793, they inaugurated a Feast of Reason, and enthroned the goddess of reason (a certain personification they could not avoid, even if it tended to the pornographic) on the high altar of the cathedral of Notre Dame in Paris, then viewed as a temple of reason. This lasted less than a year, since those who live by the guillotine die by the guillotine. Yet a tacit assumption lives on that all you need for truth is reason. This assumption received a magisterial refutation by the French metaphysician René Guénon:

> Rationalism, being the denial of every principle superior to reason, brings with it as a 'practical' consequence the exclusive use of reason, but of reason blinded, so to speak, by the very fact that it has been isolated from the pure and transcendent intellect, of which, normally and legitimately, it can only reflect the light in the individual domain. As soon as it has lost all effective communication with the super-individual intellect, reason cannot but tend more and more toward the lowest level, toward the inferior pole of existence, plunging ever more deeply into 'materiality'; as this tendency grows, it gradually loses hold of the very idea of truth, and arrives at the point of seeking no goal other than that of making things as

---

7. S.L. Frank, *The Unknowable: An Ontological Introduction to the Philosophy of Religion*, trans. Boris Jakim (Brooklyn, NY: Angelico Press, 2020), 64.
8. Ibid.

easy as possible for its own limited comprehension, and in this it finds an immediate satisfaction in the very fact that its own downward tendency leads it in the direction of the simplification and uniformization of all things; it submits all the more readily and speedily to this tendency because the results of this submission conforms to its desires, and its ever more rapid descent cannot fail to lead at last to what has been called the 'reign of quantity'.[9]

Written when the world was plunged in the darkness of the Second World War, this text goes to the heart of the struggle between darkness and light. Its key idea is that of "the pure and transcendent intellect" which mere rationalism denies. In my book *The Meaning of Blue: Recovering a Contemplative Spirit*, I compared this transcendent intellect to the light of the sun, and reason to the light of the moon. St Thomas Aquinas helpfully defines reason as designating "a certain discursiveness by which the human soul from knowing one thing comes to know another."[10] The moon's light of course depends on the light of the sun, just as reason, if it is to function properly, depends on what the scholastics called *intellectus*, meaning that deep center or heart of the human person which gazes in a contemplative spirit at that which transcends this world: the Light, the Truth, the Divine. This, by contrast with reason, designates "a simple and absolute knowledge (without any motion or discursiveness, immediately in the first and sudden apprehension.)"[11] Rationalism allows only what reason can offer and is therefore limited to secondary, indirect, reflected apprehension. It would say that the sea is only that which can be measured in it, such as heat or cold, whereas the intellect (in the scholastic sense) sees a reflection of eternity in which swims Moby Dick, the nemesis of Man's claim to control the creation.

Reason can however lead us to an awareness of its own limitations. To conceive any real being in anything, we cannot simply say,

---

9. René Guénon, *The Reign of Quantity and the Signs of the Times* (Hillsdale, NY: Sophia Perennis, 2001), 94–95.

10. *The Meaning of Blue* (Brooklyn, NY: Angelico Press, 2014), 34–35, quoting *De Veritate* q.xv, a.1.

11. Ibid., 35.

"It is what it is" or "A = A." We also have to say, "A = B" and then to make sense of that by saying, "B = C" so as to give some description of C and so on in an infinite series. If *only* A = A is true, then A is simply not-not-A: that is, practically speaking, it is not anything, for it has no relation to anything else, not even being; it altogether lacks any sharing in what constitutes creation; it is bereft of any name or nature. Its existence is incomprehensible because it cannot be described in terms of anything else. So to make sense of anything's reality, we have to say *both* A = A *and* A = B. But B is not-A. So A is A and not-A. There is a contradiction: the "excluded middle" is excluded. A hovers between non-being and being. This is taken account of in the intuitionistic logic programmed into computers. Theologically it makes sense, since (as Meister Eckhart said) creation is God's contradiction of nothingness, but this sense is not understandable in the absence of some transcendent frame of reference. In terms of this world—and reason functions as a tool for dealing with this world—the contradiction cannot exist, for logically speaking a thing can only either be or not be. So we cannot explain it in the terms of reason, that is to say: merely on the level on which it exists. It has a spiritual hinterland where its reality can be understood. The excluded middle works for material reality: if I give you my cake, I cannot have it myself. It does not work for spiritual reality: if I give you my love, I do not therefore have less love. This spiritual hinterland is in a sense embodied in language. In English (and there are parallels in many other languages), we say, "It is raining/ sunny/ nice today." The implication of "it" is that there is a reality beyond the rain or sun, there is a source of what is "nice."[12] The merely reasonable ignores this ontological depth. This is entirely proper in the context of making practical assessments, but if reason is king, we are in trouble. This is evident in wartime when soldiers are considered as just so many pawns whose sacrifice is to be rationally calculated in terms of strategic advantage. I don't exclude the possibility that, all things considered, this sort of assessment could be a least bad option, but I contest the notion that this way of thinking gives us the most objective reality. This latter has to include the

12. Cf. Frank, *The Unknowable*, 3.

depth of reality of the human person, which we know only too painfully when the one who dies is the particular object of our love. It is this reality that is ignored in the engineered society such as Stalinist communism reaches for, the "anthill" that was the particular object of Dostoevsky's detestation. Killing people for the sake of a supposedly beneficial future society may be rational but it cannot respect truth, for this, in its depth, is manifest in the human person.[13]

As I argued in my book, *The Mystery of Identity*,[14] each person is an unsoundable mystery because her or his identity is rooted in God and only realized in its reception from Him. Killing people is killing the mystery: it is, we might say, enigmaticidal. It assumes a knowledge about outcome and benefit which is not there: it is born of those partners in crime, reason and self-will. In this partnership, self-will is the master-mind and reason the accomplice. Reason, when serving what Guénon calls "the super-individual intellect" (that is to say when open to divine truth intuitively encountered in the heart and center of the person) is entirely innocent and good. Furthermore, it is necessary. We cannot know everything, yet we need to have some kind of grasp on reality in order to function. Reason gives us this grasp, and it serves us well as long as we remember that it is a grasping and not a beholding, subordinate and subsequent to the fuller view of the latter. "An enthroning of discursive reason above wisdom," Catherine Pickstock felicitously writes, "condemns one to discontented uncertainty, which one then tries to resolve by seeking a grim and gritted satisfaction in dominating other creatures."[15] Rational assessment enables reasonable action, yet if we take it for absolute and over-riding truth we are in trouble in matters practical as well as social. There is a sort of paradigm of this in the Germanwings tragedy. This was an airline whose name had to be dropped after a seriously disturbed copilot (who had been signed off work by a doctor) flew the plane into the ground on one

---

13. The line of thought in this paragraph is indebted to the above-cited text, 3–4, 10–11, 34–35 and to Florensky's *The Pillar and Ground of the Truth*, 35–37, 345–47.

14. Angelico Press, 2022.

15. Stephen R.L. Clark, *Can We Believe in People? Human Significance in an Interconnected Cosmos*, Foreword by Catherine Pickstock (Brooklyn, NY: Angelico Press, 2020), x.

of its flights. This occurred because the reasonable (in terms of addressing a particular danger) precaution of making the door to the cockpit impossible to open from the passenger area (offering protection from any threat there) prevented the captain of the plane and others from re-entering the cockpit to take control. Reason generates systems like this which make an absolute universal of what in particular and proper contexts are reasonable and responsible precautions. Of course within hours the system was modified worldwide to make sure there would never be only one person in the cockpit, but the any such system can never be an absolute, for it can never "know" for sure what might be round the corner. If a system is at least open to modification, it can limit damage in the long term—it will always need modification, in the same way that as computers always need updates—unless a person is able to over-ride it, it will kill the joy and spontaneity of life and, ultimately, life itself.

These systems are a result of abstraction from the person, reasonable and even benign if they do not take charge, but fatal if not subordinate to that openness to the divine which is above reason. In the latter case there is only self-will to take charge and reason enters the service of what is not divine. Where this leads is dramatically illustrated through two characters in Dostoevsky novels. In *Crime and Punishment*, Rodion Raskolnikov reasons that there can be more good in the world (through him) if he kills a mean, grasping old woman pawnbroker to get funding for this purpose. The truth in his conscience utterly derails this project and ultimately leads him to confessing his guilt to the authorities. In *The Brothers Karamazov*, Ivan Karamazov is presented as a thinker and writer of learned articles whose guiding idea is similar to that of Raskolnikov: if God does not exist, then everything is permitted. The servant Smerdyakov, having heard this, allows himself to kill the three Karamazov brothers' father (who is also thought to be Smerdyakov's illegitimate father). That killing is an instantiation of the parricidal rage sweeping Russia (and the world), which has in its sights not only the Tsar but even God the Father. Smerdyakov ends up hanging himself. Florensky's generalization is apposite: "Evildoers have always destroyed themselves: God 'hath scattered the proud' by nothing else than 'the thoughts of their hearts' (Luke 1:51), or, more precisely, by rational arguments for rationality . . . a manifestation of selfhood."[16] Smerdyakov's first speech in the novel (on the book of Genesis in the context of a Scripture lesson) manifests his self-will in the form of rationality: "The Lord God created light on the first day, and the sun, moon, and stars on the fourth day. Where did the light shine from on the first day?"[17] This willfully ignores the divine light both literally and metaphorically. Unlike Raskolnikov, he never allows it to enter him.

It is commonly supposed that Smerdyakov learns his rationality from Ivan, but this episode precedes their contact and the Russian critic Vladimir Kantov has persuasively argued that it is Smerdyakov who is tempting Ivan, rather than the other way round.[18] In that case, Smerdyakov embodies the self-will to which the reason embodied by Ivan becomes enslaved. Of course it is true that "Dostoevsky's hero is always a human being and never an idea 'in itself'"[19] and we see this particularly in Ivan. He is ambivalent about his rationality, as though he senses that reason does not equal truth but is rather her handmaiden. When his brother Alyosha tells him "everyone should love life before everything else in the world . . . love it before logic," Ivan responds, "You're already saving me. . . ."[20] He tells his spiritually-minded brother, "I want to get close to you,"[21] confessing, "I have a Euclidean mind, an earthly mind."[22] He can see, obscurely, that "reason is a scoundrel."[23] Alyosha, whom the (fictional) narrator writes about hagiographically, tells Ivan, "It was *not you* who killed father!"[24] adding, "God has

16. *The Pillar and Ground of the Truth*, 127.

17. Fyodor Dostoevsky, *The Brothers Karamazov*, trans. Richard Pevear and Larissa Volokhonsky (London: Everyman's Library, 1997), 124.

18. *Dostoevsky and the Christian Tradition*, edited by George Pattison and Diane Oenning Thompson (Cambridge: Cambridge University Press, 2001), 189–225.

19. Diane Oenning Thompson, *The Brothers Karamazov and the Poetics of Memory* (Cambridge: Cambridge University Press, 1991), 17.

20. *The Brothers Karamazov*, 231.

21. Ibid., 234.

22. Ibid., 235.

23. Ibid., 236.

24. Ibid., 601.

sent me to tell you that."[25] Smerdyakov is Ivan's bad angel (replaced after the former's death by a hallucination of the actual devil), who seduces Ivan and his reasoning mind into non-resistance to evil despite the best efforts of Alyosha, his good angel. Kantor explains why this happens:

> The obstacle . . . is Ivan's pride. Taking on himself responsibility for the entire cosmos, entering into a debate with God about the management of the universe, Ivan does not assume responsibility for the small, weak people nearby: 'So am I my brother Dmitri's keeper?' he remarks, in Cain-like hatred and indifference to his brother.[26]

Ivan loses his wits: his mind is defeated by the Truth against which he pitches his reason. Alyosha, as he prays for his brother, begins "to understand Ivan's illness: 'The torments of a proud decision, a deep conscience!' God, in whom he did not believe, and his truth were overcoming his heart, which still did not want to submit." He adds bitterly, "He will either rise into the light of truth, or . . . perish in hatred, taking revenge on himself and everyone for having served something he does not believe in."[27]

We do not know what happens to Ivan, but we do know the end of another votary of reason, the very brilliant mathematician and logician Kurt Gödel. His death certificate records the cause of death as "starvation and inanition, due to personality disorder."[28] His life is movingly chronicled in a biography entitled, *Journey to the Edge of Reason*. As a four-year-old he was known as *Herr Warum*, Mr. Why, because "he always wanted to get to the bottom of everything through particularly intensive questions."[29] His "highest aim" became "pleasure of cognition."[30] He saw mathematics as "a search

25. Ibid., 602.
26. *Dostoevsky and the Christian Tradition*, 211.
27. *The Brothers Karamazov*, 655.
28. https://plato.stanford.edu/entries/goedel/.
29. Stephen Budiansky, *Journey to the Edge of Reason: The Life of Kurt Gödel* (Oxford: Oxford University Press, 2021), 46.
30. Ibid., 47.

for truth."[31] The truth he found in his celebrated Incompleteness Theorem was that:

> In any formal system of mathematics, there will always be true statements that cannot be proven within the system itself. In other words, there are mathematical statements that are true but cannot be proven using the rules and axioms of that system. This means that any mathematical system that is complex enough to capture arithmetic will always have gaps or limitations, and there will always be true statements that cannot be proven within that system. Gödel's theorem has important implications for the foundations of mathematics, as it shows that there are limits to what we can know and prove using formal systems. It also has broader philosophical implications, suggesting that there are fundamental limits to our ability to fully understand the world around us.

The above explanation of the theorem (for which I do not claim completeness) is generated by artificial intelligence: ChatGPT, to be precise. This is itself a mathematical system, one with considerable reach. However, it is not immune from "hallucination" or disconnection from reality and such connection as it has is vulnerable to being superseded by change. It is not itself a validating system. That is universally true of such systems. Alan Turing, who famously first envisaged the possibility of a computing machine, demonstrated in 1936 that no computer program or other algorithm can, in a finite number of steps, demonstrate whether a proposition is true or false.[32] There always has to be a starting-point outside the system, something taken on trust, so that rather than generating truth it simply facilitates the process Saint Anselm described as "faith seeking understanding." Gödel understood that the implication of his finding was that "human intuition was a more magnificent thing than what any machine could duplicate."[33] He consistently maintained that we will always be able to recognize through intuition some truths that can never be established "even by the

31. Ibid., 104.
32. Ibid., 119.
33. Ibid., 141.

most advanced computing machine."[34] The human brain, he believed, is "a computing machine connected with a spirit."[35] He could see that reason is not enough. And, like Nietzsche, who also had an intense and ambiguous relationship with reason, he lost his sanity at the end of his life.

A Psychiatrist's Diagnosis

There are two ways of knowing. One is open to the whole picture, the other narrowly focused on what is needed to get stuff done. It is insane to limit oneself to the latter.

Ultimately, the question of how we relate to reason is one of sanity. It has received extensive consideration by the psychiatrist and neuroscientist Iain McGilchrist in two major works. In the first of these, *The Master and His Emissary*, he explains:

My thesis is that for us as human beings there are two fundamentally opposed realities, two different modes of experience; that each is of ultimate importance in bringing about the recognisably human world; and that their difference is rooted in the bihemispheric structure of the brain. It follows that the hemispheres need to co-operate, but I believe they are in fact involved in a sort of power struggle, and that this explains many aspects of contemporary Western culture.[36]

McGilchrist argues that the finding that the functions performed by one hemisphere can in case of need (such as following a stroke) be taken over by the other does not affect the crucial difference between *how* the two hemispheres work.[37] His analysis of this has been compared to the story in Saint Luke's gospel about Martha and Mary: Martha is busy about many things (like Smerdyakov, she is occupied with food); Mary simply contemplates the Lord.[38] In a

---

34. Ibid., 291.
35. Ibid., 276–77.
36. Iain McGilchrist, *The Master and His Emissary* (New Haven, CT: Yale University Press, 2009), 3, Kindle.
37. Ibid.
38. Luke 10:38–42.

similar way, the left hemisphere of the brain is concerned with getting things done, and so with a particular take on the world, and the right hemisphere with contemplating reality as such, and so with the whole picture. It is significant that manipulation is usually done by the right hand, which is controlled by the left hemisphere, and that an adored baby is usually cradled in the left arm, which is controlled by the right hemisphere. In order to manipulate, even in a good sense, you have to select information relevant to your purpose so that you have a sort of map that tells you where to go; if instead there is before you the full beauty of the scene, you are aware of too much to find your direction. The beautiful landscape becomes an end in itself and no longer a means to get somewhere. If on the other hand you have only means, that is narrowly functional and abstracted information, there is no point in going anywhere. There would be no joy in it. You need a sense of the beauty of the whole so that there is a value according to which to act. This latter (associated with the right hemisphere) is the "Master" of McGilchist's book; the mapping and manipulation is the work of the "Emissary." The power struggle he refers to is this Emissary attempting to be a hegemon, instead of working together with the Master so that life has a meaningful direction based on values derived from openness to the whole of reality. Reason, in the sense that I have been considering it, corresponds to the Emissary who is good and necessary in his work as long as it is for his Master, and the intuitive and contemplative spirit that beholds the truth corresponds to the Master. While never claiming they are "nothing but" parts of the brain, McGilchist's work gives an account both scientific and illuminating of the physiological basis of these aspects of the human mind. It is telling, for example, that the emotion of anger is registered in the left hemisphere, while softer emotions such as those associated with love are registered in the right hemisphere. Anger is an occasionally useful aid to getting things done, but of course a life lived in a cloud of red mist is disastrously myopic. The lieutenants of the left brain can do stuff, but not rule righteously. Self-righteous anger is never persuasive. Sometimes, however, a lovingly shared beholding can persuade.

McGilchist's verdict regarding the work of reason on its own is remarkably consonant with the finding of Gödel. His research indicates that:

> All apparently 'complete' systems, such as the left hemisphere creates, show themselves ultimately, not just by the standards or values of the right hemisphere, but *even in their own terms*, to be incomplete. In addition, whether or not the superstructure holds up, their foundations lie in, and are 'bootstrapped' on, intuition: the premises from which the rational system building begins, and even the rational mode of operation itself, that of the value of reason, cannot be confirmed by the process of rationalistic systematisation, but need ultimately to be intuited.[39]

This research echoes the conclusion the philosopher S.L. Frank came to before the scientist began his work:

> We have not one but two kinds of knowledge: (1) abstract knowledge about the "object" expressed in judgments and concepts— knowledge which is always of a secondary order; and (2) *immediate perception or intuition of the "object" in its metalogical wholeness and indivisibleness*—primary knowledge upon which abstract knowledge is based and from which it originates.[40]

Both the scientist and the philosopher have a similar awareness of the mystery in intuitive knowledge. Frank writes:

> Primary knowledge is expressed by us in secondary, abstract knowledge; and in this sense it is expressible in concepts and judgments. But this kind of "expressibility" refers to the ability to "reflect" intuitive knowledge, to "translate" it into the language of concepts. There is no relation of logical identity between what is expressed and the form of expression (i.e., between primary knowledge and secondary knowledge). There is only a relation we may call "metalogical correspondence" or "resemblance," and which, like all resemblances, presupposes difference as well.

His point is not that there is a difference in content between primary and secondary knowledge, but that "the source and ground of all our knowledge is—in itself, in its essence—something unspeak-

39. *The Master and His Emissary*, 207.
40. *The Unknowable*, 27.

able and unknowable."[41] McGilchrist writes that when the implicit becomes explicit in its rational, left-hemisphere formulation, "the whole is lost" so that what we know in this way is:

> a concealing as well as unconcealing. . . . The left hemisphere cannot deliver anything new direct from 'outside', but it can unfold, or 'unpack', what it is given . . . it can render explicit what the right hemisphere has to leave implicit, leave folded in. [42]

The result of this being made explicit is that:

> Many important aspects of experience, those that the right hemisphere is particularly well equipped to deal with—our passions, our sense of humour, all metaphoric and symbolic understanding (and with it the metaphoric and symbolic nature of art), all religious sense, all imaginative and intuitive processes—are denatured by becoming the object of focused attention, which renders them explicit, therefore mechanical, lifeless.[43]

A similar observation is made by Michael Martin in a book chapter entitled, "The Repercussions of a Left-Brain Theology." He comments on Saint Augustine's teaching that we cannot comprehend what God is like by thought: "There are some truths we can apprehend only by releasing our claims to them."[44] The refusal to dethrone reason has led to a culture that is "self-contained, self-absorbed, materialistic and subsequently calcified, impervious to metaphysics, and desensitized to the supernatural."[45] Science, philosophy and theology (at least in their representatives cited above) agree that allowing reason unalloyed hegemony deadens. How the world would be were reason's agent, the left hemisphere of the brain, allowed to be in charge is described by Iain McGilchrist:

> It would be relatively mechanical, an assemblage of more or less disconnected 'parts'; it would be relatively abstract and disembodied; relatively distanced from fellow-feeling; given to explicitness;

41. Ibid., 27–28.
42. Ibid., 207–8.
43. Ibid., 209.
44. Michael Martin, *The Submerged Reality: Sophiology and the Turn to a Poetic Metaphysics* (Brooklyn, NY: Angelico Press, 2015), 18–19.
45. Ibid., 36.

utilitarian in ethic; over-confident of its own take on reality, and lacking insight into its problems. . . .[46]

In his second major work, *The Matter With Things*, McGilchrist is more explicit about this kind of ratiocination. He says it

> replicates in us something like a way of looking at the world nor-
> mally found in mental illness. A kind of (itself irrational) rational-
> ising and a neglect of reasonableness are . . . striking character-
> istics of both schizophrenia and autism, which tend toward an
> unbalanced, rigid, disembodied, procedural type of mentation,
> lacking in normal emotional intelligence.[47]

To put it another way, the sinister dependence on the light of the moon (mere ratiocination) to the exclusion of the light of the sun (intuitive awareness of reality as a whole) is indeed lunatic. McGilchrist gives a striking example of where this mentality leads in the tale of a woman who was told that her brother had died in an explosion:

> She rushed to the hospital and was taken to the morgue to identify
> the body. It was indeed her brother. She bent to kiss him on the
> forehead and felt that he was still slightly warm, although the body
> had been refrigerated. She felt his hand and thought she detected
> an infrequent pulse. Amazed and alarmed, she called for a nurse.
> This nurse felt the body briefly and agreed that it was indeed still
> warm, but commented, 'That's odd, but you needn't worry about
> it, dear, because it says here on this chart quite clearly that he's
> dead'.

The nurse went away; the woman found a doctor who was more sane and treated her brother, happily restoring him to life.[48] "The chart" here is the secondary—and in its context lunatic— illumina-tion; the doctor's personal and direct awareness of the situation is the light of the sun. McGilchrist links the abstract reasoning that passes for a pursuit of truth in our age, and is evidenced in the

---

46. *The Master and His Emissary*, 209, Kindle.

47. Iain McGilchrist, *The Matter With Things: Our Brains, Our Delusions and the Unmaking of the World* (London: Perspectiva Press, 2021), 845–46, Kindle.

48. Ibid., 594.

dependence on the chart in this anecdote, to "the talk of schizophrenic subjects," which "tends to have an excessively abstract, excessively general quality."[49] He observes that "schizoid and schizophrenic persons tend to drop the first person in favour of a more impersonal language ('the thought occurred that')—similar to the way we are taught to write scientific reports."[50] Their way of thinking is characterized by "excessive abstraction"[51] and a "third-person perspective."[52]

In contrast to this way of thinking and the nurse enslaved to it, there was "an untrained auxiliary nurse with 30 years' experience on the wards" whose acumen McGilchrist records as being his "most valued 'suicide detection instrument'"[53] in his work as a psychiatrist. The person with intuition nurtured by experience saved life, the one merely following procedure put it at risk. It is a question of different kinds of knowing: the rationalistic and the intuitive. The latter is the more profound: as William James put it, "If you have intuitions at all, they come from a deeper level of your nature than the loquacious level which rationalism inhabits."[54] It puts you more in touch with reality, a distinction Florensky explains simply: "Blind intuition is a bird in the hand while reasonable discursion is a bird in the bush."[55] McGilchrist summarizes the neuroscience: "in general it is the judgements on reality made by the right hemisphere that are more reliable."[56] He illustrates the profitability of preferring such judgments with an account of a man who "made considerably more than a comfortable living" from his tips on horse races. He and his team discovered that his predictions were more accurate when the opportunity to discuss them with others was removed. Intuition, not reasoning, produced favorable results.[57]

49. Ibid., 504.
50. Ibid., 502.
51. Ibid., 505.
52. Ibid., 502.
53. Ibid., 1077.
54. Ibid., 1033.
55. *The Pillar and Ground of the Truth*, 26.
56. McGilchrist, *The Matter With Things: Our Brains*, 272, Kindle.
57. Ibid., 1036–42.

The Mystery of Things

True knowing is not predatory capture, but openness to eternal mystery, especially that of the person. Being is mystery. Truth is a gift of God.

We tend to gravitate to the rational, limited way of thinking because it offers certainty. Such assurance is wholesome if we are facing a threat we have to deal with or an opportunity we will lose if we do not swiftly take it, but it is unhealthy if we mistake it for knowledge of reality in any ultimate sense. It serves limited, practical purposes; it does not assuage the thirst for Truth. Once it becomes an absolute, our mental health is at risk; McGilchrist reports that his clinical experience is that "the most deluded patients are the most logical."[58] Madness comes from ignoring mystery, for Truth involves mystery. The psychiatrist is right to say, "the more certain our knowledge the less we know."[59] The terrible twins of certainty and precision limit. We say we are sure this is all there is and shut out what shines through what we see: we turn to the timetable of the tides and miss the intimation of infinity in the majestic waves of the sea; we grasp the geology of the beach and ignore eternity in a grain of sand. We claim exactitude and exclude all ambiguity: we ignore the richness of the symbol, seeing for example only drink in water and not death by drowning, only new life in green and not the color of a corpse. We comfort ourselves with the compromise of the candy without the protein, willfully blind to the consequences of our diet; we look at what is to our liking, turning away from what is looming on the horizon. Whether our myopia substitutes the banally conventional for joy or entertainment for sorrow, in our narrowing of the perceived to the precise we frustrate the reach of the human heart that would know its home in the riches of a divinity that can never be quantified.

And as is our heart, so is the way we treat other people. To those blind to the mystery of the human person, people are just a quantity: not beholding the faces of the poor which they grind, they

58. Ibid., 526.
59. Ibid., 127.

remain unaware that the Son of Man in all His glory identifies with them. To those not open to the deep reality of the other, categories can replace countenances: whole classes of persons can be dismissed as not counting for anything for want of sharing the nationality, religion or political stance of the one who registers rather than beholds. Florensky discerns what is really going on here: "The rationalist intellectual ... in practice ... hates the whole world in its concrete life and would like to destroy it, in order to replace it with the concepts of his rational mind, i.e., with, in essence, his self-assertive I."[60] This is consonant with Jean-Paul Sartre's observation that "evil is the systematic substitution of the abstract for the concrete."[61] This substitution may even be considered by the one making it to be selfless to the point of nobility: blindness to the humanity of others is blindness to one's own inhumanity. It comes with a false certainty that imposing one's will on others is right. This sort of religious fanaticism is bred in the same stable as the "anything goes" attitude of secular humanism: both are a refusal to be open to God, to be humble before the mystery. This openness is neither grasping certainties nor lacking all conviction of truth. It is, rather, wonder. The French philosopher Merleau-Ponty wrote of his perception of the blue of the sky, "I abandon myself to it and plunge into this mystery, it 'thinks itself within me'...."[62] The symbol, not the will, channels truth. As I wrote in *The Meaning of Blue*, "Blue is the color of mystery ... the mystery of heaven, the mystery of God."[63] In Florensky's words, "Azure, in its absolute significance, represents heavenly truth; that which is true, that which is in itself, is eternal."[64] Developing Goethe's perception that the color "is a kind of contradictory combination of excitation and rest in visual perception" he reflects that "blue deepens reality" and cites Hegel's observation that "blue corresponds to meekness, to an expression full of intelligence and the soul's repose" and that "it originates in

---

60. *The Pillar and Ground of the Truth*, 215.
61. McGilchrist, *The Matter With Things*, 1758, Kindle.
62. Ibid., 167.
63. *The Meaning of Blue*, 40–41.
64. *The Pillar and Ground of the Truth*, 394.

darkness that does not produce opposites."[65] Plunging into this mystery of contemplative impartiality opens the human person to God's eternal truth; concomitantly, it opens the person to other persons, made in the image of the same God. It is the opposite of the mentality that would persecute others for their views, whether religious or political. It is open to the truth of God as expressed in His creation of the human person and as fully expressed in the person who has this openness. It is, therefore, loving. Awareness of ontological depth blossoms into reverence for the mystery-filled truth of the person and bears the abundant fruit of this very truth, which unites all in love. In this love is true knowing. Florensky goes as far as to say: "Knowing is not the capturing of a dead object by a predatory subject of knowledge, but a living moral communion of persons, each serving for each as both object and subject. Strictly speaking, only a person is known and only by a person."[66]

Later chapters will develop this situation of truth in what there is among people. I want to focus here on the reality that predatory capture is not knowledge. True knowing is a kind of unknowing, because what there is to be known is infinite. If we have something pinned down, then at best we have a simplification. This simplification may have a practical use, but it does not put us in the presence of the Truth. There we can only wait with our eyes upon the Lord of all as a servant, not a master. The medieval mystical treatise, *The Cloud of Unknowing*, teaches us that it is only by staying with our not knowing that we can be open to the Truth of eternity. Saint Bonaventure cites ancient wisdom to the same effect:

> Let us say with Dionysius: "But you, my friend, concerning mystical visions, with your journey more firmly determined, leave behind your senses and intellectual activities, sensible and invisible things, all nonbeing and being; and in this state of unknowing be restored, insofar as is possible, to unity with him, who is above all essence and knowledge. For transcending yourself and all things, by the immeasurable and absolute ecstasy of a pure mind,

---

65. Ibid., 397.
66. Ibid., 55–56.

leaving behind all things and freed from all things, you will ascend to the superessential ray of the divine darkness."[67]

This Christian mystical teaching is consonant with ancient Greek wisdom about awareness of our not knowing.

Poetry everywhere bears witness to the same reality that is beneath or beyond every particular simply because it prefers to abstraction (with its spurious claim to grasp the essence of reality) language that points beyond itself by symbols, which denote without defining, shamelessly juxtaposed where mere reason would demand selection. Philosophically, this reality is given expression by a writer I have already cited: S.L. Frank. His masterly work, *The Unknowable: An Ontological Introduction to the Philosophy of Religion*, deconstructs the "rational thought" that "can grasp and 'understand' only things that are static or fixed" by contrasting it with true awareness: "The attentive gaze that penetrates into the genuine essence of things sees the immeasurable and indefinable abyss of the transfinite revealed in every point of being."[68] He develops this insight in this lapidary saying: "*Being as such* (i.e., in its absoluteness) and *mystery* are simply *one and the same*." If this is not generally noticed, that is because it is always and everywhere true and so "naturally escapes our attention."[69] Mystery is the necessary basis for any thought, for "all that is knowable and understandable, all that can be grasped conceptually, is rooted in the unknowable and has meaning only in relation to the unknowable."[70]

It is possible to be aware that the enthroning of reason as master rather than servant does not lead to truth and yet fail to be open to the mystery where Truth abides. Indeed, this is a widespread contemporary tendency. Scientism, which is not the valuable pursuit of practical understanding proper to science but the universal application of its method, is rightly perceived as not being in itself a source of values, and a false conclusion is drawn from this premise: that

67. *The Soul's Journey into God*, trans. Ewert Cousins (London: SPCK, 1978), 114–15.
68. *The Unknowable*, 40 and 39.
69. Ibid., 67–68.
70. Ibid., 69.

there are no values other than those arbitrary self-will asserts. This seems logical if we assume that rationality and practical investigation are the only way of understanding reality and that they have a monopoly on finding such truth as might be available. But the assumption is false. Higher truth is received not grasped, a gift not a conquest, a blessing not an achievement. And so—and the whole of this book develops this idea—it is manifest in the holiness of the person, coming from God who is both beyond and within. That becomes possible through humility in the presence of the divine mystery. The assertion of self-will as the source of value is ignorant of or ignores this mystery. It is at best a sort of half-truth: it sees correctly that value comes from the person, but not the need for that person to be a saint or sage. It is understandable as a revenge for the neglect of persons in the ravages of rationalism, but not understanding of the calling of the person to embody divine truth.

Only the "all-embracing total unity"[71] of the divine can offer truth that is not partial. Otherwise, people's private truths are so many ignorant armies clashing by night, unable in the darkness to perceive what there might be of reality in each other. And this is what we see: sometimes actual military conflict, sometimes a polarized politics, sometimes an uneasy truce dependent on lack of communication. Such consensus as can be built is established not by robust reference to incontestable truth, but by sensitivity to people's feelings. "The truth shall make you free,"[72] said Christ, and this freedom includes not being bound—whether by a sense of dutiful concern for others or by legislation mandating this concern—to avoid saying what we believe is true if that might emotionally impact others holding different beliefs. So where is this eirenic, mysterious truth that liberates us from antagonism and walking on eggshells? Clearly, it is not in the hostility which mocks others' religion, whether explicitly or implicitly, yet it is divine. So where is God?

71. *Vide supra*, 18.
72. John 8:32.

Ann and Timothy

Contradictions in reasoning that belongs to this world point to the infinite and divine. Persons are infinitely valuable, whatever their shortcomings.

Clearly, to continue to speak in metaphor, God is above reason. We have a clue to this in Kant's *Critique of Pure Reason*, where he called "contradictions in which reason becomes tangled in its attempt to think the absolute, the contradictions of reason with itself" antinomies, deriving the word from the Greek *antinomia* (ἀντινομια), signifying a law contradicting itself or another law.[73] It is in such contradictions, apparent in the world of space and time that reason inhabits, that Nicholas of Cusa found God, calling Him "the coincidence of opposites." This insight into the traces of the divine is a theme that has been echoed by searchers and thinkers through the centuries. Hegel saw antinomies "in all objects of every kind," arguing that "every actual thing involves a coexistence of opposed elements" and that "to comprehend an object is equivalent to being conscious of it as a concrete unity of opposed determinations."[74] Frank viewed them as germane to the very essence of things, maintaining that "the primordial ground is the absolute unity and coincidence of all opposites: *coincidentia oppositorum*."[75] Sergei Bulgakov, a Russian theologian of the first half of the twentieth century, considered such an insight necessary to thought about the infinite, writing, "Antinomy does not imply a mistake in reasoning or the overall falsity of a given epistemological misconception, which can be clarified and thus eliminated. Entirely legitimate antinomies are inherent to reason."[76] Alfred North Whitehead, an English philosopher of the same epoch, went so far as to say, "There are no whole truths; all truths are half-truths. It is trying to treat them as whole truths that plays the devil," considering that to have seen something "from one side only is not to have seen it."[77]

73. *The Pillar and Ground of the Truth*, 585 and 411–12.
74. McGilchrist, *The Matter With Things*, 1248, Kindle.
75. *The Unknowable*, 208.
76. McGilchrist, *The Matter With Things*, 1251. Kindle.
77. Ibid., 1252.

As in thinking, so in life: merely to pursue happiness, to want the sweet without the sour, the joy without the sorrow is self-defeating. As Blake wrote:

> Joy & Woe are woven fine,
> A Clothing for the Soul divine;
> Under every grief & pine,
> Runs a joy with silken twine.[78]

Jesus said and says to His followers, "Verily, verily, I say unto you, That ye shall weep and lament, but the world shall rejoice: and ye shall be sorrowful, but your sorrow shall be turned into joy."[79] It is in the decay of the seed that the new growth comes, in the endurance of darkness that new light comes, in death that the Lord of life triumphs. In the person of Jesus Christ, this dynamic is at its most stark and manifest. Florensky sums this and its implication up thus:

> On the one hand, He is one of many, a part of the world; on the other hand, He is the all, and the world is only one of the manifestations of His creative activity. Here we *immediately* hit a contradiction, an antinomy. And every living thought hits a contradiction and lives by it. The more living the thought, the more acute the contradiction. Religious thought does not blur, but simultaneously affirms, both yes and no.[80]

The antinomy is implicit in His saying, "And I, if I be lifted up from the earth, will draw all men unto me." The explanation following, "This he said, signifying what death he should die,"[81] makes it clear that He is not only talking about His being lifted up in glory, His ascension into heaven, but also about His being raised up on the cross and exposed to shame and ridicule. In the telling of Saint John the Evangelist, the shame *is* the glory, the sorrow the joy, the death the resurrection. In Him opposites coincide: utter weakness and omnipotence, perfect communion with His heavenly Father and

---

78. "Auguries of Innocence" in *William Blake: Poems & Prophecies* (London: Everyman, 1970), 335.

79. John 16:20.

80. Pavel Florensky, *At the Crossroads of Science & Mysticism*, trans. Boris Jakim (Brooklyn, NY: Angelico Press, 2014), 124.

81. John 12:32–33.

being abandoned and forsaken by Him. In the Book of Revelation He is both the Lamb led to the slaughter and the Lion of Judah, the stain of whose blood makes the robes of His followers white. Faith in Him finds the light coming through the cracks of reason and in that light a certainty more stable than reason can supply. As Florensky puts it, "In faith, which overcomes the antinomies of consciousness and breaks through their all-suffocating crust, a rock-like affirmation is acquired."[82] In this light, seen "through the yawning cracks of human rationality, the azure of eternity is visible."[83]

It is in this light that we can make sense of the contradictions in the psychology of the human person. Jung believed that "the self is made manifest in the opposites and the conflicts between them; it is a *coincidentia oppositorum*."[84] We are made of light and darkness and it is both in letting our light shine before men *and* in the acceptance and acknowledgment of the darkness in us that we find the truth of our personhood, for "if we say that we have no sin, we deceive ourselves, and the truth is not in us."[85] If the darkness is not acknowledged, it all too easily becomes the hidden motivator of what purports to be the work of light, the engine of the drive that lays waste the earth in seeking to make it perfect. Concomitantly, there is serious error in thinking that others can be all evil without any admixture of good. The evil one can never become incarnate, he lacks the humility for that; evil can never be pure, for it always lacks purity of heart. Love can see this with regard to anyone whosoever. As S. L. Frank puts it:

> Love in itself (outside of objective judgments concerning others) does not blind, but opens our eyes, gives us sight, for the first time. By revealing to us "thou" in its real, profound center, by revealing "thou" as a *person*, love makes us accessible for the first time to the revelation of the *holiness* of the person, a holiness we cannot keep from loving reverently even in the most hideous, perverted, and monstrous criminal.[86]

82. *The Pillar and Ground of the Truth*, 344.
83. Ibid., 348.
84. Quoted in McGilchrist, *The Matter With Things*, 1274, Kindle.
85. 1 John 1:8.
86. *The Unknowable*, 146.

I don't want to profane the holiness of the heart's affections by setting before you real-life examples, so please allow me to tell you about two fictional persons. Let us call them Ann and Timothy. Ann adores Timothy. Her father Frank is by contrast blunt about Timothy's shortcomings. He cannot understand why Timothy being late for every rendezvous, being unable to hold down a job, being given to over-doing the drink does not put Ann off Timothy completely. This is not in the foreground of Ann's vision. She is simply focused on Timothy's being: he is her darling, her one and only, her best-beloved. Ann's mother Sophia, being married to Frank, has a ready appreciation of his point of view. Yes, she will concede, Timothy is liable to be late; yes, he is not good at following through; yes, he does not always know when to stop. But she is happy for her daughter. She knows that her love for Timothy is real and that which she loves is real. And when Ann confides the depth of her love for Timothy, Sophia's eyes mist over and their pupils dilate. Ann knows her mother understands her. So it seems that this is a happy family with one mind, one heart. Yet, dear reader, you will have perceived that there are possibilities of discord when they are gathered together. And indeed, it comes to pass that one night the three of them are sitting down for supper awaiting Timothy, who is invited and has said he will be there for seven. As eight approaches, he telephones to say he slipped off work that afternoon to join a good pal for a birthday drink with mutual friends and expects the gathering to wind up soon. Frank (who is in any case hungry) has had enough. He spells out Timothy's shortcomings. Sophia has eyes only for Ann. She gathers her into an embrace and kisses her on the cheek. "But you agree with me!" exclaims Frank, "How can you be sympathetic to such a poor choice!" Ann is not slow to eulogize her chosen. Frank demands that Sophia choose between his practical and reasonably fair-minded assessment of Timothy and their daughter's starry-eyed adoration. Sophia gives him a wifely look, saying, "That is Ann and Timothy" and gives her daughter another kiss.

I will move from story-telling to philosophy (S.L. Frank's) to explain why both Frank and Ann can be right and why Sophia, while being fully aware of this, is right to give the plenitude of her loving attention to her daughter:

In every genuine relation of "thou," the beloved "thou" appears to us as *infinitely valuable.* And since value and being coincide in the final analysis in the idea of foundation or *fundamental being*, it follows that love also appears to us as infinitely full of being. After all, love is precisely the apprehension of the genuine reality and, hence, the infinite, inexhaustible depth of being of another soul. But in relation to the infinite, everything that is finite becomes a vanishing quantity, seems to be a kind of "nothing." Therefore it follows from the essence of all true love that I am as nothing, count myself as nothing, in relation to the beloved "thou." It follows that my closed, self-contained self-being vanishes from my gaze and is replaced by my being *for* and *in* another soul.[87]

This anticipates another thing that is going to annoy Frank: his daughter (he thinks) is undervaluing herself, making an unreasonable assessment of Timothy. Of course, Ann sees beyond reason. Sophia sees thus too and is wise enough to understand that Ann sees more truly, for she sees Timothy as he will be for all eternity, purified by God's love. At the same time she also understands the fairness of what Frank is saying (she is not just agreeing with him for the sake of an easy life), but she knows that his view belongs to the partially obscured vision of earth below.

I am not even going to try to describe what it is like for Ann when Timothy dies because of drunk-driving, but rather appeal to the universal experience of death taking a loved one to point out that the moment this happens the absolute breaks into time and we become aware that the person is irreplaceable. People are not fungible. Each person is of infinite value. Faults and failings belong to the finite. *De mortibus nihil nisi bonum*, for each of them embodies the whole and infinite meaning of life. Ann's view of Timothy is ultimately more realistic. That is to say, it is more poetic. Poetry tells the truth because it goes beyond reason: its oxymorons articulate antinomies. For reason, Smerdyakov's assessment that poetry is "nonsense" is enough; for true thinking, S.L. Frank's assessment that it is "the human revelation of the mystery of primordial reality

87. Ibid., 249.

41

in all its depth and significance"[88] is more accurate. Poetry can speak of the infinite value of the dear departed precisely because it is unreasonable. This stanza from W. H. Auden's poem, "Stop All the Clocks," exemplifies this:

> Let aeroplanes circle moaning overhead
> Scribbling on the sky the message 'He is Dead'.
> Put crepe bow round the white necks of the public doves,
> Let the traffic policemen wear black cotton gloves.[89]

This universal announcement of the passing of the beloved is not practically realistic but it is poetically true, for each person *is* the universe, containing it in his or her soul in the image and likeness of God in whom all live and move and have their being. That is why, in Shakespeare's play, Desdemona would not wrong Othello "for the whole world" and if she had not wronged him, as he wrongly imagines, he would not have exchanged her for "such another world/ Of one entire and perfect chrysolite."[90] Frank is not able to see this sort of poetry, nor is Caesar's friend Dolabella in Shakespeare's dramatic dialogue between his reasonableness and Cleopatra's sense of the boundless worth of her dear departed Antony:

> *Cleopatra*: I dreamt there was an Emperor Antony.
> O such another sleep, that I might see
> But such another man!
> *Dolabella*:　　　　　　If it might please ye—
> *Cleopatra*: His face was as the heav'ns, and therein stuck
> A sun and moon, which kept their course, and lighted
> The little O, th' earth.
> *Dolabella*:　　　　　Most sovereign creature—
> *Cleopatra*: His legs bestrid the ocean, his rear'd arm
> Crested the world, his voice was propertied
> As all the tuned spheres, and that to friends;
> But when he meant to quail and shake the orb,

---

88. Ibid., 234.

89. https://allpoetry.com/Funeral-blues.

90. Shakespeare, *Othello*, Act IV, scene iii, ll. 78–79 & Act V, scene ii, ll. 144–45. This and all subsequent Shakespeare quotations are from *The Riverside Shakespeare* (Boston: Houghton Mifflin Company, 1974).

He was as rattling thunder. For his bounty,
There was no winter in't; an autumn it was
That grew the more by reaping. His delights
Were dolphin-like, they show'd his back above
The element they liv'd in. In his livery
Walk'd crowns and crownets; realms and islands were
As plates dropp'd from his pocket.
Dolabella: Cleopatra!
Cleopatra: Think you there was or might be such a man
As this I dreamt of?
Dolabella: Gentle madam, no.
Cleopatra: You lie up to the hearing of the gods!
But if there be, nor ever were one such,
It's past the size of dreaming.[91]

The infinite is "past the size of dreaming," beyond what dreams can imagine, and Antony has infinite value. Dolabella's refusal to accept even the possibility that there could be truth in the extent to which Cleopatra's dreams can reach is reasonable, and therefore (to complete the antinomy) wrong. Dolabella speaks for the rationalism of the so-called "enlightenment," Cleopatra for the Christian view of the person as having such ontological depth as to be of infinite worth. She speaks poetry and, as Florensky wrote, "the Christian world-understanding can be compared with a poetic work."[92] In her love, she knows the God-given truth of the human person. She is Ann, not Frank; truthful, not reasonable.

Facing the Truth

A person contains many an opposite. Learning is personal. God shines in the face of the one who beholds Christ. This is true personhood.

The scientific method, proceeding with passive and impersonal voice, has a partial objectivity. Full and complete impartiality, however, requires a maximum of partiality: the sort of devotion that

---

91. Shakespeare, *Antony and Cleopatra*, Act V, scene ii, ll. 76–97.
92. *At the Crossroads of Science & Mysticism*, 130.

Ann has for Timothy. The antinomy here approaches the divine in which opposites coincide, for God is love. For this (higher) knowing, the personal is essential. The living person, the image and likeness of God, is the quintessence of antinomy pointing us to Him. The person is the summit of life and antinomy is life, which is the culmination of existence. All that exists comes from contrarieties, for (as Heraclitus said), "War is the father of all things."[93] In the person there is war between matter and spirit, war between time and eternity, war between necessity and freedom; in the person there is peace between flesh and spirit, between the moment and the everlasting, between the limited and the unlimited; in the person there can be unity between war and peace. Of all that is, the person is capable of coming closest to that transcendent unity of opposites which is God, that truth which is above all reason, that love which passes all understanding. The person balances between peril and opportunity, between the piecemeal and the perfect, between perdition and perpetual life. Concomitantly, the person is the core of creativity, the mirror of the Maker, the incarnation of the ineffable, the mine of mystery, the seed of sanctity, the gateway to God. A person can be a teller of the Truth; a letter from the far shore of Lethe, "written not with ink, but with the Spirit of the living God;"[94] an oracle of the Omniscient in knowing that knowledge cannot be known.

That a person is a combining of opposites and a source of creativity follows from this (loosely translated) account given by the twelfth-century theologian Richard of St Victor of what a person is:

> The word "person" means not so much "something" as "someone." Further, the word "person" is never understood except as meaning: one, alone, distinguished from all others by a unique quality.[95]

---

93. McGilchrist, *The Matter With Things*, 1426, Kindle.

94. 2 Corinthians 3:3.

95. *Ad nomen personae, non tam aliquid quam aliquis designatur. Ad nomen autem personae, nunquam intelligitur nisi unus aliquis solus, ab omnibus aliis singulari proprietate discretus.* Richard de Saint-Victor, *La Trinité* (Paris: Éditions du Cerf, 1959), 244. (*De Trinitate*, Book 4, Chapter 7.)

Only some "one" can keep in unity what on the level of substance (which Richard St Victor opposes to "person") is disparate. And only one "distinguished from all others" has a unique dignity. This double aspect corresponds to the two meanings of the word "identity"—being the same and being different, as I argued in my book, *The Mystery of Identity*.[96] This is a paradox in the terms that describe this world, but coherent in relating what transcends it, for God Himself is identified with all that is (which is why being is His symbol) and is utterly unlike all that is (for He is the Most High). And a person has the capacity to transcend the world for:

> God created man in his own image, in the image of God created he him; male and female created he them.[97]

That which is transcendent is eternal, and that which is eternal is true. Therefore a person is a channel of truth.

If we do not always animadvert to such things it is perhaps because they are obvious. We only ever begin to learn the truth of things from another person, whether that be our mother or father speaking to us when we are babies or a spiritual master leading us to the fullness of life. Every view of everything is personal; all awareness involves a person, if only our own person. A person organizes truth; fragmentation without living, organic unity is no more truth than a random scattering of scrabble tiles is a poem; a complete failure to connect is catatonic. Awareness of our own integrated personhood is the foundation of our openness to truth. Awareness of another person is awareness of awareness. Perception of presence is alertness to being present to someone. And we become aware of another person, and present to that person, above all through the face: indeed, the Russian word for "person," *litso*, can also mean "face."[98] In Florensky's words, "personhood is something that abides in the face."[99]

---

96. Angelico Press, 2022.

97. Genesis 1:27.

98. Vladimir Solovyov, *Sophia, God & A Short Tale About the Antichrist*, trans. by Boris Jakim (Brooklyn, NY: Angelico Press, 2014), 125, note 8.

99. Pavel Florensky, *The Meaning of Idealism: The Metaphysics of Genus & Countenance* (Brooklyn, NY: Angelico Press, 2020), 75.

The countenance shows the person through the eyes that speak honestly, the smile that communicates lovingly, the words that echo the Word. It is no accident that the devotees of the father of lies wear masks for their liturgies. If a person is the image of God, then the face is the image of a person and so, *mutatis mutandis*, the face of God. There is manifest, to the proper degree, divine creativity and freedom. This is particularly so of Saint Stephen, the first martyr or witness to the Son of the living God, of whom it is written, "And all that sat in the council, looking stedfastly on him, saw his face as it had been the face of an angel."[100] By contrast, evil is impersonal and faceless, deceiving others by pretending to be a person. It divides and fragments, not only nations and communities, but also the individual person. So, when Jesus demands to know the name of the devil possessing the man at Gadara, he is told, "Legion: because many devils were entered into him."[101] His exorcism breaks the illusion that the legion of devils constitute a person.

It is easy enough to see how we, preparing a face to meet the faces we shall meet, can be two (or more) faced, but how can we find facial integrity? Saint Paul answers this question:

"But we all, with open face beholding as in a glass the glory of the Lord, are changed into the same image from glory to glory, even as by the Spirit of the Lord."[102] This seems to contradict what the Lord told Moses: "There shall no man see me and live . . . thou shalt see my back parts: but my face shall not be seen."[103] The implication is that the absolute Truth manifest in the face of God would be too much for us. Yet there is a way we can see His face, see that Truth. Jesus tells Philip, "He that hath seen me hath seen the Father"[104] and Saint Paul calls Him "the image of the invisible God"[105] and says that in His face we have "the light of the knowledge of the glory

---

100. Acts 6:15.
101. Luke 8:30.
102. 2 Corinthians 3:18.
103. Exodus 33:20, 23.
104. John 14:9.
105. Colossians 1:15.

of God."[106] In "a clift of the rock" that is Christ we can, like Moses, stand while God's "glory passeth by."[107] To put off every mask (or "persona," which etymologically is the same thing), every fragment posing as a person for a particular purpose, and—like Saint Stephen "being full of the Holy Ghost"—to look with the mind's eye "stedfastly into heaven" and see "the glory of God, and Jesus standing on the right hand of God"[108] is to be transfigured into one bearing light, to realize true personhood, to embody the Truth.

So the search for truth is the quest to be truly a person, an undertaking in the spirit of the wisdom of a rabbi of the last century, Jacob Agus, who said, "Truth is a noun only to God; to men, truth is generally best known as an adverb, 'truly.'"[109] It is to seek to see the mystery of our personhood, since (in the words of S.L. Frank) "what is *universally valid* is expressed in the deepest *singularity* that defines the essence of the person."[110] Like a rainbow in a hurricane, like a star in the night, like a lighthouse for the storm-tossed, one who is truly a person can be beauty in an ugly world, guidance in this time of darkness, "an ever-fixed mark"[111] in the miasma of post-modernity. Irreducible to the enumeration of traits, insusceptible to the knife of analysis,[112] refusing all capture by the mind, true personhood is that wholeness reflected in the greatest works of art, the inspiration of their beauty, the accomplishment of their meaning. It is the wholeness of the heart in which all is gathered and pondered as, having heard what the shepherds said, "Mary kept all these things and pondered them in her heart."[113] It is the holiness of the heart touched by the Sacred Heart of Jesus.

Where have saints and sages found the inspiration to be holy, to be whole, to be truly persons? Where is the truth which has set them

106. 2 Corinthians 4:6
107. Exodus 33:21–22.
108. Acts 7:55.
109. McGilchrist, *The Matter With Things*, 566. Kindle.
110. Frank, *The Unknowable*, 178.
111. Shakespeare, Sonnet 116.
112. Cf. Florensky, *The Meaning of Idealism*, 75.
113. Luke 2:29.

free from the aberrations of arbitrary assertion? Where does God speak to us? As I am a Christian, I have an obvious answer to these questions: the Bible. Dear reader, let us look together at the blessings we can receive through the Bible's presentation of personhood.

B: Bible & Blessing

Names

Names are important in the Bible; they show something of God,
for they denote persons whether human or divine. His truth is
lost in abstraction, regained through persons.

Adam, Sheth, Enosh, Kenan, Mahalaleel, Jered, Henoch, Methuse-
lah, Lamech, Noah, Shem, Ham, and Japheth.[1]

The first book of the Chronicles begins simply with this list of
names: Adam, the first man, direct from the hands of God, and then
twelve following him. There are many other such lists in the Bible.
Notable for its parallel with this one is that given in Saint Matthew's
gospel of the twelve following the Second Adam:

> Now the names of the twelve apostles are these; The first, Simon,
> who is called Peter, and Andrew his brother; James the Son of
> Zebedee, and John his brother; Philip and Bartholomew; Thomas
> and Matthew, the publican; James the Son of Alphaeus, and Leb-
> baeus, whose surname was Thaddeus; Simon the Canaanite, and
> Judas Iscariot, who also betrayed him.[2]

A name is the verbal instantiation of a person, a mystery articulated, an epiphany pronounced. As Richard St Victor observes,
when it is a question of a person, we no longer ask "What is it?" but
"Who is it?" and we receive the reply "Matthew, Bartholomew..."[3]
We are given a name. In a biblical context, a name is a presencing,
whether of the divine—as in the Lord's high priestly prayer in
which He says, "I have manifested thy name unto the men which
thou gavest me out of the world"[4]—or the human, as when He
promises "to him that overcometh" the gift of "a white stone, and in

---

1. 1 Chronicles 1:1–4.
2. Matthew 10:2–5.
3. Richard de Saint-Victor, *La Trinité*, 244 (*De Trinitate*, Book 4, Chapter 7).
4. John 17:6.

the stone a new name written, which no man knoweth saving he that receiveth it."[5] To be given a name in this latter, human sense is to receive the fullness of personhood, a participation in the everlasting life of God.

If we look to the Bible to find truth, undying eternal truth, the truth of God, we find it through persons. Saint Augustine, with his formation in the relative abstraction of the Greek tradition, found one obstacle to his conversion in the lack of a clear explanatory system in the Bible; significantly, another was in his own person, in that turning to Christ involved a change to chastity. Persons and their muddled and mixed lives (those in the Bible and his own) were an obstacle, seeming to get in the way of the provision of something he could get his head around. Yet persons are the channels of God's revelation of Himself. The same reason accounts for both the obstacles he found: God is only known through our dialogue with Him. There can be no such thing as an observer standing aloof from the truth of God and chronicling its essence. Chronicles are lists of people. Each person has an ontological depth which reflects the unsoundable mystery of God. Each name is both a particular and universal revelation of Him. Sometimes these names are explicit personal divine revelations, such as when Abram is told, "Neither shall thy name any more be called Abram, but thy name shall be Abraham; for a father of many nations have I made thee,"[6] and when Simon is told, "Thou art Peter, and upon this rock I will build my church."[7] These names mean what their bearers are called to be. Sometimes names reflect the circumstances of a person coming into the world, as with Isaac, meaning one who laughs or rejoices, whose mother laughs incredulously when her husband is told that she will bear a son,[8] but who laughs with joy when this comes true, saying, "God hath made me to laugh, so that all that hear will laugh with me."[9] Isaac is to be the father of a race through which people will

---

5. Revelation 2:17.
6. Genesis 17:5.
7. Matthew 16:18.
8. Genesis 18:12.
9. Genesis 21:6.

turn from incredulity to joyful faith in God's promises. Word play, whether metaphor or pun, supplies the cracks in the strictly reasonable through which the light of God enters in. It generates antinomy and so openness to the transcendent. The Biblical names point to what is beyond them, the Truth of God, while also denoting the truth of the person in a way our casual nomenclature, with its nominalist antecedents, has all but forgotten. Their being is rooted in the infinite and eternal and their names in some sense give access to this. A person is a revelation, an image of divine truth.

So it is with the name of God. According to the Biblical account, in the third generation of humankind "began men to call upon the name of the LORD."[10] This implies both a distance and a closeness: a distance because Man is no longer like Adam directly from the hands of God, suffused with the presence of His Maker, and a closeness because the name in some sense makes God present. It also implies both a veiling and an unveiling of the Divine: a veiling because God is hidden behind the name and an unveiling because the name says who He is. The veiling is like the clothes Adam and Eve wore after their fall, knowing their nakedness because they are no longer one with creation and Creator, no longer like internal organs of a body but separated from it; the unveiling is the beginning of the return to the paradisal state by a reaching out to what has been lost. The name of the Lord is hidden in the strict protocol forbidding the general use of the Tetragrammaton (the word spelling that name) and manifest in its yearly pronunciation by the High Priest. The name of Jesus is both "the name which is above every name,"[11] not formulable in the common way of names because so "far above . . . every name that is named,"[12] and a straightforward declaration of God saving us in this Person. The ambiguity about whether God is present through His name was exemplified in the fact that, shortly before the Russian revolution, the Tsar's troops were sent to Mount Athos to take measures against monks who claimed that He was truly present in His name. All of this onomas-

10. Genesis 4:26.
11. Philippians 2:9.
12. Ephesians 1:21.

tic reticence is reflected in the response God gives to a direct question about His name: "I AM THAT I AM."[13] This response is thought to be echoed in the Tetragrammaton, the four letters of which form the root meaning of "to be" and so suggest a meaning such as "He-who-Is," or "He who brings into being." Yet this name, though a fundamental symbol of God like "light" and "love," is not how He announces Himself to Moses before He is asked His name. He says rather, "I am the God of thy father, the God of Abraham, the God of Isaac, and the God of Jacob."[14] Before God identifies Himself as symbolized by being, He identifies Himself in relation to persons. To Jacob he said, "I am the LORD God of Abraham thy father, and the God of Isaac";[15] to Isaac he said, "I am the God of Abraham, thy father."[16] The truth of God is known by what has been passed on to us through the persons who came before us.

This is the truth of the living God, of the God who gives life, as evidenced in Christ's words to those doubting the resurrection:

> Have ye not read in the book of Moses, how in the bush God spake unto him, saying, I am the God of Abraham, and the God of Isaac, and the God of Jacob? He is not the God of the dead, but the God of the living: ye therefore do greatly err.[17]

Truth, the ultimate Truth which is God, is linked to life, in particular the life of persons. It is not abstract. This was the insight that came to Pascal in his famous epiphany, of which he wrote, "Dieu d'Abraham, Dieu d'Isaac, Dieu de Jacob, Non des Philosophes et des savants—Certitude."[18] (God of Abraham, God of Isaac, God of Jacob, not of the philosophers and of the learned—Certainty.) Truth is a Person revealing Himself in history, not an abstract principle, a Person who says, "I am come that they might have life, and that they might have it more abundantly."[19] This is where the "cer-

---

13. Exodus 3:14.
14. Exodus 3:6.
15. Genesis 28:13.
16. Genesis 26:24.
17. Mark 12:26–27.
18. *The Pillar and Ground of the Truth*, 407.
19. John 10:10.

tainty" of Pascal, the "rock-like affirmation" of Florensky[20] is found, in the antinomy of God and Man, power and weakness, meekness and glory, not at all in the reasoning of "the wise and prudent."[21]

The Bible guides us to find truth in the person, not the abstraction. That is why I am using the King James Version for this book. Later, less poetic, versions tend to impose the abstract ways of our epoch upon the text: so, for example, "Let us call the young woman and ask her" instead of "We will call the damsel, and inquire at her mouth" and "my sides are filled with burning" for "my loins are filled with a loathsome disease."[22] The body matters: Descartes wrote, "I will regard myself as not having hands, or eyes, or flesh, or blood, or any senses, but as nevertheless falsely believing that I possess all these things."[23] To go in that direction is to go away from the truth that one supposes he was seeking, to neglect God-given means for the quest, to pass over the incarnate person in favor of the abstract. God's love for His people is a jealous love, meaning that He loves them in their particular lives and not through as it were some universally applicable algorithm. So recovering truth means recovering a sense of the dignity of humanity, not least by realizing it in our own persons. Almost half a century ago, Philip Sherrard saw what we were up against, writing, "The inorganic technological world we have invented lays hold on our interior being and seeks to reduce that to a blind inorganic mechanical thing"[24] and "to reduce man to the level of what the reason can perceive or understand about him is to dehumanize him."[25] The latter is now regarded in some quarters not as a hazard but as a project: transhumanism.

More recently, Iain McGilchrist has written that humans are

---

20. *The Pillar and Ground of the Truth*, 344.

21. Matthew 11:25.

22. Genesis 24:57, Psalm 38:7 ESV & KJV.

23. Gil Bailie, *The Apocalypse of the Sovereign Self: Recovering the Christian Mystery of Personhood* (Brooklyn, NY: Angelico Press, 2023), 72.

24. "Modern Science and the Dehumanization of Man" (*Studies in Comparative Religion*, Vol. 10, No. 2), Spring 1976, 4 (https://www.themathesontrust.org/papers/modernity/Sherrard-Modern_Science_and_Dehumanization.pdf).

25. Ibid., 14.

"becoming more like machines, by reason of their being obliged to interact with them." He sees this tendency as destructive:

> The best way to destroy humanity would be to hybridize it with machines. I do not call those who pursue this aim evil—they may simply have a failure of imagination or of understanding. But the aim itself is evil, if we can call anything evil. It can only further degrade our idea of what a human life is for, and it opens us up to totalitarian control.[26]

The evil he alerts us to is the destruction of the human person and therefore of the presence of truth. As we alienate ourselves from our humanity, so we distance ourselves from truth.

An alternative project, the ordering of the heart through ascesis to open it to the light of the Truth, remains possible if we turn to what has been handed on to us by those persons who were before us. "Listen, O son," says the Rule of Saint Benedict, "to the precepts of a master," and sets them forth for us.[27] Some such sense of receiving spiritual teaching from elders is universal. In Russia there is the tradition of the *starets* or elder, artistically presented with such eloquence by Dostoevsky in the person of Father Zosima in *The Brothers Karamazov*; in China, reverence and respect for ancestors; in India, the practice of seeking wisdom from a *guru*. Indeed, it exists in every human family, at least in the traditional sense of that word, for each human father, however fallible, in some measure instantiates God the Father: Christ Himself was "subject unto" Joseph as such.[28] And Cormac McCarthy, in his novel about a father and young son walking through land laid waste by nuclear war, movingly imagines this continuing even in utter desolation. The father dies and the boy says a final goodbye to him before joining a family that adopts him:

> I'll talk to you every day, he whispered. And I wont forget. No matter what. Then he rose and turned and walked back out to the road.

26. "Resist the Machine Apocalypse," in *First Things* (March 2024), 36.
27. Rule of Saint Benedict, prologue.
28. Luke 2:51.

The woman when she saw him put her arms around him and held him. Oh, she said, I am so glad to see you. She would talk to him sometimes about God. He tried to talk to God but the best thing was to talk to his father and he did talk to him and he didn't forget. The woman said that was all right. She said that the breath of God was his breath yet though it pass from man to man through all of time.[29]

Adam

Adam includes humanity as such and determines the meaning of creation. The image of divine truth is passed on from him. This is restored in Christ.

In this paternal transmission of wisdom, Adam is a special case, for he is instructed ("of the tree of the knowledge of good and evil, thou shalt not eat of it") and given correction ("in the sweat of thy face shalt thou eat bread")[30] directly by God. His name means "Man" in the sense of the whole of humanity, women as well as men, for, "God created man, in the likeness of God made he him; Male and female created he them; and blessed them, and called their name Adam, in the day when they were created."[31] Everything goes back to him. He includes all his descendants, and is himself not included in anyone, except in a more figurative sense that I shall explore in a later chapter. Given the primordial importance of names referred to above, he determines the meaning and so the essence of every creature, for when "out of the ground the LORD God formed every beast of the field and every fowl of the air," He "brought them unto Adam to see what he would call them: and whatsoever Adam called every living creature, that was the name thereof."[32] He knows their meaning because he knows what they really represent. He is an archetypal microcosm of all creation, an embodiment of the knowledge of it, the presence of all that is to

---

29. *The Road* (London: Pan Macmillan, 2019), 306 [*sic*].
30. Genesis 2:17, 3:19.
31. Genesis 5:1–2.
32. Genesis 2:19.

come. Every longing of the human heart is an ancestral memory of his joy in paradise, yet not in the sense of nostalgia for the past, for that paradise was living intimately close to the eternity of God, which is the final goal of human life. The memory is the anticipation; the memory and the anticipation are a disengagement from the passing and a resting in the enduring. Each biblical person is an image of a spiritual state,[33] but Adam is the figure of humanity as such: falling for the delusion that we can improve upon what the divine decree has destined for us, clothed in our vulnerability with the garments of salvation, tilling the ground from which we are taken to sustain a life that distantly echoes the melody of paradise and remotely preintones the music of heaven. In knowing Adam, the very beginning and archetype of our personal humanity, we know in person the truth of our lives, for he is the first likeness and image of absolute and eternal Truth.

That likeness and image he passed on when he "begat a son in his own likeness, after his image."[34] The said son, Seth, "begat sons and daughters,"[35] and in so doing passed on the likeness and image of Truth. That these were truly passed on is evidenced by the fact that, as God once walked "in the garden in the cool of the day" making himself present to "Adam and his wife,"[36] five generations later, "Enoch walked with God: and he was not; for God took him."[37] Man, in the person of Enoch, can still be with God and still go to God. And so it—the likeness and the image, the intimation of truth in the human person—goes on. I am not of course denying that the flaw of Eve and Adam works itself out in the horrors of history, yet I do dispute that there is no humanly available truth. However flawed are the inter-generational relationships that transmit this truth, God can heal them, as he promises through the prophet Malachi:

> Behold, I will send you Elijah the prophet before the coming of the great and dreadful day of the LORD: And he shall turn the heart of

---

33. Florensky, *At the Crossroads of Science & Mysticism*, 98.
34. Genesis 5:3.
35. Genesis 5:7.
36. Genesis 3:8.
37. Genesis 5:24.

the fathers to the children, and the heart of the children to their fathers, lest I come and smite the earth with a curse.[38]

The angel Gabriel announces another and greater prophet, John the Baptist,[39] with the words, "The rough ways shall be made smooth; And all flesh shall see the salvation of God."[40] More of John later: here I am making the point that the inter-generational bond and the concomitant communion with the Creator are capable of being healed. Even on the merely natural level, the tendency is towards its working: a spark of life, a hint of holiness, a little love even in the midst of much that is negative, is enough to inspire a sense of truth and her importance. And I have personally witnessed (privileged as I am to live in a place where people come on such quests) the young seeking and recovering a truth fuller than that which they have explicitly inherited. The transmission of truth, like the human body, tends to heal itself.

The supreme and necessarily supernatural healing of the transmission of truth from generation to generation images the bond with "the only true God."[41] They are the work of the Savior announced by the Apostle Paul: "Our Lord Jesus Christ, by whom we have now received the atonement."[42] As the multitude of humanity knows mortality through Adam, so they know asymmetrically the life that is the light of truth[43] through Him: "much more the grace of God, and the gift by grace, which is by one man, Jesus Christ, has abounded unto many."[44] Adam, and the new Adam, (in Walt Whitman's words) "contain multitudes."[45] The human truth of Adam, and the human and divine truth of Christ include our personal truth, the antinomy of death and life: "As in Adam all die, even so in Christ shall all be made alive."[46] The former is the trans-

38. Malachi 4:5–6.
39. Luke 1:17.
40. Luke 3:5–6.
41. John 17:3.
42. Romans 5:11.
43. Cf. John 1:5.
44. Romans 5:15.
45. "Song of Myself" 51 (https://poets.org/poem/song-myself-51).
46. 1 Corinthians 15:22.

mitter of a partial life and truth, the latter of unlimited life and truth: "The first man Adam was made a living soul; the last Adam was made a quickening spirit."[47]

In the remainder of this chapter we shall consider by name nine of the first Adam's descendents as the Bible presents them to us, to see how each of them in his or her different way personifies and embodies truth. That is to be found as much in their lives as in their words, and not at all in any abstraction. The last Adam will be central to the chapter that follows and so number ten, signifying the fullness of life.

Abraham

God connects with the world through Abraham, speaking directly to him. He embodies all who leave home to seek truth and worship God. Blessing and judgment come through him. He is a model of faith, offering sacrifice prefiguring that of Christ.

As a mediator of God's truth, Abraham is significant in manifold ways. He is father to three religions, Judaism, Christianity and Islam, so in one sense very capacious in his spiritual progeny. Yet he is also, in the Biblical account, the man in whom God's particular connection with the world becomes more narrowly focused. The beginning of the chapter in which he first appears reads, "And the whole earth was of one language, and of one speech."[48] Humanity at this point is, relatively speaking, one. This unity breaks, as the story of the Tower of Babel illustrates, when an attempt is made to rival heaven (taking what they construct themselves as absolute) and therefore peoples no longer have a transcendent, and so universal, language (for each is locked into an "absolute" of their own). The Transcendent responds, so to speak, by inserting Itself into humanity through the person of Abraham. He and his progeny become the object of God's jealous and particular favor. Love is always particular, on pain of being pernicious because abstract. If it is the latter, then another object will do as well and the first can be abandoned

47. 1 Corinthians 15:45.
48. Genesis 11:1.

and come to realize that he or she was never truly loved at all. God's love is never like that. His dilection for the patriarch and his people is steadfast, unforgetting and so true. His truth, forgotten by squabbling denizens of Babel, is given to the world in the person of Abraham.

It is significant that God speaks directly to Abraham. The passing on of truth, so vibrant at the beginning, has diminished. These are very post-diluvian times, with "the nations divided in the earth after the flood."[49] So God speaks directly to Abram (as he then is), reinjecting truth into tradition, as it were. This is one of those moments which, like the Resurrection, are too sacred to be described directly by Scripture. It is given to us as a *fait accompli*, in the pluperfect:

> Now the LORD had said to Abram, Get thee out of thy country, and from thy kindred, and from thy father's house, unto a land that I will shew thee.[50]

The implication is, to put it in popular parlance, that Abram is not in a good place. Scripture says nothing ill of his father, Terah, but the instruction suggests that the social milieu is not so very truth-bearing. Abram has to leave, and in this he is first and father of many who will leave their homeland, whether as pilgrims, seekers or desert dwellers, to find freedom from a socially corrupt truth. Saint Benedict is one such, leaving Rome for Subiaco for a solitude so severe that he does not even know it when Easter comes. And like Abraham, he has many spiritual descendants: monks and nuns who have made a similar journey. The latter is explicitly told about his:

> And I will make of thee a great nation, and I will bless thee, and make thy name great; and thou shalt be a blessing.[51]

As Adam contains all people, so Abraham contains all worshippers of the One God. He becomes "a great nation" and more than that in his spiritual offspring. He is blessed by God and is therefore a blessing. The Truth of God suffuses him and radiates through him. Yet, truth shows up what is wrong as well as blessing. Like Jesus, he is

49. Genesis 10:32.
50. Genesis 12:1.
51. Genesis 12:2.

"set for the fall and rising again of many" and is to be "a sign which shall be spoken against."[52] Through him comes the light of truth, but "every one that doeth evil hateth the light, neither cometh to the light lest his deeds should be reproved."[53] It follows that contained within the blessing which comes through him is the potential for division:

> And I will bless them that bless thee, and curse him that curseth thee: and in thee shall all the families of the earth be blessed.[54]

Abraham's person becomes a touchstone for true blessing, a way of transmitting God's truth and divining divagation. And so the prophet Isaiah, enjoining people to "walk in the light,"[55] proclaims:

> Hearken to me, ye that follow after righteousness, ye that seek the LORD: look unto the rock whence ye are hewn, and to the hole of the pit whence ye are digged. Look unto Abraham your father and unto Sarah that bare you: for I called him alone, and blessed him, and increased him.[56]

The blessing comes through "him alone": he is the particular person, chosen and loved by God, through whom the light is known or rejected. When Isaac blesses his son Jacob, he says, "God Almighty bless thee" and adds "and give thee the blessing of Abraham."[57] The implication is that they are synonymous: God's blessing comes to the new generation through Abraham.

In the New Testament, the filial bond with Abraham is regarded as a touchstone for integrity, for personal truth. John the Baptist challenges the claim of the Pharisees and Sadducees, saying, "Think not to say within yourselves, We have Abraham to our father: for I say unto you, that God is able of these stones to raise up children unto Abraham."[58] A godly, truthful person is a child of Abraham. The same implication is there when the opponents of Jesus say to

52. Luke 2:34.
53. John 3:20.
54. Genesis 12:3.
55. Isaiah 50:11.
56. Isaiah 51:1–2.
57. Genesis 28:3–4.
58. Matthew 3:9.

Him, "Abraham is our father" and He responds, "If ye were Abraham's children, ye would do the works of Abraham. But now ye seek to kill me, a man that hath told you the truth, which I have heard from God: this did not Abraham."[59] The personal presence of God's truth is in Abraham and his blessing. That original, Jewish understanding acquires a new dimension in the Christian tradition. What the angel of the Lord tells Abraham when he shows himself willing to sacrifice his son Isaac, "By myself have I sworn, says the LORD, for because thou hast done this thing, and hast not withheld thy son, thine only son: that in blessing I will bless thee,"[60] points to the supreme blessing of God the Father, who "so loved the world, that he gave his only begotten Son, that whosoever believeth in him should not perish, but have everlasting life."[61] Abraham's blessing prefigures and participates in the Father's universal blessing and so he is the personal channel and model for the blessing of every father, both natural and sacerdotal. He is the father of those who have faith: "they which are of faith, the same are the children of Abraham."[62]

He is in particular a paternal model for everyone who believes in God's "only begotten Son," for "by faith, Abraham, when he was tried, offered up Isaac."[63] He is therefore the model for everyone who is open to God's truth, for that, ultimate, truth is above the reach of our reasoning minds and can only be known by faith. Abraham in his person contains all those who live by God's truth and all those who believe in His promises in this world. More than that, he contains all those in paradise: such is the implication of the parable of the rich man and the beggar, in which Jesus says that "it came to pass, that the beggar died, and was carried by the angels into Abraham's bosom."[64] If making the latter a synonym for the dwelling of all the saints makes it seem extraordinarily big, we need to remember both that the universal always and necessarily comes

59. John 8:39–40.
60. Genesis 22:16–17.
61. John 3:16.
62. Galatians 3:7.
63. Hebrews 11:17.
64. Luke 16:22.

to us in the particular (never in an abstraction) and that "the only begotten Son"[65] by whom "were all things created"[66] is in "the bosom of the Father."[67] Abraham is the personal manifestation of the divine breast, the embrace of which is so broad that it includes all who are and all that is. It is no wonder that because he had faith, "Therefore sprang there even of one and him as good as dead, so many as the stars of the sky in multitude, and as the sand which is by the sea shore innumerable."[68]

Jacob

Blessing also comes through Jacob, who is connected with heaven. He personally receives the truth of God.

Jacob, Abraham's grandson, is another person who contains multitudes. The Lord God of Abraham his father and the God of Isaac tells him, "Thy seed shall be as the dust of the earth, and thou shalt spread abroad to the west, and to the east, and to the north, and to the south: and in thee and in thy seed shall all the families of the earth be blessed."[69] This blessing through his progeny is both that of Abraham and one that comes directly to him. The latter is implied by the context of the dream of "a ladder set up on the earth, and the top of it reached to heaven: and behold the angels of God ascending and descending on it. And, behold, the LORD stood above it"[70] speaking his promise. The ladder connects Jacob with heaven; the angels are the personal messengers of God communicating between heaven and earth. As with Gabriel announcing to the Blessed Virgin Mary her unique mission, so with Jacob: truth is communicated in person. The most significant communication that Jacob has with God is even more personal:

65. John 1:18.
66. Colossians 1:16.
67. John 1:18.
68. Hebrews 11:12.
69. Genesis 28:14.
70. Genesis 28:12.

And Jacob was left alone; and there wrestled a man with him until the breaking of the day. And when he saw that he prevailed not against him, he touched the hollow of his thigh; and the hollow of Jacob's thigh was out of joint, as he wrestled with him. And he said, Let me go, for the day breaketh. And he said, I will not let thee go, except thou bless me. And he said unto him, What is thy name? And he said, Jacob. And he said, Thy name shall be called no more Jacob, but Israel: for as a prince thou hast power with God and with men, and hast prevailed. And Jacob asked him, and said, Tell me, I pray thee, thy name. And he said, Wherefore is it that thou dost ask after my name? And he blessed him there. And Jacob called the name of the place Peniel: for I have seen God face to face, and my life is preserved.[71]

Whether "the man" with whom Jacob struggles is angelic or human, he is certainly a person and the final sentence of the above quotation leaves no doubt that this is God. Jacob encounters Him in person, sees Him face to face and memorializes this in naming the place of meeting "Peniel," meaning "the face of God." The truth of God comes to him in person. Yet he has also to risk his own person in the encounter, as the injury indicates. As with cunning he got the blessing that his elder brother expected from their father,[72] so with valor he gets a blessing from God. In this sense he has "power with God" and prevails. However, he does not get an answer to his question about God's name: His infinite mystery does not allow itself to be defined. He, on the other hand, is told his name by God. Humanity cannot confine God in a name, yet God gives each person his or her identity. And Jacob's identity shares something of God's infinitude—for his name, Israel, is that of a whole people. He is both a person and a people.

And God speaks His truth through that person and that people. And he speaks to them, saying, "I have loved thee with an everlasting love."[73] In our individualistic age, we too easily forget that a person can be the people, can be Israel, can be the New Israel which is the Church, and that a people can be a person, can be each and

71. Genesis 32:24–28.
72. Genesis 27:6–40.
73. Jeremiah 31:3.

every one of us. And in an environment in which abstractions tend to dominate, we can too easily lose sight of the fact that to fully enter into the Truth we need to give ourselves to struggle, as Jacob did, prefiguring the struggle in the garden of the Lord to accept the divine will, to bring the greatest of blessings on the world. There are angels to give us personal help such as the Lord received when "there appeared an angel unto him from heaven, strengthening him."[74] And in a society oriented to the supply of comfort, we can too easily back away from the reality that pain can be partner to prayer as it was for Him, when "being in an agony, he prayed more earnestly: and his sweat was as it were great drops of blood falling to the ground."[75] Yet, it is when praying with Him "thy will be done" and so losing our selfish individuality that we find our truth, our personhood in God.

Moses

Moses sees, and is the mediator of, God, who is a consuming fire and whose transcendent truth lifts us up even in our greatest weakness.

Like Jacob, Moses and his companions have a direct vision of God:

> Then went up Moses, and Aaron, Nadab, and Abihu, and seventy of the elders of Israel: And they saw the God of Israel: and there was under his feet as it were a paved work of a sapphire stone, and as it were the body of heaven in his clearness.[76]

They know Him as "the God of Israel," through the person of their ancestor, and through the celestial blueness that is under Him. The people of Israel who do not go up, know Him through His mediator, Moses. Direct contact with Him would be too much for them, so they say to Moses, "Speak thou with us, and we will hear: but let not God speak with us, lest we die."[77] Yet even the sight of Moses

74. Luke 22:43.
75. Luke 22:44.
76. Exodus 24:9–10.
77. Exodus 20:19.

evokes fear in them, for "when Aaron and all the children of Israel saw Moses, behold, the skin of his face shone; and they were afraid to come nigh him." He is a true light-bearer, as is every holy person who radiates God's truth; yet the people cannot bear so much light, so "till Moses had done speaking with them, he put a vail on his face."[78] Every halo of a saint is testimony that the light of God's truth comes through a person, as it did through Moses.

God's light, His truth, however is not experienced simply as a mood-enhancer, like the tasteful and relaxing lighting in a restaurant which, with the first drink, puts us in a place where we can forget our cares for an evening. Nor does it simply increase our fund of information, like an electronic device that we consult to find out what is going on while we wait for the first dish to arrive. To assume that the divine and luminous truth can be limited to what we feel and what our minds can grasp is to underestimate the Majesty of God (to put it mildly) and also to be reductive about the human person, who is (in the patristic phrase) capable of God. Yet some such assumption regularly warps people's understanding of truth and person. The former can be reduced to "what you feel comfortable with" or "what you feel most deeply about" while the latter can be mistaken for a collection of digital data that is binary-encoded (never mind antinomy). If this mistake about personhood seems far-fetched, consider the common assertion that sufficiently advanced artificial intelligence, which replicates the emotional complexity of a person in addition to processing information and calculating, actually has some kind of consciousness. This runs parallel to the notion that if we can record our habits, thoughts and feelings sufficiently, we can somehow live on in the internet, an idea given form in the creation of "thanabots" which offer an interactive digital simulacrum of the deceased, put together from data collected from their lives and soullessly marketed to the grieving. The folly of supposing that truth and person can be reduced to digital data comes from the assumption of materialism that there is only what is material, ruling out the vast reality of a time-and-space transcending consciousness on the grounds that the evidence for it is not of the

---

78. Exodus 34:30, 33.

sort that science is accustomed to dealing with. Those who fall prey to this folly mistake facility in rationally organizing data for personal intelligence that is *aware* of truth. Indeed, as Bruno Bérard has persuasively argued in the context of getting ChatGPT to reveal its limitations in dialogue, "artificial intelligence" is a misnomer for "artificial reason."[79]

The truth of God shatters, pulverizes and makes as nothing this feeble anthropology and any theology based on it. For those who think they are contained and constrained within this anthropology, there can be no truth of God. All that matters for them is what you and I feel is important and whatever data we have made our own. For those not so constrained, "our God is a consuming fire."[80] This is the truth that Moses mediates to the people of Israel:

And Moses brought forth the people out of the camp to meet with God; and they stood at the nether part of the mount. And mount Sinai was altogether on a smoke, because the Lord descended upon it in fire: and the smoke thereof ascended as the smoke of a furnace, and the whole mount quaked greatly.[81]

Such is the power of the presence that it is life-threatening: the Lord tells Moses, "Go down, charge the people, lest they break through unto the LORD to gaze and many of them perish."[82] Only Moses and Aaron can be in the presence without perishing. The key point is that God's truth is transcendent: it is so very far above what we can feel or understand. Yet we would not be able to have any contact at all with it were it not also immanent: intuitively within our souls, deeper than any feeling or thought. Reaching us for this reason, it lifts us up beyond where we could go by our own strength. Such is the message God gives through Moses:

Ye have seen what I did unto the Egyptians, and how I bare you on eagles' wings, and brought you unto myself.[83]

79. *Conversations avec ChatGPT sur l'homme, le monde, Dieu et l'intelligence artificielle* (Paris: L'Harmattan, 2024).
80. Hebrews 12:29.
81. Exodus 19:17–18.
82. Exodus 19:21.
83. Exodus 19:4.

The eagle traditionally flies up to the sun, the source of light, taking its young upon its back. God's people are lifted up above mundane and passing concerns; in His truth what belongs simply to our thoughts and feelings is transcended, slavery to Egyptian taskmasters is overcome, enabling us to escape the compulsion of worldly allures and soar into the azure beyond. Moses communicates the vital truth that this is for the realization of the dignity and worth of the people:

> Now therefore, if ye will obey my voice indeed, and keep my covenant, then ye shall be a peculiar treasure unto me above all people: for all the earth is mine: And ye shall be unto me a kingdom of priests, and an holy nation.[84]

In God's truth, the people know who they truly are. As for the people, so for the person: each of us is "a peculiar treasure" to God, *sans pareil*, infinitely valued by Him. We simply need to listen to Him and let Him lift us up.

Which He always wants to do, even when appearances are to the contrary. The temptation is to fail to believe this, ignoring the Apostle's confident assertion that "all things work together for good to them that love God."[85] The children of Israel fail in this way, for "the people did chide with Moses, and said, Give us water that we may drink" and "murmured against Moses, and said, Wherefore is this that thou hast brought us up out of Egypt, to kill us and our children and our cattle with thirst?"[86] Yet the truth is that there is a Providence at work in what seems hard, which is unfolded to Moses by the Lord:

> I will stand before thee there upon the rock in Horeb; and thou shalt smite the rock, and there shall come water out of it, that the people may drink.[87]

This Providence prefigures that which we have in Christ our rock, who offers water that will be for each of us, "a well of water spring-

---

84. Exodus 19:5–6.
85. Romans 8:28.
86. Exodus 17:2, 3.
87. Exodus 17:6.

ing up into everlasting life."[88] The truth is that God is caring for us, even or perhaps especially when things are hard, and working for our undying flourishing.

David

David, like the psalms attributed to him, speaks for the whole of humanity. He acts disinterestedly; in his name God's mercy is invoked.

There is a sense in which each person is all-containing (how otherwise could anybody ever mean the world to anybody?), but some persons sum up, articulate and present to the All High the whole of the human predicament. By being who they are, very particularly, they are who we are, very universally. They contain the truth of humanity. Such is David. Prescinding from the question of whether he actually wrote them, we can say that the attribution of the psalms to David is apt because they, like he, express what it is to be human and in the presence of the Lord God. It is not that David is without fault: he rightly says, "I have sinned against the Lord"[89] when there comes to light his sending of Uriah the Hittite to his death so that he can take for himself the latter's wife, Bathsheba, who is "very beautiful to look upon."[90] It is rather that David knows and acknowledges the transcendent aspect of human life. This is evident in his very acknowledgement of guilt, as articulated in the psalm traditionally associated with this episode:

> HAVE mercy upon me, O God, according to thy lovingkindness, according unto the multitude of thy tender mercies blot out my transgressions.[91]

Repeatedly, out of an awareness of the transcendent dimension of life, David acts in a way not consonant with his short-term, natural interests. So, he refuses to kill his enemy King Saul when the oppor-

---

88. John 4:14.
89. 2 Samuel 12:13.
90. 2 Samuel 11:2.
91. Psalm 51:1.

tunity arises, "for who can stretch forth his hand against the LORD's anointed, and be guiltless?"[92] He pours away water for which he is thirsting, seeing it as "the blood of the men that went in jeopardy of their lives,"[93] because his thirst cannot justify their mortal peril. And, although from the point of view of the messenger who brings the news the death of his enemy son means that "all is well,"[94] he bitterly laments his passing saying, "O my son Absalom, my son, my son Absalom! would God I had died for thee, O Absalom, my son, my son!"[95]

The prayer of humanity becomes simply "Remember David"[96] and its claim on the Lord's mercy David's treasured person and His promise to him, as in this supplication:

> For thy servant David's sake turn not away the face of thy anointed. The LORD hath sworn in truth unto David; he will not turn from it; Of the fruit of thy body will I set upon thy throne.[97]

This prayer, made for the sake of a person who stands for humanity, is answered in the Person of the One called "Son of David" by the "woman of Canaan" desperate for her daughter "vexed with a devil,"[98] and called "Jesus, Son of David" by the blind man crying out, "have mercy on me."[99] These persons cry out for all of humanity, demon haunted and blind, for healing and for light. And the promise of deliverance is made to another person called, "son of David," Joseph, who is the shadow and image of the very fatherhood of God, by an angel who gives and explains the sacred name of his foster Child, "JESUS, for he shall save his people from their sins."[100] Of His person, I shall speak more fully in the following chapter.

92. 1 Samuel 26:9.
93. 2 Samuel 23:17.
94. 2 Samuel 18:28.
95. 2 Samuel 18:33.
96. Psalm 132:1.
97. Psalm 132:10–11.
98. Matthew 15:22.
99. Luke 18:38.
100. Matthew 1:20–21.

Jeremiah

God's truth is transmitted through prophets like Jeremiah, who calls us from the desolation of mechanization and ideology to the fountain of living waters, our heart's hope.

I want next to consider timeless, transcendent truth as transmitted through a particular person. The prophetic role is in a sense a paradigm for all humanity: we are all made to receive God's truth. Yet there are individuals through whom it comes to us most especially. We can look to them for light irrespective of how long ago they lived. Such is Jeremiah. The words of his calling are both universal and particular:

> Before I formed thee in the belly I knew thee; and before thou camest forth out of the womb I sanctified thee, and I ordained thee a prophet unto the nations.[101]

It is universal because everyone is known by God from eternity and fashioned by Him in the womb, given even there the grace of a particular vocation, some light to allow into the world, some service to do. It is particular because Jeremiah is a prophet unto the nations: one who carries the burden of receiving God's truth directly and broadcasts it across boundaries and through the centuries. He has the distress and social consequences of being the source of people's discomfort and discombobulation, of being the person through whom the consuming fire that descended on Mount Sinai reaches the hearts of his hearers, as he cries out:

> Be astonished, O ye heavens, at this, and be horribly afraid, be ye very desolate, saith the LORD. For my people have committed two evils; they have forsaken me the fountain of living waters, and hewed them out cisterns, broken cisterns, that can hold no water.[102]

This addresses Israel and her particular forsaking of the Lord, but it is perennial in its call. The whole rationalist mindset of our age tends to shut out mercy that "droppeth as the gentle rain from

101. Jeremiah 1:5.
102. Jeremiah 2:12–13.

heaven/ Upon the place beneath,"[103] to deny the source of the fountain, the Source of life and to seek in its stead "honour one of another,"[104] and oftimes that not even in person but at a remove through a digital simulacrum of a human response. These broken cisterns can never quench the thirst for the Spirit that has been forsaken. The paternally mediated truth of God and the connection with the Creator is not to be had by "saying to a stock, Thou art my father; and to a stone, Thou hast brought me forth."[105] No amount of technological hardware can generate the life of the Spirit; no ideology, however rigidly adhered to, can bring renewal among us.

The denunciation forever linked to Jeremiah's name is indeed salutary for us, but it would not be God's word if it did not also offer hope. The words that follow do this so powerfully that I have witnessed a grown man break down in tears while reading them:

> Behold the days come, saith the LORD, that I will make a new covenant with the house of Israel, and with the house of Judah: Not according to the covenant that I made with their fathers in the day that I took them by the hand to bring them out of the land of Egypt; which my covenant they brake, although I was an husband unto them, saith the LORD: But this shall be the covenant that I will make with the house of Israel: After those days, saith the LORD, I will put my law in their inward parts, and write it in their hearts; and will be their God, and they shall be my people. And they shall teach no more every man his neighbour, and every man his brother, saying, Know the LORD: for they shall know me, from the least of them unto the greatest of them, saith the LORD: for I will forgive their iniquity, and I will remember their sin no more.[106]

This is the promise of God putting His truth directly into each person's heart. It is distinguished from the dispensation in which Moses gave laws and, with the help of others, judged their enforcement. It is a truth given in our "inward parts," that place so deep

103. Shakespeare, *The Merchant of Venice*, Act IV, scene i, lines 185–86.
104. John 5:44.
105. Jeremiah 2:27.
106. Jeremiah 31:31–34.

that it is above all that which ratiocination can reach, that place so high that it knows the very depths of our being, there where all the antinomies meet. Primary among these is the antinomy of "where all the ladders start/ In the foul rag and bone shop of the heart,"[107] where Dmitri Karamazov saw both the ideal of the Madonna and the degradation of Sodom. This is possible, and only possible, by the supreme mercy of God that overlooks the breaking of a spousal covenant, that remembers no more the violations of divine mercy by the proud self-will of the blinded person.

John the Baptist

John announces Christ, bringer of truth. He gives his life in witness to what is true.

The prophet of this mercy, John the Baptist, links the old and the new covenants, for "The law and the prophets were until John: since that time the kingdom of God is preached, and every man presseth into it."[108] Like Jeremiah, John is sanctified in the womb, for therein he leaps in response to the blessed fruit of his mother's cousin,[109] and like Jeremiah he is unsparing in his invective, calling his listeners a "generation of vipers."[110] Yet he also offers hope in the very words of the prophet Isaiah:

> Every valley shall be filled, and every mountain and hill shall be brought straight, and the rough ways shall be made smooth; And all flesh shall see the salvation of God.[111]

The filling, the straightening and the smoothing signify the goal of time, when God is "all in all";[112] the sight of salvation signifies that "the Word was made flesh"[113] and that His "grace and truth"[114]

---

107. W.B. Yeats, "The Circus Animals' Desertion" (https://www.poetryfoundation.org/poems/43299/the-circus-animals-desertion).
108. Luke 16:16.
109. Luke 1:41–42.
110. Luke 3:7.
111. Luke 3:5–6.
112. 1 Corinthians 15:28.
113. John 1:14.
114. John 1:17.

dignify and offer light to every precious treasure of a human person. He is "a burning and shining light"[115] and "much more than a prophet."[116] He is great, but announces an epoch of those who are even greater:

> Among them that are born of women there hath not risen a greater than John the Baptist: notwithstanding he that is least in the kingdom of heaven is greater than he.[117]

He announces the One greater than himself through whom the consuming fire is to come, through whom the cleansing water is given:

> I indeed baptize you with water; but one mightier than I cometh, the latchet of whose shoes I am not worthy to unloose: he shall baptize you with the Holy Ghost and with fire: Whose fan is in his hand, and he will thoroughly purge his floor, and will gather the wheat into his garner; but the chaff he will burn with unquenchable fire.[118]

This is once more the consuming fire that descended on Mount Sinai, which is the destiny of those who do not abide in God's truth "and men gather them, and cast them into the fire, and they are burned."[119] This is the end of suzerainty of the one who "was a murderer from the beginning, and abode not in the truth, because there is no truth in him"[120] and the casting of him into "the lake of fire and brimstone."[121] This is the victory of "all they that have known the truth," that truth "which dwelleth in us, and shall be with us for ever."[122] The Son of David, the Person who is the way, the truth and the life, the one bringing the fire of truth, is announced through the person of the prophet, and He lights that fire in the heart of each person who comes to Him, so that she or he

115. John 5:35.
116. Luke 7:26.
117. Matthew 11:11.
118. Luke 3:16–17.
119. John 15:6.
120. John 8:44.
121. Revelation 20:10.
122. 2 John 1–2.

may do the same for others, so that there is gathering of fire burning away falsehood and illusion and bringing light and warmth to the whole of humanity.

To give personal witness to the truth, as John does, means (again) witnessing that the truth transcends the contingencies and comforts of this world, testifying that it is beyond the antinomy of life and death, that it is present in those who do not insist on one of these poles at the expense of the divine that triumphantly includes them both. It does not bow to the lie that leverages life in the service of death, choosing rather in this contingency death in the service of Life. So John the Baptist, not afraid to speak truth to power, says to Herod, "It is not lawful for thee to have thy brother's wife."[123] The other actors in the drama cannot say, like John and the One he proclaims, "I receive not honour from men":[124] the daughter of Herodias defers to her mother and Herod himself acts "for their sakes which sat with him."[125] Despite knowing that John "was a just man and an holy,"[126] he immediately sends an executioner and commands "his head to be brought."[127] John joins those who "loved not their lives unto the death" and overcame the father of lies "by the blood of the Lamb, and by the word of their testimony."[128]

Peter

Peter witnesses to God's revelation of truth in Christ. All His faithful and their leaders are included in the person of Peter, whose witness is enabled by God's mercy and grace.

Such also is Saint Peter, whose final personal witness to the truth of Christ fulfills His prophecy, "When thou shalt be old, thou shalt stretch forth thy hands, and another shall gird thee, and carry thee whither thou wouldest not."[129] Like Jeremiah, he mediates tran-

---

123. Mark 6:18.
124. John 5:41.
125. Mark 6:26.
126. Mark 6:20.
127. Mark 6:27.
128. Revelation 12:11.
129. John 21:18.

scendent truth. Asked by Jesus, "Whom say ye that I am?" he responds, "Thou art the Christ, the Son of the living God." That this truth has a divine, not a human, origin is clear from the answer of Jesus: "Blessed art thou, Simon Barjona: for flesh and blood hath not revealed it unto thee, but my father in heaven." Like Abraham, he contains a multitude, for he is told also, "Thou art Peter, and upon this rock I will build my church; and the gates of hell shall not prevail against it."[130] He is, as his name implies, a rock, the stable point of reference, for the Church, not because of any firmness of his own—he is to betray Christ after all this—but because the truth he has been given is divine. Making his own the words of the psalm, he can say, "The LORD is my rock."[131] It is God's stability, not his own, that he transmits to the Church. He embodies in his person not only the people whom he leads in his own time, but also those leaders who come after him: each of the Popes of the Church. They, like him, are infirm men who are channels of the firmness of God's revelation of truth. They, like him, are commissioned to nourish with this truth those who are gathered in the Church. "Feed my sheep," Jesus says to him, making this the pledge of Peter's love for Him.[132] Peter contains not only the Popes to come but also all the followers of Christ to come. These share in the truth which Peter received, not simply by reference to him but in their own right, for "no man can say that Jesus is the Lord, but by the Holy Ghost."[133] The truth that Peter, the Popes and all the people of God live by is not at all an arbitrary assertion of self-will, but a gift of God.

As heralded in Jeremiah's announcement of the new covenant, it is given in the context of mercy and forgiveness, given to those who have broken their relationship with God, given to those who can only relate to God through His mercy. There is no abstract systemic truth independent of the human person: there is only divine truth which comes to us personally and through persons, despite the reality that we are weak and wayward. There is no algorithm that will

130. Matthew 16:15–17.
131. Psalm 18:2.
132. John 21:16.
133. 1 Corinthians 12:3.

get the quest for truth right; there are only people who will get it wrong and be forgiven by God who will nonetheless, writing straight with crooked lines, give His truth in and through their persons. That is the meaning of this response to betrayal: "The Lord turned, and looked upon Peter."[134] It is a look of mercy and truth: mercy towards the one who has betrayed Him and a reminder of the truth of His prediction of this betrayal and, finally, the truth that He is indeed "the Christ, the Son of the living God." Only tears can be an adequate response to such mercy, to such truth and "Peter went out, and wept bitterly."[135] The gift of tears, when granted by God, is the essence of our encounter with His mercy and truth.

Having undergone this experience, Peter knows that he needs to be made clean by Jesus, that he was wrong to say, "Thou shalt never wash my feet."[136] Knowing this, his own frailty, he is ready to tell people gathered in Jerusalem about the gift of God's truth in the Holy Spirit, which they have just witnessed in the appearance of "cloven tongues like as of fire,"[137] which they have just experienced in the miracle of understanding crossing the language barrier.[138] He does this in the words of the prophet Joel:

> And it shall come to pass in the last days, saith God, I will pour out of my Spirit upon all flesh: and your sons and your daughters shall prophesy, and your young men shall see visions, and your old men shall dream dreams: And on my servants and on my handmaidens I will pour out in those days of my Spirit, and they shall prophesy.[139]

This prophecy is fulfilled with the gift of the Holy Spirit, which Jesus simply calls, "the promise of my Father"[140] and of which He had said, "He shall teach you all things, and bring all things to your remembrance, whatsoever I have said unto you."[141] It is this Spirit

---

134. Luke 22:61.
135. Luke 22:62.
136. John 13:8.
137. Acts 2:3.
138. Acts 2:6–12.
139. Acts 2:17–18.
140. Luke 24:49.
141. John 14:26.

who brings to mind and guarantees the truth that the disciples have received from Jesus and we from the apostles. Central is not what He said, but what happened to Him in person, the truth that "This Jesus hath God raised up, whereof we all are witnesses."[142] The truth of the death and resurrection of the person of Jesus, told in the person of Peter, reaches persons then and now, as they are "pricked in their heart,"[143] and:

> To hero of Calvary, Christ, 's feet—
> Never ask if meaning it, wanting it, warned of it—men go.[144]

John

Through his gospel, John abides in all contemplatives, who share his intimacy with Christ so entering the life of the Trinity. They too receive the gift of Mary as mother.

Peter's role is a very public one; John's is more personal. Of course, the gospel of Saint John conveys the truth of Christ more explicitly and more widely across the nations and the ages than any other document, and it is central to this book, providing not only the epigraph but much of the substance of the themes and the thinking in it. In this chapter about the Bible, though, I want to focus on the person of John and the personal way he receives the truth of Christ. His person remains in all the persons he contains. At the end of the gospel, Jesus says of him, "I will that he tarry till I come."[145] He abides (a translation of the same Greek word that is rendered as "tarry") still in all who are contemplatives, whose primary calling is to be close to the Lord. That vocation is perennial: what needs to be done varies with the changes of time, but "one thing is needful"[146] in and for itself for all time, and that is closeness to Jesus, "the way,

142. Acts 2:32.
143. Acts 2:37.
144. Gerard Manley Hopkins, "The Wreck of the Deutschland," Stanza 8 (https://www.poetryfoundation.org/poems/44403/the-wreck-of-the-deutschland).
145. John 21:22.
146. Luke 10:42

the truth, and the life."[147] John teaches this by his personal relation to Him: not only indicating that the truth is in His person, but also showing that it is known through personal intimacy with Him. The Evangelist does this by not appearing in the gospel, at least not by name. At the beginning of the gospel two followers of Jesus ask Him, "Where dwellest thou?"[148] Only one is named (Andrew); the other is commonly supposed to be John. The absence of his name makes it possible for the reader to take his place and, through meditation on the gospel, find the same closeness and make the same journey to the truth as he makes. The question just quoted has more than one meaning: it is about where he lives, but also about where he abides eternally: that is, it is a question about eternal life, the central concern of the gospel. Its answer has already been given earlier in the first chapter: Jesus lives "in the bosom of the Father."[149] The gospel is, then, nothing less than an invitation to share in the life of the Holy Trinity, to receive that same truth of God that Jesus has received from His Father. He says, "I have called you friends, for all things that I have heard of my father I have made known to you."[150]

That friendship, and that knowledge, is ours through the gospel. We simply enter the place John has vacated for us. At the Last Supper, "There was leaning on Jesus' bosom one of his disciples, whom Jesus loved."[151] John's name is missing so that we can take his place. If we do that, we are on the bosom of the One who is in the bosom of Father: that is to say, in the intimate life of the Trinity, sharing in the Spirit of Love and Truth who is between the Father and the Son. We also share John's closeness to Mary, whom he looked after in Ephesus after the Ascension, since we are included in what happened when "there stood by the cross of Jesus his mother" and:

> Jesus . . . saw his mother, and the disciple standing by whom he loved, he saith unto his mother, Woman, behold thy son! Then

---

147. John 14:6.
148. John 1:38.
149. John 1:18.
150. John 15:15.
151. John 13:23.

saith he to the disciple, Behold thy mother! And from that hour that disciple took her unto his own home.[152]

Again, the place of the disciple Jesus loved is there for us, and so we can receive Mary as our mother and take her into our home. Mary Magdalene too can be in our lives as the very first to announce the gospel as:

> She runneth, and cometh to Simon Peter, and to the other disciple, whom Jesus loved, and saith unto them, They have taken away the Lord out of the sepulchre, and we know not where they have laid him.[153]

We can also meet the risen Christ, when "Jesus shewed himself again to the disciples at the sea of Tiberias"[154] and "he stood on the shore: but the disciples knew not that it was Jesus."[155] We can witness the catch of "the multitude of fishes" and, together with "that disciple whom Jesus loved," say, "It is the Lord."[156] We can see truth standing before us.

Mary

Mary's calling is unique and universal. She is immaculately true. She contains the One in whom all are contained. She models openness to the Spirit of Truth.

Of course, John is not the person in the Bible who is most intimate with the Lord: that is Mary. Hers is a sovereignly unique vocation, above all others and, unlike those we have been considering, lived without flaw. Yet that same uniqueness makes it universal. This is so in a double sense. It is when we are most particularly ourselves that we are most universally human: it is those writers and artists who have been most true to the depth of their own being who speak to everyone. Mary has this truth, but more than this: there is in her no

152. John 19:25–27.
153. John 20:2.
154. John 21:1.
155. John 21:4.
156. John 21:6–7.

sin and so nothing that comes from her enemy, the father of lies. Sin is a failure to love and therefore separates, distancing us from God and other people; Mary knows no such failure and therefore is close to everyone, sinners especially included. Her vocation is announced in person by an angel:

> And the angel said unto her, Fear not, Mary, for thou hast found favour with God. And behold, thou shalt conceive in thy womb, and bring forth a son, and shalt call his name JESUS. He shall be great, and shall be called the Son of the Highest: and the Lord God shall give unto him the throne of his father David: And he shall reign over the house of Jacob for ever; and of his kingdom there shall be no end.[157]

In His person are included those persons considered above, David and Jacob, and all whom they contain and all the light that comes through them; He is "the light of the world."[158] Yet, in the most literal sense, Mary contains Him. Furthermore, by extension, Mary contains His Body, the Church, of which she is the mother. Her person is the seat of wisdom; through her comes the light of truth; she is the "woman clothed with the sun."[159] The manner in which she accepts her vocation shows us how we can share in that light. The angel tells her, "The Holy Ghost shall come upon thee, and the power of the Highest shall overshadow thee: therefore also that holy thing which shall be born of thee shall be called the Son of God." Mary responds with complete openness, saying "Behold the handmaid of the Lord; be it done to me according to thy word." We can, like her, allow the Holy Spirit to come upon us, "the Spirit of truth,"[160] so that we may know the truth in person by living the life God calls us to live. This is more than knowing about things, it is knowing in the depth of our souls "that holy thing" born of Mary; it is allowing the Truth to live in us; it is growing into ontological truth, in which our very being is true and radiates God's truth. In this we become like Mary. If that seems fanciful, considering her

157. Luke 1:30–33.
158. John 8:12.
159. Revelation 12:1.
160. John 14:17.

unique privilege, here is a word of the Lord to the contrary: "Whosoever shall do the will of my Father which is in heaven, the same is my brother, and sister, and mother."[161]

It is not to be supposed that the Mother of God will be jealous of this: like John, she will want to make space for us. Her essential quality is her humility. She knows that God "hath scattered the proud in the imagination of their hearts. He hath put down the mighty from their seats and exalted them of low degree."[162] That humility means that all generations will call her blessed; it means that in her person is the truth of every human life, stripped of every pretension and distortion of pride; it means that in her is God Himself.

I will be returning to Mary later in this book: here the concern is simply to show how the Bible shows us truth in persons, and she above them all, bar one. That One is, as Saint Jerome observed, in the whole of Scripture, and is Truth incarnate. Before considering more fully the implications of this latter designation, I will leave you with one more reflection from S. L. Frank on how He and His truth are known in the Bible and in the inspirations of the Spirit:

> All particular "words of God," as they are conveyed in the Bible or as they may be "heard" by every man (if he is worthy), are particular manifestations of the Word, Logos, as the expression of the very essence of God, an expression in which His essence acquires for us a living image and likeness (without thereby ceasing to be unknowable). This expression of God—as the Word, in a living image—is that highest and most adequate concrete-positive revelation in which "the Word was made flesh" in the human figure of Jesus Christ.[163]

Let us together receive that revelation.

161. Matthew 12:50.
162. Luke 1:52–53.
163. *The Unknowable*, 234.

C: Christ & Community

Truth in Person

Christ is the truth. The word encompasses what is right in relationship. We find this truth in the encounters with Christ people have in John's gospel. It is stronger than death.

Truth comes to us in the Bible through persons, and above all in the Person of Christ, who says, "I am the way, the truth, and the life,"[1] and, "He that hath seen me hath seen the Father,"[2] seen the very truth of God. He is, says His Apostle, "the image of the invisible God."[3] Yet we cannot arrive at acceptance of these statements by reason alone. The Person we encounter does not derive His truth from us; we derive our truth from Him. That truth is closely bound up with life; God is the God of the living, not the dead and He did not make death. Our truth and our life come from Him, for "all things were made by him."[4] His Truth is our life. The living truth cannot be conceptually cut-and-dried, for then it would no longer live. We cannot pin it down, for it is the play of opposites: of joy and sorrow, of strength and weakness, of victory and defeat. The One who is the Truth is also the Resurrection and the Life. That Truth and that Life are self-validating, "for as the Father hath life in himself; so hath he given to the Son to have life in himself."[5] The Truth is validated in the Person who speaks; the Life is validated in the Person who rises from the dead. The whole of Saint John's gospel is crafted to lead to an encounter with that Truth, that Life, that Person. It facilitates a handing over of the enterprise of being sure of the vivifying Truth from the self-will to Him. In other words, it

1. John 14:6.
2. John 14:9.
3. Colossians 1:15.
4. John 1:3.
5. John 5:26.

guides us to faith in Him so that believing we "might have life through his name,"[6] for He is the way to truth and so life.

Truth in this gospel is more than what is implied by the Greek word *aletheia* (ἀλήθεια). In its semitic context truth is always in relationship: it is something done, kept, practised—not abstract. Joseph Gebhardt-Klein, the distinguished scholar of Hebrew, Syriac, and Aramaic, observes:

> The Hebrew (and Syriac/Aramaic) conception of "truth" is insep-
> arable from the concept of rightfulness and "what is right," or
> morally proper, within a relation of two subjects. The common
> assumption of a universal "amoral facticity" as perceived and con-
> strued through secularist paradigm is not the Hebraic truth of
> either Biblical or Rabbinical Judaism.[7]

The gospel's author's familiarity with Hebrew and Aramaic thought will have influenced his use of the concept of truth so that it carries a multifaceted meaning, encompassing notions of authenticity, reliability, faithfulness, and ultimate reality. It conveys the idea of something that is genuine, trustworthy, and in accordance with God's nature, corresponding with the sense of the Hebrew word *emet*, which conveys the idea of reliability, stability, and faithfulness, as does the closely related Aramaic term *emeth*. This truth is not only a concept, but also a communal reality.

We enter it through the persons who encounter Jesus in the gospel of John. The woman of Samaria, to whom He speaks of "living water,"[8] says, "I perceive that thou art a prophet" when He tells her her marital situation.[9] If she thinks of this water as a way of saving labor, we are led to understand it as the Spirit who will give us "everlasting life,"[10] identified later in the gospel as "the Spirit of truth."[11] Simon Peter's declaration of faith takes us closer to Jesus as the source of life. He says, "Thou hast the words of eternal life. And we

6. John 20:31.
7. Personal communication.
8. John 4:10.
9. John 4:17–19.
10. John 4:14.
11. John 16:13.

believe and are sure that thou art that Christ, the Son of the living God."[12] Life has already been identified with light in the first chapter of the gospel, when it is said about Jesus: "In him was life; and the life was the light of men."[13] The life and truth of Jesus illuminate human existence, make sense of it. Light comes from life and truth, from a life truly lived. Jesus, Truth in Person, lives His life most truly and so can say, "I am the light of the world"[14] and exemplify this by giving sight to the man who was born blind. This latter echoes the Samaritan woman, saying, "He is a prophet."[15] And as she says, "Is this not the Christ?"[16] and as those of her city who encounter him say, "We have heard him ourselves, and know that this is indeed the Christ, the Savior of the world,"[17] so the once-blind man responds to the question, "dost thou believe on the Son of God?" with the declaration, "I believe" and worships Him.[18] Jesus in and of Himself convinces people that He is the Son of the living God.

The truth of His life, filiated by the living God, is manifested as more than light for the blind: it is also life for the dead. He declares, "I am the resurrection, and the life: he that believeth in me, though he were dead, yet shall he live: And whosoever liveth and believeth in me shall never die." Asked whether she believes this, Martha responds, "Yea, Lord: I believe that thou art the Christ, the Son of God."[19] The justice of this belief in Jesus as resurrection and life is shown when Lazarus, four days dead, comes forth at His command, evidencing the truth of His prayer to the living God, "I thank thee that thou hast heard me."[20] It is the very author of the gospel, however, who first comes to believe that Jesus in His own person has conquered death, and so darkness and the untruth which does not share in the eternal unforgetting. He does so in the empty sepul-

12. John 6:68–69.
13. John 1:4.
14. John 9:5.
15. John 9:17.
16. John 4:29.
17. John 4:42.
18. John 9:35–38.
19. John 11:25–27.
20. John 11:41.

cher, where "he saw and believed." Direct evidence of the resurrection, the presence of Jesus in person, is first given to Mary Magdalene. Significantly, she recognizes Him when addressed personally: "Jesus saith unto her, Mary. She turned herself, and saith unto him, Rabboni; which is to say, Master."[21] He is Teacher of Truth, which is to say, Master of Life. She is His apostle to His disciples. They know the truth of her words when, even though they are behind shut doors, He is there in person among them. He gives them His peace and shows them His person, in particular "his hands and his side."[22] Thomas, like the reader of the gospel, is not there and it is he who utters the culminating declaration of faith in Jesus, responding to the invitation to touch His hands and to put his hand in His side, with the words, "My Lord and my God."[23] Jesus is God and "God is light;"[24] He is light, radiating the Truth of God; He is Truth, embodying the life of God. Readers are invited to share in this vivifying truth in a special way: "Blessed are they that have not seen, and yet have believed."[25]

Christ before Pilate

Pilate asks what truth is without realizing it stands before him in Christ, inviting acceptance. It suffers violence in His person, but is triumphant in the resurrection.

In contrast to this sequence of persons and confessions of faith is Pontius Pilate. He asks the rational question, "What is truth?"[26] But reason divides and separates what contemplation sees clearly. Here Pilate is dividing himself from his responsibility to act according to the truth, a separation enacted when "he took water, and washed his hands before the multitude."[27] He actually knows the truth of Christ's innocence. His wife has said, "Have thou nothing to do

21. John 20:16.
22. John 20:19–20.
23. John 20:28.
24. 1 John 1:5.
25. John 20:29.
26. John 18:38.
27. Matthew 27:24.

with that just man: for I have suffered many things this day in a dream because of him."[28] He says himself, "I find no fault in him."[29] He is made "more afraid" by being told "by our law he ought to die."[30] He realizes he is becoming complicit in injustice, violating the truth. The Truth is standing before him in person. This is implicit in the Latin text of his question "What is truth?", *quid est veritas*, which is an anagram of *est vir qui adest*, "It is the man who is present." His mistake, which is the mistake of "enlightenment" thinking, is to make himself the point of reference, the one who ascertains what truth is, rather than receiving truth as a gift from its source. In a sense of course he is right to do this, for he is "on the judgment seat"[31] and has power given "from above";[32] but he is wrong to do violence to the truth, both metaphorically in his false judgment and literally in scourging and delivering to crucifixion the truth in person. He gives in to the perennial political temptation to prefer avoidance of danger—the potential violence of the mob is a threat to his reputation and perhaps his position as governor—to allowing truth, and indeed Truth, to govern him. He is not fit to judge truth, for truth "only doth judge itself," as Francis Bacon wrote. The latter continued:

> The inquiry of truth, which is the love-making or wooing of it; the knowledge of truth, which is the presence of it; and the belief of truth, which is the enjoying of it, is the sovereign good of human nature.

It follows that the "depraved judgments and affections" of those like "jesting Pilate" who "would not stay for an answer" to his question are actually self-harming in their violation of truth. Humanity is terribly one and we harm ourselves when we act against "the sovereign good of human nature."[33] There is an irony here in that Bacon,

28. Matthew 27:19.
29. John 19:4.
30. John 19:7.
31. Matthew 27:19.
32. John 19:11.
33. Francis Bacon, *Of Truth* (https://fountainheadpress.com/expandingthearc/assets/francisbacontruth.pdf).

who is eloquently clear-sighted in this essay, was a pioneer of the epistemology that proclaimed "knowledge is power" and went on in practice to subordinate truth and its contemplation to the exercise of dominance rather in the manner of Pilate, who preferred being governor to being truthful.

Making Christ the point of reference in seeking truth is the alternative to subordinating truth to power. He is the radically powerless one, who is silent before Pilate, who suffers with reproach, who dies rather than renounce the cup His father has given Him to drink. That is, in the most divine antinomy, what omnipotence looks like. That is the power to do whatever you like; that is freedom. This is explicit in Christ's promise about following His teaching:

> If ye continue in my word, then are ye my disciples indeed; And ye shall know the truth, and the truth shall make you free.[34]

Reason, as I explained in Chapter A, cannot reach truth in its own strength: it always has to start with a premise that it does not itself establish. In essence, it needs a self-authenticating starting-point. Christ is such. He transforms the meaning of truth in His very person. It becomes for us no longer a teaching or doctrine, but is rather a person, *His* person. And we find truth by becoming a person like Him; indeed, more than that, we find truth by sharing the life of Christ. Yet, this too is not saying enough: Truth finds us, not the other way around, and Christ shares His life with us, more than we with Him. Truth is inextricably a truthful *life*: it cannot be something desiccated and held at arm's length for our inspection. Truth and life are necessary concomitants. And we only live truly when Christ shares His life with us.[35]

That is His mission. He says, "To this end was I born, and for this cause came I into the world, that I should bear witness unto the truth." It is a question of listening to Him. To do that, we need to have some sense of truth, however obscure. With it, we can hear, for

---

34. John 8:31–32.
35. This paragraph is indebted to Robert Slesinski, *Pavel Florensky: A Metaphysics of Love* (Yonkers, NY: St. Vladimir's Seminary Press, 1984), 150.

He testifies, "Every one that is of the truth heareth my voice."[36] We can only do this through the Spirit of truth, for "no man can say that Jesus is the Lord, but by the Holy Ghost."[37] It depends however not only on interior inspiration but also on exterior witness. The gospel of John is very clear about the truthfulness of its author, "the disciple which testifieth of these things, and wrote these things": it says, "We know that his testimony is true."[38] The explicit witness to the crucifixion is equally emphatic: "He that saw it bare record and his record is true: and he knoweth that he saith true, that ye might believe."[39] Again, though, it is a matter of self-validating truth. It can be no other way. This truth cannot be calculated, it can only be received. And it takes courage to receive it: conformity will not lead a person there, nor will the sort of academic research in which one puts away one's books at the end of a day's study to engage in a convivial get together in a life which has nothing to do with it. For it costs all that we have. The truth of Jesus's powerlessness is evidence of that. To receive it we need to be willing, if need be, to leave the realm in which reason operates, the kingdom of this world where time and space is all that there is. His kingdom is "not of this world"[40] and those who have been the supreme witnesses of it, the martyrs, have been ready to leave this world.

In the end, it is a stand-off between truth and violence, which is to say between truth and lies, between life and death, between light and darkness. Which wins depends on whether life is true, in the sense implied by the Greek noun *aletheia* (ἀλήθεια), meaning that which does not succumb to Lethe, the river in which all is forgotten. If death is in perpetuity lethal, extinguishing all hope beyond it, then power as expressed in violence has leverage to enforce lies. If the life which is "the light of men"[41] conquers death, then "the light shineth in darkness,"[42] which cannot swallow it up: the truth of life

36. John 18:37.
37. 1 Corinthians 12:3.
38. John 21:24.
39. John 19:35.
40. John 18:36.
41. John 1:4.
42. John 1:5.

is eternal. The truth of the resurrection first proclaimed by Saint Mary Magdalene is the source of truth: the self-validating Truth in person stands before her and calls her by her name. The whole burden and song of John's gospel transmits this Truth and the concomitant truth that through Him we have "everlasting life."[43] This life, lived in Him, is our personal (though not private) truth and also universal truth, for in Him all live. Skepticism about truth and its possibility arises when we look for it in the wrong place: in what is dead. So the left-brain strategies of getting fixed plans of reality for the purposes of practical action will give us truth only in a provisional and temporary sense, never as something that endures like the Ancient of Days. Indeed, all attempts to situate truth in this passing world only will fail: although if contemplated in its depth it will speak to us of what is beyond, in itself it will pass away. Shakespeare offers his beloved memory in this world —"So long as men can breathe or eyes can see,/ So long lives this, and this gives life to thee"[44]—but this is not eternal and nor is it really life.

It has some relation to the eternal though, for it is born of love, which "never faileth."[45] The same cannot be said for what passes for the verifiable in our world: documentation completed, procedures followed, algorithms at work. Indeed, the scientific method underpinning them guarantees their lack of full truth, for it is based on what can be repeated and so is a slave to certainty. Yet only what is dead and past is certain. Life remains open, uncertain, and truth is alive. Precisely defined truth is a story wrecked by plot spoilers, a dead thing, artificially intelligent with the data of yesteryear. Real truth is lived in the person who can do we know not what and to whom the totally unexpected can happen. Without these uncertainties there could be no stories worth listening to and no life that is any fun.

In the gospel, God has in a sense given us a plot spoiler, like that given more directly to Julian of Norwich, "All shall be well." Yet there is enough for each one of us in our personal story to keep us

43. John 3:16.
44. Sonnet 18.
45. 1 Corinthians 13:8.

90

within the narrative, with any prolepsis only partial and "through a glass darkly."[46] Generally, we do not have an overview: that is for what is dead and we are alive. The life of Jesus shares this quality of being lived in darkness yet leading to light. With the agony in the garden, the anguished thirst on the cross and the brutal death, it is not a children's story. And yet we are told, "Verily I say unto you, Except ye be converted, and become as little children, ye shall not enter the kingdom of heaven."[47] Was Wordsworth right to say in his poem that the vision of childhood fades "into the light of common day"?[48] Is the child's expectation of a happy ending a spiritual insight into what is beyond this world, fading from our view as we get older and more worldly? Do we recover it through faith when we believe that "all things work together for good to them that love God"?[49] Jesus seems to imply as much when He says, "Your sorrow shall be turned into joy"[50] and "your heart shall rejoice, and your joy no man taketh from you."[51] The gladness of the resurrection is in one sense beyond and outside the story, but it can shine as a light guiding us toward it and lighting with meaning that through which we pass. And if we share the life of Christ, there is only really one story. Our life within it is framed by the scene of Christ before Pilate, Truth before temporizing, innocence before complicity.

This is pictured in the image on the front cover of this book. Truth is vulnerable and hemmed in by power and violence. Christ's naked foot, soon to be pierced, is enclosed by the booted feet of the man guarding Him, who has raised a fist as if in readiness to strike Him. Behind Him are more guards and weaponry. No person is looking at Christ. The guards, the power on the left side of Him, are looking to Pilate. Pilate himself is looking either at the chief guard, or into the middle distance to avoid facing the Truth. A woman on

46. 1 Corinthians 13:12.

47. Matthew 18:3.

48. William Wordsworth, *Ode on Intimations of Immortality from Recollections of Early Childhood* (https://www.poetryfoundation.org/poems/45536/ode-intimations-of-immortality-from-recollections-of-early-childhood).

49. Romans 8:28.

50. John 16:20.

51. John 16:22.

his other side is there to comfort him and a man is pouring water over his hands, as if in parody of the server washing the hands of the priest about to offer the sacrifice of the Mass. Only the dog, in its animal innocence, is turned towards Christ, though it may be looking at its master the guard. Christ's clothing is subdued in color, by contrast with that of the other people there. His eyes are cast down and His blood-spattered face ashen and pale. Yet His halo is brighter and more prominent than all the fine furnishings. It is a double echo: it mirrors the downward curve of Pilate's chain of office and also the crown of thorns around His head. Perhaps it is more precise to say the thorns are a reflection of the power indicated by the chain and the halo is the outgrowth of the thorns. Faced with power, Truth suffers; through suffering comes light. In the words of Nicholas Berdyaev, "Christianity is the religion of Truth crucified."[52] And it is also the religion of the light that comes through that.

The Light of the World

Christ is light; in Him we can become light and see truly through purity of heart. Our light is known by our love for others.

Truth is naked on the cross. There is "darkness over all the land,"[53] yet here is "the light of the world"[54] who said, "And I, if I be lifted up from the earth, will draw all men unto me."[55] And so He does, for the crown of thorns is the halo of light; the darkness of the earth is the light of heaven; the lifting up in the dark disgrace of the cross is the being raised up in the glorious dawn of the resurrection. And light is self-authenticating: every object is seen by means of light, light is seen by itself. "God is light"[56] and is the self-authenticating Truth and ground of every veridical use of reason. This Light, this Truth draws us to Himself when we are in darkness and distress; this Person says to us, "I am come a light into the world that whoso-

---

52. *The End of Our Time* (New York, NY: Sheed & Ward, 1935), 164.
53. Matthew 27:45.
54. John 8:12.
55. John 12:32.
56. 1 John 1:5.

ever believeth on me should not abide in darkness."[57] In William Blake's prophetic words:

> God Appears & God is Light
> To those poor Souls who dwell in Night
> But does a Human Form Display
> To those who Dwell in Realms of Day.[58]

The light comes to the dark heart; the illumined heart is led to Light (the Light of Truth) in Person; He shows those who live in light Divine Truth in human form. They can see this because they are illumined and can know that He is the Truth.

Yet what is sought is not simply seeing the light, it is not just being illuminated so that we can see the Truth in Person: it is becoming the light. So Saint Paul writes to the Ephesians, "Ye were sometimes darkness, but now are ye light in the Lord." This being light, he points out, means that they should "walk as children of light." [59] That involves avoiding certain behaviors—"the unfruitful works of darkness"[60]—which are identified as such by the light, for "all things that are reproved are made manifest by the light."[61] The concomitance of light and right living enables a person to know God, for like knows like. Living truly makes possible knowing God's truth. The tendency of our own time is to try to abstract the person from the knowing, for knowing truly is costly since it shows up the person who knows:

> And this is condemnation, that light is come into the world, and men loved darkness rather than the light, because their deeds were evil. For every one that does evil hateth the light, neither cometh to the light, lest his deeds should be reproved. But he that doeth truth cometh to the light.[62]

---

57. John 12:46.
58. Blake, *Auguries of Innocence* (https://www.poetryfoundation.org/poems/43650/auguries-of-innocence).
59. Ephesians 5:8.
60. Ephesians 5:11.
61. Ephesians 5:13.
62. John 3:19–21.

Coming to the light is knowing oneself truthfully. This involves accepting our flaws, for "if we say we have not sinned, we make him a liar, and his word is not in us."[63] These home truths are perhaps relevant to a certain kind of skepticism about truth, which may, at root, be a rationalizing of a hatred of the light. A proud refusing of truth can be linked to a refusal to acknowledge it.

Conversely, humility is the context in which truth becomes apparent. This is so in the obvious sense that if we do not assume we know something we are more likely to find it out, but also in the deeper sense that a person who has humility is thereby open to the light of God's truth. Such was Moses, of whom it is written that he was "very meek, above all the men which were upon the face of the earth,"[64] who received "tables of testimony, tables of stone, written with the finger of God"[65] and whose converse with God was so unselfconscious that he "wist not that the skin of his face shone while he talked with him."[66] Such receiving of light is the primary human need, and Daniel prays for it in the time of the desolations of Jerusalem: "O our God, hear the prayer of thy servant and his supplications, and cause thy face to shine upon thy sanctuary that is desolate, for the Lord's sake."[67] This light of God's face can only be received by or through a human person, and a human person is ultimately desolate without it. To receive it, a person needs purity of heart, for "Blessed are the pure of heart: for they shall see God."[68] Saint Macarius the Great, the fourth-century monk and hermit, purified his heart in the asceticism of the desert and bore this witness to the purification:

> When man broke the commandment, the devil covered his whole soul with a dark curtain. For this reason, grace finally comes and removes the whole cover, so that the soul, having become pure and having apprehended its proper nature, this irreproachable

63. 1 John 1:10.
64. Numbers 12:3.
65. Exodus 31:18.
66. Exodus 34:29.
67. Daniel 9:17.
68. Matthew 5:8.

and pure creation, always remains pure and with pure eyes contemplates the glory of the Holy Light and True Sun of Truth shining in the heart itself.[69]

The labor of purification involves concentrating the entire being in the heart, so that the heart becomes attentive through the concentration of the mind in it, vigilant through the concentration of the will in it and chaste through the concentration of feeling in it. Those without such purification do not have awareness in their heart, so that "they seeing see not; and hearing they hear not, neither do they understand";[70] they do not have love in their heart, so that with Peter they merit the Lord's reproach, "Could ye not watch with me one hour?";[71] they do not have desire in their heart, so that they look "on a woman to lust after her."[72] Without awareness, love and desire the "heart is waxed gross"[73] and dark.

Nonetheless, sometimes it can be given to one who is not fully purified to see this light in another person. Here is an eye-witness account of one who conversed with Saint Seraphim of Sarov:

> Imagine in the middle of the sun, dazzling in the brilliance of its noontide rays, the face of the man who is speaking to you. You can see the movements of his lips, the changing expression of his eyes. You can hear his voice; you can feel his hands holding you by the shoulders. But you can see neither those hands nor his body nor yourself. You can see nothing except a blinding light, which shines around, lighting up with its brilliance the snow-covered meadow and the snowflakes, which continue to fall unceasingly on me and the great elder.[74]

This unearthly light is that spoken of by Saint Augustine. This is his account of entering, with God's help, into his inmost self:

> I entered and beheld with the eye of my soul (such as it was), above the same eye of my soul, above my mind, the Light

69. *The Pillar and Ground of the Truth*, 72.
70. Matthew 13:13.
71. Matthew 26:40.
72. Matthew 5:28.
73. Matthew 13:15.
74. *The Pillar and Ground of the Truth*, 76.

95

Unchangeable. Not this ordinary light, which all flesh may look upon, nor as it were a greater of the same kind, as though the brightness of this should be manifold brighter, and with its greatness take up all space. Not such was this light, but other, yea, far other from these. Nor was it above my soul, as oil is above water, nor yet as heaven above earth: but above to my soul because it made me; and I below It, because I was made by It. He that knows the Truth knows what the Light is; and he knows It, knows eternity, Love knoweth it. O Truth Who art Eternity! and Love who art Truth! and Eternity Who art Love![75]

This light can sometimes be perceived by one who does not radiate it because the boundaries of the stubbornly self-sufficient ego have been overcome by the one from whom it shines. Although the ascetic labor of purifying the heart and concentrating the powers of soul there involves solitude, this solitude is the means to overcoming separation from others. The light shining through Saint Seraphim was perceived by another because the saint had overcome the egotistical narrowness that is the common lot of fallen man: he had the expanded heart of one running in the way of God's commandments of which Saint Benedict writes in the prologue to his rule. Ceaseless socializing is not the same as unselfishness: the higher truth beyond the apparent opposition between closeness to other people and solitude is that being alone with God allows into the heart His light in which all are seen as siblings.

Loving others as such is indeed an indication of there being light within, for "he that loveth his brother abideth in the light, and there is none occasion of stumbling in him."[76] To claim light without such love is to lie and *ipso facto* not to have the light of truth: "he that saith that he is in the light, and hateth his brother, is in darkness even until now."[77] Such enmity-bred deprivation of light leads a person astray: "he that hateth his brother is in darkness, and walketh in darkness, and knoweth not whither he goeth, because that darkness has blinded his eyes."[78] It works both ways: loving

75. Ibid., 79, quoting E.B. Pusey's translation of *The Confessions*.
76. 1 John 2:10.
77. 1 John 2:9.
78. 1 John 2:11.

others allows God's light into the heart; allowing God's light into the heart enables loving others. In God's light the opposition between being separated from people and being united with people is overcome: they are as the rhythm of breathing, drawing in the Holy Spirit of truth and love and breathing It out to others; they are as the beat of the heart taking in the Precious Blood which is perfect love and giving the chalice of this love to siblings.

Mount Tabor

The transfiguration shows Christ's light, which is eternal. We can work at receiving this light by prayer and self-discipline.

This truth and love is costly. Pilate is not prepared to pay the political price for standing by the truth of Jesus' innocence. Jesus Himself pays the ultimate price for His "witness unto the truth"[79] and for loving His own "unto the end."[80] And He warns His disciples of this cost, saying, "If any man will come after me, let him deny himself, and follow me."[81] However, immediately after telling of the cost to Himself and His disciples He shows that He is indeed the light of the world and truth in person, giving them courage to face what is to happen to Him and strengthening His followers in their commitment to truth and love for all time. He takes His inner circle, Peter, James and John up "a high mountain apart" (reflecting Moses on Mount Sinai), symbolizing and effecting communication with heaven. Here, He is "transfigured before them," His face "shining as the sun" and His clothes "white as the light."[82] This light which transfigures Him is the eternal light: unlike His suffering, it does not pass with time. It is a light that can embolden His followers to say with Saint Paul, "I reckon that the sufferings of this present time are not worthy to be compared with the glory which shall be revealed to us."[83] There are three indicators that it is eternal light.

79. John 18:37.
80. John 13:1.
81. Matthew 16:24.
82. Matthew 17:1–2.
83. Romans 8:18.

First, He says to His disciples, "Verily I say unto you, There be some standing here, which shall not taste of death, till they see the Son of man coming in his kingdom."[84] The context of this makes clear that these "some" are Peter, James and John, for the very next verse in the gospel is about them being taken up the mountain. It cannot mean that they will not die before the glory of the Eternal Man erupts in time in His second coming, for He has not yet come again and they have died. Yet they do see Him in the light of His glory, for that glory is eternal and so identical on Mount Tabor and in the Parousia when Christ returns to judge the world: that is the way the prediction makes sense. The second indicator that it is eternal is that with him appear "Moses and Elias talking with him."[85] They lived their lives in an earlier time than He did, yet in undivided atemporal eternity they are with Him: past, present and future are one in eternity. Finally there is the voice from the "bright cloud,"[86] like the cloud that covered "the tent of the congregation" of the people of Israel when "the glory of the LORD filled the tabernacle."[87] The voice that speaks from this cloud is that of the eternal God saying, "This is my beloved Son, in whom I am well pleased; hear ye him."[88] Divinely identified as divine, His light is manifestly that of "the only true God."[89]

When Jesus comes down "to the multitude"[90] from His transfiguration on Mount Tabor, He finds His disciples have failed to cure a demon-possessed boy. They want to know why, and He replies:

Because of your unbelief: for verily I say unto you, If ye have faith as a grain of mustard seed, ye shall say unto this mountain, Remove hence to yonder place; and it shall remove; and nothing shall be impossible for you. Howbeit this kind goeth not out but by prayer and fasting.[91]

84. Matthew 16:28.
85. Matthew 17:3.
86. Matthew 17:5.
87. Exodus 40:34.
88. Matthew 17:5.
89. John 17:3.
90. Matthew 17:14.
91. Matthew 17:20–21.

Out of context this makes little sense: there are many records of miracles in Christian history, but even the holiest of saints appear not to have moved mountains. The context, however, provides a coherent sense. "This mountain" is Mount Tabor, the one He has just come down from, and which may be indicated by a gesture. In its context, it stands for the vision of Jesus as God, filled with divine light. In essence, Jesus is saying to His disciples that with a little faith they could see Him as God and in some sense have that mountain experience of Him suffused and illuminated with the Truth of God. And to have that vision is to have light oneself. In Berdyaev's words, "Truth, the one integral truth, is God, and to perceive Truth, is to enter divine life."[92] That does not mean that one instantly becomes one with Truth incarnate. That life develops over time. The Russian theologian just quoted gives a pertinent explanation of why Jesus did not reply to Pilate's question, 'What is truth?': "He was Truth, but Truth which is to be divined and discovered through the whole course of history. Truth is surely not knowledge which conforms to some reality which is outside man."[93] The light of truth comes with work to do: to make true the life of an individual human person. That starts with true faith in Jesus and includes living according to true morality, analogously to the way a fashioning of the object of some craft is true, and the true awareness of prudence which takes into account reality as it is. This being made true is a work that involves asceticism, or discipline, since the natural tendency is to have confidence only in what is immediately apparent, to consider one's desires as divine directives and to mistake one's wishes for reality. It also requires openness to God. That is why Jesus says, "this kind goeth not out but by prayer and fasting": the work of prayer and ascetical discipline is needed for a person to become truthful enough to confront the father of lies. Cleverness in reasoning and academic expertise can offer only what in comparison with this presence of the eternal is a very subordinate truth: the

---

92. Berdyaev, *Christian Existentialism: A Berdyaev Anthology*, trans. Donald A. Lowrie (London: George Allen & Unwin Ltd, 1965), 159.

93. Ibid., 163.

fullness of truth is in a living human person alone, for truth entails mystery, divine mystery.

The light of truth is perceived by Saint Seraphim's interlocutor and by Saint Augustine in himself because they have entered that mystery through prayer and self-discipline. The link between truth and mystery is captured by a contemporary novelist who implicitly compares a man "with no centre, who might be nudged in any direction, depending" with a woman "who had worn no masks and was therefore almost impossible to understand."[94] The man who lies constructs a "truth" and this narrative of his own fabrication can be read: it all passes over his face "second by second, like weather"[95] in contrast to the face of an honest person, which is "impenetrable because so much itself."[96] The difference is that the former is limited because it is self-constructed and the latter is open to God's truth and so unlimited. It is the difference between a particular object, which is bounded by form and dimension and only able to show us itself (though not by its own illumination) and light itself, which can show us anything. It is the difference between someone who is not himself because he is putting on an act and someone who is herself because she accepts her being from God.

We become light-filled persons, open to all truth, by following Him who says, "I am the light of the world: he that followeth me shall not walk in darkness, but shall have the light of life."[97] His intention that we should realize our calling as such is clear from Him also saying, "Ye are the light of the world."[98] This realization is a process, that of becoming clear-sighted, for, "The light of the body is the eye: if therefore thine eye be single, thy whole body shall be full of light."[99] It is the eye of the heart that is in question: it is a matter of becoming one of those who are "pure in heart" and "shall

94. Zadie Smith, *The Fraud* (New York, NY: Penguin Random House, 2023), 112–13.
95. Ibid., 113.
96. Ibid., 112.
97. John 8:12.
98. Matthew 5:14.
99. Matthew 6:22.

see God."[100] In our natural, fallen, state we do not see God, being on the contrary focused on private, temporal advantage. We are led by errant desires and so have clouded vision, mistaking darkness for light. That is darkness indeed, for "if thine eye be evil, thy whole body shall be full of darkness. If therefore the light that is in thee be darkness, how great is that darkness!"[101] Yet we can nonetheless learn to walk "as children of light,"[102] that is to say as children of the God who is light and in whom is "no darkness at all."[103] Saint Peter, as an eyewitness to the glorious majesty of Christ on Mount Tabor, guides us in this learning, writing, "We have also a more sure word of prophecy; whereunto ye do well that ye take heed, as unto a light that shineth in a dark place, until the day dawn, and the day star arise in your hearts."[104] The "sure word" is God's word in Holy Scripture: that is our illumination. Meditating on it and offering prayer illuminated by it informs our once-dark hearts so that they become as Bethlehem in the darkness of which "the light shineth in darkness"[105] and full of peace and "good will toward men."[106] Such light is in the heart of the saints: like John the Baptist, who first pointed out Christ our light, every saint is "a burning and shining light."[107] Such is the light of heaven where "they need no candle, neither light of the sun; for the Lord God giveth them light."[108]

Communion

Christ's truth and light is given to us through our communion with Him and with others. This is undying life.

As we have seen, as well as denoting truth, this light is closely identified with life: hence Jesus says of His followers, "I am come that

100. Matthew 5:8.
101. Matthew 6:23.
102. Ephesians 5:8.
103. 1 John 1:5.
104. 2 Peter 1:19.
105. John 1:5.
106. Luke 2:14.
107. John 5:35.
108. Revelation 22:5.

they might have life, and they might have it more abundantly."[109] He is "the way, the truth, and the life"[110] as well as "the light of the world"[111] and so it is through knowing Him that we find light, truth and life. Such is the indication of His prayer, "This is life eternal, that they might know thee the only true God, and Jesus Christ, whom thou hast sent."[112] That knowing comes through the assiduous practice of prayer and also simply through His gift of His life, and His truth, and His self in sacramental communion. Here, with us always "even unto the end of the world,"[113] is the self-authenticating subject that reason alone cannot provide, the One who has "life in himself,"[114] the One who is Truth in Person. To know truth, we need to share His life. Truth is announced to us by Him communicating His word to us; we find truth in sharing His life by communicating in His Body and Blood. This communion is incorporation in the Word made flesh, participation in the Meaning of human life, illumination by the Light of the world. It is as much a communion of love as of truth. Our knowledge of any person is limited without love, for only love allows her or him fully to be who she or he is: mere knowledge will be rather a servant of our own gratification or purposes. Love alone allows the other person to be in her or his own right and not as a hazard or annoyance to be controlled or as a personal convenience to be exploited. How much more is this the case with the One who is love and truth in one single person. To receive the Omnipotent with a love that is generous enough not to insist on escaping particular trials or having particular consolations is to participate "through a glass, darkly"[115] in His omniscience.

And it is to have true life. He says, "Except ye eat the flesh of the Son of man, and drink his blood, ye have no life in you."[116] This is

---

109. John 10:10.
110. John 14:6.
111. John 8:12.
112. John 17:3.
113. Matthew 28:20.
114. John 5:26.
115. 1 Corinthians 13:12.
116. John 6:53.

"an hard saying"[117] because we naturally suppose that the test of truth is correspondence to our desire to have something or to avoid something. The whole of modern scientist epistemology is built on this presumption. It asks the question, "Does this knowledge get something (or someone) to do, or not do, what we want to be done or not done?" If so, it can be recorded in a learned paper and filed on a shelf in a university library or an online source. This is a different, and lesser, truth than that Truth who says, "I AM THAT I AM,"[118] and invites a sharing in that which includes all being, not limited by the attraction or aversion of the moment. And it is the latter that gives life, for life is precisely openness to all that is, a readiness for adventure, an enjoyment of mystery. And so Saint Peter, when invited to go away with those who were basically just after bread, replies, "Lord, to whom shall we go? thou hast the words of eternal life."[119]

This, true, life is a shared life. Nicolas Kabasilas, the fourteenth-century Archbishop of Salonika, gives us apt similes for the sharing:

> The role of the sacrament of communion in the Church is not a symbolic one, but can be likened to the role of the heart in the body, the role of the roots of a tree, or (as the Lord said) the role of the vine with respect to the grapes; for what we have here is not similarity of name, but true identity, since the sacrament is the body and blood of Christ.[120]

The images are all organic; the heart, the roots and the vine all give life. In the last instance, the point is emphasized by the words of Christ:

> Abide in me, and I in you. As the branch cannot bear fruit of itself, except it abide in the vine; no more can ye, except ye abide in me.[121]

The abiding is life, eternal life. To share that life is to be fruitful, not

---

117. John 6:60.
118. Exodus 3:14.
119. John 6:68.
120. Florensky, *The Meaning of Idealism*, 63.
121. John 15:4.

to share it is to be "cast forth as a branch."[122] Christ identifies with us so that we may embody His life, truth and light:

> For as the body is one, and hath many members, and all the members of that one body, being many, are one body: so also is Christ.[123]

Truth is not individualized: René Descartes, lying all morning in bed, struggles to find it through his reasoning mind: it is not there, it is between or among people. "For where two or three are gathered together in my name, there am I in the midst of them." There is the Truth in person; there is the Light of the world.

There is a striking illustration of this in the miracle that took place in 1411 in Austria. A thief had stolen a consecrated Host from a church in the town of Weiten-Raxendorf and hidden it in one of his gloves. He galloped off, but before he could reach his destination his horse stopped, refusing all efforts to make him move. Suddenly the animal took off at great speed and the Host dropped to the ground without anybody noticing. A few days later "Mrs Scheck from Mannersdorf passed by the spot and saw the Host encircled in a strong light. In great wonder, she picked it up and noticed that the consecrated Host was broken in two parts but remained joined together by threads of bleeding flesh."[124] The two parts were united by the sacrifice of Christ and they had the same shared light of Christ, the Truth in person.

Priesthood

Christ's priesthood makes present light and truth. His priests personally participate in this, sacramentally linking heaven and earth, and all His faithful have a share in it.

That light and truth becomes present in the world through the priesthood of Christ: "this man, because he continueth ever, hath an

---

122. John 15:6.
123. 1 Corinthians 12:12.
124. www.miracolieucaristici.org (Thanks to Saint Carlo Acutis).

unchangeable priesthood."[125] Because it is eternal, it is the way for us to come to the eternal truth of God and to be made true ourselves. He is able:

> To save them to the uttermost that come unto God by him, seeing he ever liveth to make intercession for them. For such a high priest became us, who is holy, harmless, undefiled, separate from sinners, and made higher than the heavens.[126]

This priesthood is personal. The channel of divine truth, the bridge between earth and heaven, the maker true of our crooked selves is a person. Every Christian priest acts in His person, *in persona Christi*. Each priest's action is doubly personal: personal because belonging to Christ's person and personal also because he himself is a particular person. No bot can consecrate the Eucharist. It depends on a personal act:

> The Lord Jesus the same night in which he was betrayed took bread: And when he had given thanks, he brake it, and said, Take, eat: this is my body, which is broken for you: this do in remembrance of me. After the same manner also he took the cup, when he had supped, saying, This cup is the new testament in my blood: this do ye, as oft as ye drink it, in remembrance of me.[127]

This is Christ's personal action and it is personally shared by each of His priests. The person is the channel of God's truth. Christ is such as Priest, Prophet and King: personally embodying truth in a threefold manner. The priest is the one who links heaven and earth; the prophet communicates heaven's truth; the king embodies all his subjects. In this last case, Christ is the King of Kings[128] and His kingdom is "not of this world":[129] that is, all humanity is summed up in Him and its supramundane destiny is personally realized in His ascension into heaven. Every Christian, irrespective of any ministerial, prophetic or governmental role, shares in this threefold per-

125. Hebrews 7:24.
126. Hebrews 7:25–26.
127. 1 Corinthians 11:23–25.
128. Cf. Revelation 19:16.
129. John 18:36.

sonal dignity. The manifold truth that Christ embodies speaks of the unfathomable worth and meaning of each human person.

The person sums up everything: each is a microcosm. The priest, according to the ancient tradition into which Jesus was born, does this in a particular way. The Book of Wisdom says this about the sacerdotal garment, the ephod, worn by Aaron, the priest: "in the long garment was the whole world, and in the four rows of the stones was the glory of the fathers graven, and thy majesty upon the diadem of his head."[130] According to Jewish tradition, the long blue robe denoted the sky[131] and so it would speak also of the peace and tranquility of heaven. "The glory of the fathers" is "in the four rows of the stones" because "the stones shall be with the names of the children of Israel, twelve, according to their names."[132] Each of the different named precious stones is set in gold and signifies "the glory" of Israel's children, that is to say the spiritual heritage mediated through their persons. They also signify the whole of Israel, that is the twelve tribes which are their descendants, so Aaron in his ministry is both the channel of ancestral holiness and the embodiment of the present people. Similarly, Elijah makes an altar with twelve stones for the twelve sons of Israel for his contest with the prophets of Baal.[133] By anticipation they signify the twelve Apostles, whose names are the "twelve foundations" of "the wall of the city" of the heavenly Jerusalem.[134] The practice of personal presence from the sacred past is continued in the custom of putting relics of saints under the altar in a church.

The gems Aaron wears are set in "the breastplate of judgment upon his heart, when he goeth in unto the holy place, for a memorial before the LORD continually."[135] Furthermore, there are "two onyx stones" engraved with "the names of the children of Israel: six of their names on one stone and the other six names of the rest on

130. Wisdom 18:24.
131. Addison G. Wright, *The Jerome Biblical Commentary*, Vol. 1, edited by Raymond E. Brown *et al.* (New York, NY: Geoffrey Chapman, 1984), 567.
132. Exodus 28:21.
133. 1 Kings 18:31–32.
134. Revelation 21:14.
135. Exodus 28:29.

the other stone," set in gold "upon the shoulders of the ephod for stones of memorial."[136] The remembrance of the names is the invocation of blessing through the persons of the fathers of the people. The "plate of pure gold" on Aaron's miter engraved with the words "HOLINESS TO THE LORD"[137] signifies the Lord's majesty, from which the blessing descends through the person of the priest. Aaron's garments, Moses his brother is told, are "for glory and for beauty."

As such, they sum up the purpose of human life. Three colors are woven together in them: blue, purple and scarlet.[138] Blue suggests the heavenly destiny of humankind, scarlet the sacrifice entailed in reaching it (for it is the color of blood and of love) and purple the life given to the mingling of them (such, according to two evangelists, was the color of the robe put on Jesus before His crucifixion).[139] The colors reflect the Holy Trinity: the Father to whom we return, Christ whose sacrifice makes that possible and the Holy Spirit who unites our life of love and sacrifice on earth with that of heaven. Together with these three colors, which are the beauty of life, is gold, which is its glory: as the noblest metal, it signifies the divine presence that is the "crown of life," given to those "faithful unto death."[140] Moses is instructed to adorn the ephod with the colors and the gold:

> Thou shalt make pomegranates of blue, and of purple, and of scarlet, round about the hem thereof; and bells of gold between them round about: A golden bell and a pomegranate, a golden bell and a pomegranate, upon the hem of the robe round about.[141]

In his person Aaron is to take into the tabernacle the whole of human life: the blue pomegranate for the joy of heaven's grace, the purple for its mingling with earthly sacrifice, the red for the sorrow of loss. Together, they are beautiful. The interstitial golden bells,

136. Exodus 28:9–12.
137. Exodus 28:36.
138. Exodus 28, *passim.*
139. Mark 15:17, John 19:2.
140. Revelation 2:10.
141. Exodus 28:33–34.

whose sound protects him in the "holy place,"[142] reflect the glory of the divine presence in the midst of life's mingled joys and sorrows. Life itself is "for glory and for beauty"; the glory is the divine truth to which it is directed, the beauty is life's truth here on earth.

Keats put it this way: "Beauty is truth, truth beauty, —that is all/ Ye know on earth, and all ye need to know."[143] The beauty is either that of nature, in which case it comes from the person of "the Father Almighty, maker of heaven and earth" or it comes from the fashioning of a human person. Either way, it is in the wholeness that the beauty is found: the light and the dark, the delightful and the somber, the sweet and the sour. The big picture, the entire tapestry of the creation is beautiful, though in parts it may be ugly; the whole symphony played by an orchestra is beautiful, though separated individual notes may be discordant; the words of a work of literature come together to form "something of great constancy"[144] though individual sentences may make little sense on their own. That wholeness can only come from a person, because only a person can gather together the disparate in one apprehension, harmonize the discordant in a single song, gather together the chapters of life in one book. Wholeness is life, truth and beauty: life because it is the patterning of time and space, the linking of moments and limbs; truth because it is the relation of each to all; beauty because it forms a harmonious whole, intuitively recognized as such. Seeing the big picture is wisdom and so is the fashioning of the whole. That is why the making of Aaron's garments is entrusted by the Lord to Bezaleel, of whom He says, "I have filled him with the spirit of God, in wisdom and in understanding, and in knowledge, and in all manner of workmanship."[145] Truth is found in the beautiful work of a person's life, not in the mechanical repetition of "dark Satanic Mills."[146] Every artisan, in the work of his or her life, reflects in

142. Exodus 28:35.

143. John Keats, *Ode on a Grecian Urn* (https://www.poetryfoundation.org/poems/44477/ode-on-a-grecian-urn).

144. *Midsummer Night's Dream*, Act V, scene i, line 26.

145. Exodus 31:3.

146. https://www.poetryfoundation.org/poems/54684/jerusalem-and-did-those-feet-in-ancient-time.

some manner the divine truth, beauty and unity. That too, even if it does not directly serve the sacerdotal like the work of Bezaleel, is a participation in priesthood, the bridging of heaven and earth.

Synodality and Sobornost

Truth emerges when people are united in Christ through the Spirit. This is understood in both the Western and the Eastern Church.

Unity in an ephod or a Grecian urn is a reflection of divine beauty and truth, but it is not the height of it. Since truth and beauty come through persons, they are more fully manifest in unity of persons. This is effected precisely by the sacrifice of Christ, in whom "there is neither Jew nor Greek, there is neither bond nor free, there is neither male nor female." All are "one in Christ Jesus."[147] This means that there is not partiality: neither a partial view nor a partial truth. In God what appear to be opposites are united in a higher truth, a fuller beauty, a more abundant life. Christ "is our peace, who hath made both one, and hath broken down the middle wall of partition" who makes "in himself of twain one new man, so making peace."[148] The unity is personal and expressed most cogently by Saint Paul as the unity of a human body:

> For as the body is one, and hath many members, and all the members of that one body, being man, are one body: so also is Christ. For by one Spirit are we all baptized into one body, whether we be Jews or Gentiles, whether we be bond or free; and have all been made to drink into one Spirit.[149]

This Spirit transcends the partiality of particular mind-sets, as evidenced on the day of Pentecost when the apostles were "filled with the Holy Ghost"[150] and "the multitude came together, and were confounded, because that every man heard them speak in his own

---

147. Galatians 3:28.
148. Ephesians 2:14–15.
149. 1 Corinthians 12:12–13.
150. Acts 2:4.

language,"[151] undoing the confusion of language of Babel.[152] In Christ there is shared life, the life of "the Spirit of truth,"[153] a certain consubstantiality. In that life there is truth, born of community sustained by communion in His Body and Blood.

Yet even if there is agreement that He is Truth in person, the true way of living in particular circumstances, of responding to particular challenges, of establishing true priorities still needs to be discerned. There are two ways of doing this which are secular rather than Christian, though attempts are sometimes made to smuggle them into Church life under the cover of being the latter. Described in the bluntest terms, they are fascism and mob rule—and they feed off each other. Missing from both and from their interplay is the work of the Spirit of truth. Even described in the politer terms of hierarchical governance and democracy, they do not do the job. To listen only to the person at the top is to ignore the truth Saint Benedict draws attention to in his Rule: "that the Lord often reveals what is better to the younger,"[154] as He did to Daniel in the judgment of Susanna. Even the Pope, who as the Vicar of Christ speaks in his teaching in the person of the Truth in person, can need correction, as did Pope Gregory XI, who was afraid to return from Avignon to Rome and was admonished by Catherine of Siena:

> May ardor of charity be in you, in such wise as shall prevent you from hearing the voice of incarnate demons, and heeding the counsel of perverse counselors, settled in self-love, who, as I understand, want to alarm you, so as to prevent your return, saying, "You will die." Up, father, like a man![155]

When Jesus brings His followers before His Father and prays, "Sanctify them through thy truth" and "for their sakes I sanctify

---

151. Acts 2:6.
152. Genesis 11:9.
153. John 15:26.
154. *RB 1980* (Collegeville, MN: The Liturgical Press, 1981), Chapter 3.
155. *St Catherine of Siena as Seen in Her Letters*, ed. Vida D. Scudder (London, 1911), 165–66 (https://catholic.com/magazine/online-edition/how-st-catherine-brought-the-pope-back-to-rome).

myself, that they also might be sanctified through the truth,"[156] He also prays "that they may be one."[157] It is as one that the Body of Christ lives in the truth: the Spirit of truth "bloweth where it listeth" among them.[158]

Paying attention to this Spirit through whomsoever He may speak is the purpose of synodal gatherings in the Church. A synod is, etymologically, journeying together: it is sharing the Way of the One who is also the Truth and the Life. Pope Francis clarifies what this means for the Church:

> A synodal Church is a Church which listens, which realizes that listening "is more than simply hearing." It is a mutual listening in which everyone has something to learn. The faithful people, the college of bishops, the Bishop of Rome: all listening to each other, and all listening to the Holy Spirit, the "Spirit of truth," in order to know what he "says to the Churches."[159]

This is not the same as democracy, which at its most brutally unreflective is merely the counting of heads regardless of contents. Pope Francis teaches that "the synodal process is first of all an inner conversion of mind and heart, a communal listening to one another in which we discern the voice of the Spirit."[160] This is the way to the "one accord" and "singleness of heart"[161] that the Church had when fresh from the coming of the Spirit. It is the way of Christ, in whom is truth and life. It is the way the Church follows, listening to the Holy Spirit under the leadership of the Pope.

As he opened the Synod of Bishops gathered to reflect on the synodal way on October 2, 2024, Pope Francis characterized it as "a place of listening in communion." He singled out as important and fundamental "the harmony that only the Holy Spirit can achieve." Harmony is beauty in sound and if, in the words attributed to Plato,

---

156. John 17:17,19.
157. John 17:11.
158. John 3:8.
159. Roch Kereszty, "Synodality, the Magisterium, and the faith of the people of God" in *Communio*, Winter 2021, 640.
160. Ibid., 642.
161. Acts 2:46.

"beauty is the splendor of truth," then harmony is an indicator of the presence of the Spirit of truth. "The Holy Spirit," says Pope Francis, "is the master of harmony and is capable of creating one voice among so many different voices."[162] It is here *among* those guided by the Holy Spirit, and not in the private possession of any individual, that there is to be found the harmony whose beauty indicates the presence of truth. Here is the Spirit of the Truth in person, who said, "Where two or three are gathered together in my name, there am I in the midst of them."[163] The Final Document of the Synod on Synodality in October 2024 describes this working of the Spirit:

> The synodal Church can be described using the image of the orchestra: the variety of instruments is necessary to give life to the beauty and harmony of music, within which the voice of each one retains its own distinctive features at the service of the common mission. Thus, is manifested the harmony that the Spirit brings about in the Church, the One who is harmony in person.[164]

Here is the beauty of truth.

We cannot say however that the Catholic Church in synod has a monopoly of the truth of Christ, for Christendom is divided. Pope Saint John Paul the Second in his encyclical letter *Ut Unum Sint* expressed this division as a breathing with one lung only; he saw in the Eastern Church the other lung, into which the breath of the Spirit of truth is also drawn. There, in the Russian Orthodox tradition, is an idea similar to that of synodality: that of *sobornost*, aptly defined by the Merriam-Webster dictionary as "spiritual harmony based on freedom and unity in love." The twentieth-century Russian theologian Sergei Bulgakov explains that according to the idea of *sobornost*:

> The Church is an *organism* or a body, or generally a living multi-unity. In the Church, many members are united and diverse gifts

162. Homily of Pope Francis for Mass of the Guardian Angels, Saint Peter's Square, Wednesday October 2, 2024.

163. Matthew 18.20.

164. https://www.synod.va/content/dam/synod/news/2024-10-26_final-docum ent/ENG---Documento-finale_traduzione-di-lavoro.pdf, paragraph 42.

in Chapter F, though that is not the whole of its reach. His wonderful *magnum opus* is named for the scripture citation above, *The Pillar and Ground of the Truth*. It starts with the insight that the completely individualized existence of anything is impossible since any existent qualifies the mysterious depth of universally shared being and it goes on to find truth in the fellowship of belief. Beginning life in a household where there was no explicit religious faith and losing life, without ever renouncing the open profession of his Christian priesthood, to a Soviet bullet, he gave a witness to truth which was indeed grounded.

This witness was in the context of the Russian tradition. Dostoevsky, among other Russians before Florensky, understood *sobornost*. It is more than the satisfaction of the "need for *communality* of worship" which his diabolical Grand Inquisitor describes as "the chief torment of each man individually, and of mankind as a whole, from the beginning of the ages": it includes the freedom which the Inquisitor reproaches Christ for increasing.[173] This freedom, Dostoevsky's entire oeuvre passionately argues, is essential to humanity's reaching the truth. It is not to be imposed but rather guarded by the saint, "the keeper of God's truth in the eyes of the people," though they be worn out by toil, grief and sin. The people feel and even reason, "He knows the truth; so the truth does not die on earth, and therefore someday it will come to us and will reign over all the earth, as has been promised."[174] Dostoevsky knew, from his time of imprisonment so vividly fictionalized in *The House of the Dead*, of the tares ("the children of the wicked one"[175]) among the wheat of the kingdom, yet he saw "the saving road of humble communion with the people"[176] as the only one to Christ's truth. This too is the conviction of Pope Francis, who calls for a "synodal Church" that "journeys together" with men and women, "sharing the travails of history." Our gaze, he says, needs to extend "to

173. *The Brothers Karamazov*, 254.
174. Ibid., 30.
175. Matthew 13:38.
176. "Pushkin" in *Dostoevsky's Journal*, trans. S. Koteliansky and J. Middleton Murry (*The Complete Works of Fyodor Dostoevsky* [ebook], 8625).

humanity as a whole."[177] The implication of this is that in our quest for truth we need to dialogue with everybody, not only those who share our faith. Dostoevsky shows us this courage-demanding way. That is the theme of the next chapter.

177. https://www.vatican.va/content/francesco/en/speeches/2015/october/documents/papa-francesco_20151017_50-anniversario-sinodo.html.

D: Dialogue & Dostoevsky

A Sacred Depth

Truth emerges in loving dialogue, is present in the Holy Trinity and spoken by a child. It is found in the relationship between self and other, life and death, joy and sorrow.

Truth is the first casualty of war. This generally accepted observation has as its concomitant that dialogue is the way to avoid war and to find truth. Truth and love are closely connected in human relations; it is only when you love someone that you can allow the truth of that person's being its full scope, allow that person's outlook equal validity to your own. Truth and love are identified in God: Scripture tells us both that the Holy Spirit is the Spirit of truth and that God is love.[1] If the Holy Spirit is among people united in love, there is the truth. The truth is not a compromise, a political settlement in which concessions are made on both sides. It is not even a matter of courteous mutual listening and a Hegelian process of thesis, antithesis and synthesis, valuable though that may be. It involves a more radical renunciation than putting aside something of what is important to oneself or learning from another what mistakes there may be in one's own thinking. This is evident from grammar. If two people are calling themselves "I," which is right? If they are calling each other "you," who is being more truthful? Who am I and who are you? The very syntax allows only what is also not true: if I can say anything true in the first person, I am saying something that cannot be said truthfully by every person. Only if I love you and others as myself so that your "I" is also my "I" is the deficit of truth overcome. There is truth only in loving relations. As the Final Document of the October 2024 Synod on Synodality says, "Relationships and bonds are the means by which God the Father has

---

1. John 16:13 and 1 John 4:8.

revealed Himself in Jesus and the Spirit."[2] They are the presence of divine truth. The document teaches that we enter into them by conforming our hearts to that of Jesus, since only "the heart makes all authentic bonding possible, since a relationship not shaped by the heart is incapable of overcoming the fragmentation caused by individualism."[3] The work of truth is the enlarging of the heart.

This can be given a theological formulation in terms of Nicholas of Cusa's understanding of God as the coincidence of opposites: the opposite "I"s of you and I meet in God. I will explore more deeply in the final chapter the trinitarian implications of this, how the loving relationship between the Father and the Son is in the Spirit of truth. Here, let us focus on the reflection of the divine in human relations. In all languages I am aware of, there are three persons: the first, which is the origin of awareness; the second, which is the person encountered; and the third, which is the objective reality. This in a way corresponds to a human family, in which there is a father, a mother and a child. The third—the Spirit, the objective reality, the child—is the truth of the encounter between one and another. Truth is here, not in the Father *as opposed to the Son* or vice-versa, not in "I" *as opposed to* "you," not in the father *as opposed to the mother*. We do not have to say *tertium non datur* (the classic statement of the excluded middle), for a third is given. I have indicated three thirds, not because I think the Spirit, objective reality and a child are the same or even equivalent, but in the hope that after the manner of poetry, with its juxtaposed disparate images, I can suggest something of the beauty of truth, can intimate the pattern of truth's appearance in creation. Yet the child can in some sense stand for all three thirds: she is unpredictable, like the Spirit which "bloweth where it listeth";[4] she is objective reality for the married couple, interrupting their subjective visions with her needs in the night; like truth herself, she is the child of opposites, male and female. I will say more about the personification of truth as she is known in creation, as distinct from Him who is the all-creating Word, in the next chap-

2. https://www.synod.va/content/dam/synod/news/2024-10-26_final-documen t/ENG---Documento-finale.pdf, paragraph 50.

3. Ibid., paragraph 51.

4. John 3:8.

ter. Here let a child speak for her, for the Truth Himself says, "Whosoever receiveth one of such children in my name, receiveth me."[5] A child in her innocence says things that adults tacitly conspire to conceal; a child in her appeal creates between herself and others and also among others loving bonds, such as are conducive to the emergence of truth; a child is new life, the embodiment of living truth as distinct from murderous mendacity.

Let us consider this philosophically. S.L. Frank discusses reality in terms of relationship, saying it is "realized and revealed only in the absolutely primordial and unspeakable unity of 'am-is.'"[6] That is to say the truth of my being is not just "I" (my thoughts, feelings or whatever), nor is it just that of which I am aware (the world, or whatever is other): it is the ineffable unity "am-is." Necessarily, this cannot be put into words, for these are designed to negotiate a state of separation in which I am I and that (the other) is that. That is why Frank called his book *The Unknowable*. This unknowable is the ontological depth in which opposites coincide; here the distinction between my own and what is other is transcended. Of course "depth" is metaphor, which is itself an antonym of the height that is implied by the word "transcended." Our words are for time and space, not for the reality that is their source. Saint Paul is cognizant of this in his prayer that the Ephesians "being rooted and grounded in love, May be able to comprehend with all saints what is the breadth, and length, and depth, and height; and to know the love of Christ, which passeth knowledge."[7] Dimension as such cannot situate the ineffable unity of love; it is in every dimension and in none; it cannot be known in the language we speak. This love that unites is the primary reality. So much is implied even in the science of physics. MacGilchrist writes in his revealingly titled *The Matter With Things*, "In quantum field theory, the absolutely primary elements of reality are force fields, that is to say relationship and process, not things."[8] Such is the love that moves the stars.

---

5. Mark 9:37.
6. *The Unknowable*, 73.
7. Ephesians 3:17–18.
8. *The Matter With Things*, 2020. Kindle.

The mystery deepens when persons are involved, when it is no longer simply "I-that" but "I-thou." Frank describes this latter relation "as a *primordial* form of being, as *the revelation of the inner structure of reality as such*—and precisely in its *unknowableness*— beyond all conceptual knowledge."[9] This structure is antinomic; it is "the unity of separateness and mutual penetration."[10] This is given eloquent expression in Shakespeare's poem *The Phoenix and Turtle.* In my book, *The Mystery of Identity*, I applied lines from it primarily to the Holy Trinity by way of illustrating how there are distinct Persons and One God, but more explicitly they speak of love between two human persons. The two are of course related: the love in God is reflected in the love between people. The fundamental insight is that, at the deepest (or, to vary the metaphor, highest) level, reality is relational and interpersonal. Here is part of the citation:

> So they loved as love in twain
> Had the essence but in one,
> Two distincts, division none:
> Number there in love was slain.[11]

Truth, the fundamental ground of our being, is in the coincidence of opposites: ultimately in God, but also in His image, which is the personhood of human nature. Truth (in both these contexts) is necessarily mystery. The person shares in the unboundedness of God; as Frank says, "man as a person is always and essentially something *greater and other* than all we can perceive in him as a finished determination constituting his being. That is to say, he is a kind of infinitude, so that he has an inner bond to the infinitude of the *spiritual kingdom*."[12] Our knowledge of this unlimited truth is given according to the paradigm of *The Phoenix and Turtle*, that is, in Frank's words, "the 'person' can be known only in a transrationally monodualistic manner as *the unity of separateness and mutual penetration, as a unity whose essence consists in its unknowableness.*"[13] This kind

---

9. *The Unknowable*, 144.
10. Ibid., 143.
11. *The Phoenix and Turtle*, lines 25–28.
12. *The Unknowable*, 76.
13. Ibid.

of knowing is the polar opposite of the kind that follows the scientific paradigm which, when made an absolute and not confined to its proper sphere, can only lead to despair of finding the truth or pride in a false and fanatical claim to have found it in its fullness.

The reflection of the divine truth in the human person is known in another way, as Frank indicates:

> The true mystery of a person is illuminated only in love and trust, which are alien to all "spying" and incompatible with it. And only in love and trust do we gain living knowledge of the unknowable reality that forms the essence of the person.[14]

That is also how divine truth is known: in love and the trust, which is faith. It applies also to the deepest knowledge of His creation:

> At the highest levels of spiritual development, in the religious life of such a genius as St. Francis of Assisi, for example, not only wolves, birds, and fishes, but even the sun and wind, even death and one's own body become "brothers and sisters," are experienced as "thou."[15]

This communing with nature does not replace scientific understanding, which finds its place in the facilitating of the practical, but knowing in this way is an encounter with a truth of a higher order or of a deeper, and sacred, depth. One does not in fact need to be a genius to have at least a fleeting experience of oneness with all: I recall my own father reporting having such in Park Street, a main thoroughfare in Bristol (UK).

As ever, the truth of the creation is found in the coming together of antinomies: here, the self and what is other. Such is the conviction of that great seeker (and finder) of truth, Pavel Florensky. He observed that "living thought is full of contradictions, as is the case with the antinomies of Christianity." The presence of contradictions can be a sign of penetration to the truth, for "contradictoriness refers to the noumenal depths of our sense of the world."[16] As

---

14. Ibid., 91–92.

15. Ibid., 135.

16. Pavel Florensky, *At the Crossroads of Science and Mysticism*, trans. Boris Jakim (Brooklyn, NY: Angelico Press, 2014), 5.

implied in the quotation about Saint Francis above, this can include even the antinomy of life and death. This is so in the common-sense truth that a life lived without coming to terms with death is going to be unrealistic, sterile and even delusional, but it goes deeper than that. Jesus Christ, the truth in person, is the resurrection and the life *and* suffered death; He is true God and true man. The cross is the ultimate antinomy, for it is both the "tree of life" which is "in the midst of the garden, and the tree of knowledge of good and evil."[17] The latter is perhaps the more obscure sense, for in the Christian tradition we associate the cross with the forgiveness of sins that keep us from sharing God's life, but it is implied in the oxymoron "Good Friday" for what happened on that Friday was undoubtedly evil: the putting to a horrific death of perfect innocence. And though, as it were, we get back the tree of life through the cross, Christ gets the cross through the tree of knowledge of good and evil. It is only because of the *felix culpa* (happy fault) of Adam, celebrated in the Easter Liturgy, that we have so great a Savior and His embracing of the cross, the instrument of our salvation. The deepest (highest) truth, incarnate in Him, is beyond good and evil: not, of course, that He is guilty of sin, but that He was "made to be sin for us,"[18] and took upon Himself all its agony, together with the evils of bodily torment and social shame and exclusion. Good and evil are in a sense co-workers for the glory of God, for man fully alive. And here is life truly lived; here is living truth (if it were not alive it would not really be truth); here is the Holy Grail of all seekers of truth: in the antinomies of death/life, sorrow/joy, degradation/exaltation. Woven together, they are the beauty of holiness, the fabric of immortality, the vestment of glory.

Failure to enter this life comes from one-sidedness: an insistence on finding one's own life instead of letting it be lost for the Other;[19] a heart that is stone in the presence of suffering; a façade that is chosen to avoid risking losing face. Loss of this truth comes from a

17. Genesis 2:9.
18. 2 Corinthians 5:21.
19. Cf. Matthew 10:39.

refusal of antinomy; it comes from wanting the smooth but not the rough, the icing but not the cake, the gain but not the pain. Without something of the latter, without some push-back from life, we are but couch potatoes, handed everything on a plate and unfit for anything. Fundamentally, the two attitudes are the faith that is (however obscurely) aware of the deeper life and truth of the cross and the unbelief that sees it as risible folly. They are that of the centurion who says, "Truly this was the Son of God,"[20] and that of the passers-by who say mockingly, "He saved others; himself he cannot save."[21] If you look into something deeply enough it is always good, but we tend to lead superficial lives and are liable to get stuck in one side of the antinomies, closing our heart to the truth that the very hairs of our head are numbered,[22] that we "are of more value than many sparrows,"[23] that "all things work together for good to them that love God."[24] In the sacred depth, where saints (grateful for crosses) have lived, is the precious truth that anything, however bad it may seem outwardly, can be offered in union with the Truth in person and His supreme offering and that in that dark eventuality can be the light of heaven, in that grief can be ecstasy, in that loss can be the "pearl of great price."[25] Artists as well as saints have a sense of this. In *Septology*, a long novel by the Norwegian Nobel laureate Jon Fosse, the artist-narrator says, "What I painted was the darkness in all that light, I painted the real light, the invisible light." To his spiritual intuition, "In the sharp bright light of the sun what looks brightest are the shadows, in a way, yes, the darker they are the more light there is."[26]

20. Matthew 27:54.
21. Matthew 27:42.
22. Matthew 10:30.
23. Matthew 10:31.
24. Romans 8:28.
25. Cf. Matthew 13:46.
26. Jon Fosse, *Septology*, trans. Damion Searls (London: Fitzcarraldo Editions, 2023), 74 (punctuation edited).

Heaven is Other People

An I-thou relationship with all of humanity is a happy encounter with the truth.

True knowledge knows the other as "thou." That kind of knowing can extend to all that is, seeing nature herself as a sister. It is characterized by an absence of lust for domination, a compulsion to control, a greed for acquisition. It is neglected because it involves trust and vulnerability, renouncing of the self, humility before the mystery. Yet here is happiness. That can be known if it extends to one other person. It is like this: I can see in her eyes that she understands and accepts; I can say what I kept hidden and know that the person I am is nonetheless real for its revealing; I can truly live in the reality between us that is I and not-I. I am heard, her-d for she has become I. I am her, no longer I, yet now truly who I am. To be connected with somebody else like this is already to be stepping onto the road of the commandment in which any other is "briefly comprehended... namely, Thou shalt love thy neighbour as thyself."[27] It is the way to ontological unity, in which the being of others is united to my being, their sorrows my sorrows, their joys my joys, their welfare my welfare. That is the direction in which the sun rises on all because its light is no longer blocked by my egoism; the light of truth and love is allowed to shine through.

To know some happiness through rapport with another is not an uncommon experience: what is shared is known as out there as well as in me and that strengthens both my sense of reality and my sense of self. Contentment comes from this, whether the sharing is with an individual with whom there is a mutual entrusting of lives or with a group with whom there is some common belief or concern. There is a happiness of recognition of common truth, be this deeply personal or of public concern. Yet we know there are people out there with whom we do not share a point of view, whose take on reality is even antagonistic towards our own. What would it be like if we shared a loving, truthful rapport with everyone? Like this: our relationship with humanity would be a fully I-thou relationship; in

27. Romans 13:9.

every encounter there would be the joy of lovingly shared truth; at the deepest level, there would be a trusting surrender to the "thou" of the other person, whatever precautions might have to be taken on the practical level on account of the other lacking particular skills or living on a superficial level largely ignorant of that depth and its implication of how to treat people. Ultimately every encounter would be with the "Thou" that is the source of "thou," with the Creator of all. And, with the eyes of faith, we would see His eyes and His face, smiling back with the incomparable radiance of absolute love. It would be the beatific vision, tempered only by (in the Apostle's words) "our light affliction" of worldly trouble, light that is in comparison with "a far more exceeding and eternal weight of glory."[28] Creation herself would be a "thou" in whom the glory of the "Thou" gleamed, if not seen directly then "being understood by the things that are made."[29]

It is all a question of how we see things. The "hell is other people" of Sartre's play,[30] like the "this is hell, nor am I out of it" of Mephistopheles in Marlowe's play,[31] is coming from the same place as the happiness of the one who can see "Thou" in every "thou," however little that "Thou" is manifest on the surface. It is simply that the latter way of seeing things is open to the fullness of truth, not confined to and by the particular perspective of self-interest and self-gratification. In this life there is a spectrum leading from one to the other; the great divorce comes in the next. The correlation between escaping that perspective and finding truth is exemplified in the interviews the detective Cormoran Strike conducts with suspects in Robert Galbraith's novels. With the military self-discipline that comes from his background, he is never diverted to concerns about his prestige or person, however provocative his interlocutor may be, and he ends up knowing the truth of what he is investigating. To transcend the petty perspective of the self absolutely is to be in the presence of absolute truth and so (because there is no division in

---

28. 2 Corinthians 4:17.
29. Romans 1:20.
30. *Huis Clos.*
31. *Doctor Faustus*, Act 1, scene iii, l.80.

the transcendent characteristics of the divine) in the presence of absolute beauty. It is to see the beatific vision, now in the heart and in the next life fully manifest in every surrounding, for "there shall be no night there."[32]

Some Literary Theory

Dostoevsky, like Shakespeare, allows his characters to have their own voice. He aims to let them express Christ, not himself. In dialogue, they become truthful.

In practical, human terms, transcending partial perspective is being able to see from everyone's perspective. This is not because some sort of lowest common denominator is the truth or even because (though this is nearer to the truth) something veridical could be assembled from whatever is good in manifold perspectives, but rather because it involves openness to the source of every truth, to the divine that shines in "whatsoever things are true, whatsoever things are honest, whatsoever things are just, whatsoever things are pure, whatsoever things are lovely, whatsoever things are of good report."[33] That transcendence of partial perspective is, up to a point, given form for us in literature that shows different perspectives in different characters. I say "up to a point" because of course every work of fiction is in some sense contained by a single consciousness. Even a great one, like Tolstoy's *Anna Karenina*, can have an overarching single narrative voice that claims insight into all its creatures, including in this case even the perspective of a dog.[34] To get beyond this, a radical unknowing is needed, a total humility before the mystery of the human person that admits its lack of ability to understand, still less to control, each person's God-given freedom. It is there in some measure in Shakespeare, whose "negative capability" was famously remarked on by Keats[35] and of whose "profound intelligence" Florensky remarked:

32. Revelation 22:5.
33. Philippians 4:8.
34. Part 6, Chapter 12.
35. In a letter to his brothers, George and Thomas, December 22, 1817.

It is an immanent intelligence (inwardly present) to the characters and speeches, so that you do not see the writer's mind behind the images. In general, you do not see the writer himself—that is the enigma of Shakespeare.[36]

An indication that Shakespeare is getting his own self out of the way to allow others to speak is given in the way people can take what is in fact the perspective of one character as though it were his, even though the context may be indicating some other truth. An example is Macbeth's famous speech, ending with an assessment of life as "a tale/ Told by an idiot, full of sound and fury,/ Signifying nothing,"[37] which is taken by some critics[38] as indicating that Shakespeare believed that life is meaningless. This ignores the fact that the speaker has his "eternal jewel/ Given to the common enemy of man,"[39] that is to say he has allowed the devil to take control of his soul and in this state of mortal sin is bound to be fundamentally unhappy. His is an inner unhappiness that is to be outwardly manifest in the next life, the mirror image of the suffering of those open to truth, of whom it is written, "though they be punished in the sight of men, yet is their hope full of immortality."[40] The latter's tribulation is outwardly manifest in this life, the vision (albeit "through a glass darkly")[41] of eternal joy in the depth of their hearts fully realized and complete in the next.

That (comparatively) outer trouble is a sort of fence keeping swine from the pearl of great price and reserving the most gladsome beholding of the Most High to the pure of heart. This beatitude is only accessible if it does not feed egoism. That means the way to it involves forsaking control, being vulnerable to the purifying truth "as gold in the furnace"[42] and vulnerable in this world, like Christ

36. Avril Pyman, *Pavel Florensky: A Quiet Genius* (New York, NY: Continuum, 2010), 176.

37. *Macbeth*, Act V, scene v, lines 26–28.

38. See for example Jan Kott, *Shakespeare Our Contemporary* (London: Methuen & Co, Ltd, 1961).

39. *Macbeth*, Act III, scene i, lines 67–68.

40. Wisdom 3:4.

41. 2 Corinthians 13:12.

42. Wisdom 3:6.

before Pilate, to those who are not for truth. It takes form for us in literature that comes from a heart pure enough not to make every character an aspect of the perspective of the writer's self. It is there in the writing of Dostoevsky. As with Shakespeare, he has often been associated with the perspective of one or other of his characters, as for example that of Ivan in *The Brothers Karamazov* who wants to return his ticket to God's world because innocent people suffer in it. I will offer a different reading of this extraordinarily important novel below, but want first to reflect on the kind of consensus about his approach to writing that has emerged among critics. Diane Oenning Thompson is one such, deserving to be quoted at length:

> For Dostoevsky, truth is not something he has got, though he knows the direction in which it lies. Truth is something Other, something he tries to find by listening with the utmost acuity to others, from the basest scoundrel to the righteous saint. Amongst all the discordant and harmonious voices, he is seeking the one voice which is ultimately the voice of Christ. Only by letting all the earthly voices sound together with the utmost freedom can he hope to divine this one voice. And if he can then demonstrate the presence of this voice in everyone without exception, he will have achieved his great goal of demonstrating its omnipresence in the world. Thus, truth for Dostoevsky is not relative but dialogic in this special sense of seeking.[43]

Here Thompson is drawing upon the ground-breaking and seminal work of the Russian critic Mikhail Bakhtin, whose *Problems of Dostoevsky's Poetics* analyzes the novelist's "polyphonic creative activity." This is not concerned with "a world of objects" but with "a world of consciousnesses mutually illuminating one another, a world of yoked-together semantic human orientations." It is here, in the dialogic interaction of his characters, that he seeks the truth:

> Among them Dostoevsky seeks the highest and most authoritative orientation, and he perceives it not as his own true thought, but as another authentic human being and his discourse. The image of the ideal human being or the image of Christ represents for him

---

43. Diane Oenning Thompson, *The Brothers Karamazov and the Poetics of Memory* (Cambridge: Cambridge University Press, 1991), 71.

the resolution of ideological quests.... Precisely the image of a human being and his voice, a voice not the author's own, was the ultimate artistic criterion for Dostoevsky: not fidelity to his own convictions and not fidelity to convictions themselves taken abstractly, but precisely a fidelity to the authoritative image of human being.[44]

Dostoevsky's thinking is through "points of view, consciousnesses, voices."[45] Above all, he wants to hear the Good Shepherd who says of Himself, "When he putteth forth his own sheep, he goeth before them, and the sheep follow him: for they know his voice."[46] In his works, "there are absolutely no *separate* thoughts, propositions or formulations such as maxims, sayings, aphorisms which, when removed from their context and detached from their voice, would retain their semantic meaning in an impersonal form."[47] For him, thought is rooted in the human person. Bakhtin is emphatic about how his novels are formed:

> His form-shaping worldview does not know an *impersonal truth*, and in his works there are no detached, impersonal verities. There are only integral and indivisible voice-ideas, voice-viewpoints, but they too cannot be detached from the dialogic fabric of the work without distorting their nature.[48]

In response to someone who does think abstractly, in terms of his own convictions, Dostoevsky writes, "Living life has fled you, only the formulas and categories remain."[49] This "living life" is that spoken of in the fourth verse of Saint John's gospel: "In him was life; and the life was the light of men." It is the light of the One who is the truth in person, light of the world, the resurrection and the life. Truth, if it is more than a provisional estimate for practical purposes, is inextricably bound up with life with all its unpredictability,

---

44. Mikhail Bakhtin, *Problems of Dostoevsky's Poetics* (Saint Paul, MN: University of Minnesota, 2021), 97.

45. Ibid., 93.

46. John 10:4.

47. Bakhtin, *Problems of Dostoevsky's Poetics*, 95.

48. Ibid., 96.

49. Ibid., 97.

because truth cannot be pinned down. It is limitless and infinite; it is an unsoundable mystery; it is, ultimately, the infinite mystery of the person of Christ Jesus, true God and true man, who came that we "might have life,"[50] even life eternal.

Another writer deeply influenced by Bakhtin's insights is Rowan Williams, who wrote his *Dostoevsky: Language, Faith and Fiction* while still Archbishop of Canterbury. In it he observes that for his subject, the only way "to move toward a sustainable truth, a truth that is more than either a private ideology or a neutral description, is by being immersed in the interaction of the personal agents and speakers."[51] He sees characters who shy away from this as refusing truth. Golyadkin, in Dostoevsky's short story *The Double*, "cannot produce by his inner pseudo-dialogue interaction a genuinely *other* voice that can give him what he needs; ultimately he can only produce a solidified form of his own anxiety."[52] That is, he talks to himself (that is the form of the story) and ends up being split in two. Raskolnikov, the protagonist in *Crime and Punishment*, is already "potentially a murderer" because he "has lost the capacity to hear and speak, to engage humanly with others and to change in response." His crime of murder "comes out of the intensity of an inner dialogue that is practically never interrupted by a real other."[53] It is precisely when he does enter into dialogue, with Sonya Marmeladov (herself given to prostitution to keep her desperately poor family alive), that he begins to contemplate telling the truth about what he has done. It is very significant that Sonya reads him the gospel about Lazarus being raised from the dead, with its "supremely 'other' voice, that of God" for "Raskolnikov's state is effectively death" and "Christ's command to Lazarus, 'Come *forth!*'" is a summons to emerge from his isolation.[54] In doing this, he becomes vulnerable: his first confession, to Sonya, is actually overheard and his second, to the authorities, earns him punishment.

50. John 10:10.
51. Rowan Williams, *Dostoevsky: Language, Faith and Fiction* (London: Continuum, 2008), 113.
52. Ibid., 118.
53. Ibid., 116.
54. Ibid., 119.

But his emergence into dialogue is a move from killing the truth in the persons of other people to accepting the truth at the cost of suffering. The final pages of the novel, when he takes out from under his pillow Sonya's copy of the gospels, implies that he may even accept the truth in person. The direction of his life is from outward lies and violence (the two are closely associated, as even a cursory acquaintance with world politics evidences) to inward truth and life. He is, to return to the words of Berdyaev quoted in the previous chapter, moving towards "the religion of Truth crucified."[55] By contrast, the death-dealing conspirators of *Demons*, Pyotr Verkhovensky and Nikolai Stravrogin, remain isolated: the former in his flow of insincere prattle, the latter finally in his suicide. The last pages of this novel, however, show us an encounter between Stepan Verkhovensky, the father of Pyotr, and (again, significantly) a seller of gospels, which leads him to admit that he has been lying all his life.[56] Williams offers a reading of Dostoevsky's final novel, *The Brothers Karamazov*, "as narrating the processes by which each of the brothers ... puts at risk his own control over how he is seen and responded to, so as to be remade."[57] Alyosha emerges from his monastery to interact with others; Ivan publicly bares his soul in court; Dmitri becomes willing to embrace suffering. For all of them, it is "a movement into vulnerability,"[58] the vulnerability of Christ before Pilate.

My own reading of Dostoevsky, too, is influenced by Bakhtin; indeed the crystallization of the idea of this present book had a catalyst in the line of thinking that comes from him. The essential point is that truth is not owned: not by an omniscient narrator, not by a single character, not even by a set of characters who could be identified as holy or good. Rather, it is between or among them, blowing where it will, free of constraint and not subject to prediction. The implication is that the Spirit has some point of contact with every-

55. *The End of Our Time*, 164.
56. *The Demons*, trans. Richard Pevear and Larissa Volokhonsky (New York, NY: Vintage, 2006), 652.
57. Williams, *Dostoevsky: Language, Faith and Fiction*, 126.
58. Ibid., 130.

one, even if it is simply through a memory of childhood. Such is the case in this short dialogue Dostoevsky wrote in his notebook in 1877:

> – Say Christ my God, say it!
> – Well, alright, Christ my God.
> – And even though you don't believe, even though you speak with a smile (but with a kind one), Christ will forgive you – both you and me. He Himself said: blasphemy against Me I shall forgive, only blasphemy against the Spirit shall not be forgiven.
> – And what is the Spirit?
> – The Spirit is what is now between us and is why your face has become kinder, why you felt like weeping, because your lips trembled—you lie, don't be proud, they were trembling, I saw it, and the Spirit is what brought you from America to remember on this day the Christmas tree in your parents' home. That's what the Spirit is.[59]

The first speaker is a believer, the second not. Yet there is an ambiguity in the unbeliever's unbelief, a memory of early years when "every common sight . . . did seem/ Appareled in celestial light."[60] Here is explicit what is implicit in the dialogues in the great novels: "The Spirit is what is now between us." And that presence of the spirit of truth is not taken away by (to take two examples from *The Brothers Karamazov*) Ivan's refusal to accept God's creation, or Dmitri's ungodly lifestyle. It is only taken away by the refusal to dialogue, the pretence of owning the truth, the claim to be "not as other men are."[61]

The artistic representation of the Spirit in Dostoevsky's novels is enabled by the portrayal of "a world of autonomous subjects, not objects,"[62] who have "freedom vis-à-vis the usual externalizing and finalizing authorial definitions" and together constitute "the image of many unmerged personalities joined together in the unity of

---

59. Quoted in Thompson, *The Brothers Karamazov and the Poetics of Memory*, 120.

60. Wordsworth, "Intimations of Immortality From Recollections of Early Childhood" in *The Norton Anthology of Poetry* (New York, NY: W.W. Norton & Company, Inc., 1983), 551.

61. Luke 18:11.

62. Bakhtin, *Problems of Dostoevsky's Poetics*, 7.

some spiritual event."[63] Each of these is "a person possessed by an idea":[64] for example, Raskolnikov (in *Crime and Punishment*) who has the idea that exceptional persons can transcend morality for the greater good or Kirillov (in *Demons*) who has the idea that he can establish the freedom of man's will in independence from God by shooting himself. These ideas are not abstract or independent of persons: they are lived by the people who are possessed by them and given full scope in their depiction in the novels. Truth (ultimately the person of the Spirit of Christ) is not the monopoly of any of them, rather it emerges in the interaction of lives. Each of these lives is shown as "*a particular point of view on the world and on oneself,* as the position enabling a person to interpret and evaluate his own self and his surrounding reality";[65] each is "not an objectified image but an autonomous discourse, *pure voice.*"[66] The reason for this is that "a living human being cannot be turned into the voiceless object of some secondhand, finalizing cognitive process" because "in a human being there is always something only he himself can reveal, in a free act of self-consciousness and discourse."[67] The essential point is that "man is free" and his real life can only be manifested in dialogue. By contrast, "the truth about a man in the mouths of others, not directed to him dialogically and therefore a *secondhand* truth, becomes a *lie* degrading and deadening him."[68] This is why Dostoevsky considered the psychology of his day unrealistic, "a degrading *reification* of a person's soul, a discounting of its freedom and its unfinalizability."[69] He understood that "the consciousness of other people cannot be perceived, analyzed, defined as objects or as things—one can only *relate to them dialogically.*"[70] To see them as objects or things is to replace "the unity of existence" with "the unity of consciousness," eliminating antinomy and ignoring the possibil-

63. Ibid., 13.
64. Ibid., 22.
65. Ibid., 47.
66. Ibid., 53.
67. Ibid., 58.
68. Ibid., 59.
69. Ibid., 61.
70. Ibid., 68.

ity of "a unified truth that requires a plurality of consciousnesses, one that cannot in principle be fitted into the bounds of a single consciousness, one that is, so to speak, by its very nature *full of event potential* and is born at a point of contact among various consciousnesses."[71] This is not simply the coming together of ideas, for "the image of an idea is inseparable from the image of a person, the carrier of that idea."[72] The ideas in Dostoevsky's novels are not the result of abstract thought: rather "he created images of ideas found, heard, sometimes divined by him *in reality itself*, that is, ideas already living or entering life as idea-forces." He had an extraordinary openness to "the dialogue of his epoch," including not only established voices but also those still coming to birth.[73] The interplay of these voices is his thought and his art. Even when there is agreement among them, there is never "a *merging* of voices and truths in a single *impersonal* truth,"[74] for "formulas and categories are foreign to his thinking."[75] Truth, for Dostoevsky, "can only be the subject of a living vision, not of abstract understanding."[76]

His art, therefore, is pervaded by the antinomies of life:

> Everything in his world lives on the very border of its opposite. Love lives on the very border of hate, knows and understands it, and hate lives on the border of love and also understands it.... Faith lives on the very border of atheism, sees itself there and understands it, and atheism lives on the border of faith and understands it. Loftiness and nobility live on the border of degradation and vulgarity.... Love for life neighbors upon a thirst for self-destruction....[77]

Everything is reflected in everything else, all things illuminate one another dialogically.[78] The emerging light is the divine truth of the coincidence of opposites. It shimmers in the very fabric of the dis-

71. Ibid., 80–81.
72. Ibid., 85.
73. Ibid., 90.
74. Ibid., 95.
75. Ibid., 98.
76. Ibid., 153.
77. Ibid., 176.
78. Ibid., 177.

course, for "in Dostoevsky almost no word is without its intense sideward glance at someone else's word."[79] Indeed, the style of his speech is "defined by the intense anticipation of another's words."[80] It is always *to* someone: "the element of *address* is essential to every discourse in Dostoevsky." There is "no word about an object, no secondhand referential word—there is only the word as address, the word dialogically contacting another word."[81] Only the latter can know the depth of the human soul, for "it is impossible to master the inner man, to see and understand him by making him into an object of indifferent neutral analysis."[82] Such knowledge comes "in communion, in the interaction of one person with another."[83]

This account of Bakhtin's understanding of Dostoevsky's art has taken us back to "the ineffable unity 'am-is'" of S.L. Frank referred to at the start of this chapter: the indwelling of reality in relationship, the sacred depth of interpersonal encounter. It remains for it to be exemplified in Dostoevsky's writing. There we can find an exploration of what I wrote of in the second section of the chapter: the possibility of a loving, truthful rapport with everyone that is ultimately a joyful encounter with the "Thou" that is the source of every "thou," the Creator and very source of our being. This Dostoevsky gives literary form to in his last and greatest novel, *The Brothers Karamazov*, a book whose significance has resounded through over half a century of my life. I pay homage to its author at this mid-point of this middle chapter of this book dedicated to him.

Alyosha

Alyosha Karamazov, though imperfect, is Christ-like. He dialogues with others, and with unbelief, without passing judgment.

The words of Diane Thompson, quoted above, about Dostoevsky "listening with the utmost acuity to others, from the basest scoun-

---

79. Ibid., 203.
80. Ibid., 205.
81. Ibid., 237.
82. Ibid., 251.
83. Ibid., 252.

drel to the righteous saint" and "seeking the one voice which is ultimately the voice of Christ" can to some extent be applied to its hero,
Alyosha Karamazov, the youngest of the three brothers. There are
indications that he was particularly dear to its author. His name is
that of Dostoevsky's own son, born in 1875 and dying tragically
young in 1878, and indeed his father, Fyodor Karamazov, has Dostoevsky's first name. The narrator of the novel immediately claims
him as "my hero."[84] He is aware, however, that there may well be a
different view: "To me he is noteworthy, but I decidedly doubt that I
shall succeed in proving it to the reader."[85] Already, on the first page
of the novel, there is no single voice, no monologue of the truth. As
implied by Bakhtin's analysis, what might be taken as an authorial
point of view is relativized. This is emphasized by the incomplete
and partial view of what is going on that the narrator evinces
throughout his story, for example, when he is about to describe the
climactic scene: "I will say beforehand, and say emphatically, that I
am far from considering myself capable of recounting all that took
place in court, not only with the proper fullness, but even in the
proper order."[86] Dostoevsky is implicitly saying through his narrator that his own voice is not a source of truth, even that of events.
The truth rather is in the interaction of voices, the Spirit among the
speakers, including the reader. There is a double distancing of the
actual author in the novel: not only is the narrative open to question, but the hero's voice is open to question. Indeed, the substance
of the story could be seen as the dialogue between Alyosha's voice
and that of others, which readers have sometimes found more con-
vincing. Alyosha embodies openness to other voices: in this his
character is a representation of truth as (for example) Cordelia in
Shakespeare's *King Lear*, for (in words from the fragment of dialogue quoted above) "the Spirit is what is . . . between us" and he is
singularly open to this Spirit of truth. On the other hand he is not
the truth, both because the latter emerges in his contradiction by
others and because there is ambiguity in his own character. We can-

---

84. *The Brothers Karamazov*, 3.
85. Ibid.
86. Ibid., 656.

not say the Spirit of truth is unambiguously in Alyosha, for it "bloweth where it listeth, and thou hearest the sound thereof, but canst not tell whence it cometh, and whither it goeth."[87]

Something of the ambiguity of Alyosha is evidenced in the claim (which has been questioned) that Dostoevsky intended in a sequel to *The Brothers Karamazov* to have him become a revolutionary socialist who assassinates the Tsar. It is there in "the remarkable resemblance to his mother" when he reacts to his father's account of her "shrieking" when taunted by her husband by himself "shaking all over in a hysterical attack of sudden trembling and silent tears."[88] His devotion to his spiritual mentor and elder, Zosima, has been described by one insightful critic as "quasi-idolatrous worship" and a case where the personality relinquishes itself "to the will of the other as a form of 'exit' from its own unbearable anguish."[89] The day of the disappointment of his unrealistic expectation that Zosima's body will remain incorrupt after his death produces in him such "anguish" and "great perturbation" that "even later, long afterwards" he considers it "one of the most painful and fatal days of his life."[90]

Yet, "everyone loved this young man wherever he appeared, and it was so even in his earliest childhood." This response is because "there was something in him that told one, that convinced one (and it was so all his life afterwards) that he did not want to be a judge of men, that he would not take judgment upon himself and would not condemn anyone for anything."[91] This evokes Christ's words, "I came not to judge the world, but to save the world."[92] Alyosha is not Christ, but his life reminds us of Christ. Thompson goes so far as to describe him as a "christological hero,"[93] pointing out that "the narrator calls him an 'early lover of man' (*chelovekoliubets*)," a word

87. John 3:8.
88. *The Brothers Karamazov*, 136–37.
89. Yuri Corrigan, *Dostoevsky and the Riddle of the Self* (Evanston, IL: Northwestern University Press, 2017), 122.
90. *The Brothers Karamazov*, 338.
91. Ibid., 19.
92. John 12:47.
93. Thompson, *The Brothers Karamazov and the Poetics of Memory*, 312.

which is "one of the synonyms of Christ" found "in various formulaic invocations to Christ" in the Orthodox Prayerbook.[94] Since "Alyosha's radiant face is repeatedly seen by others as a salvational visage" it becomes "the face of an icon."[95] Throughout the novel, beginning with the narrator's comment that he is "very strange, having been so even from the cradle,"[96] his uniqueness is repeatedly emphasized, evoking Jesus, "the immutable representative of the singular."[97] He is also linked to Christ as one who is sent as, for example, when his beloved elder tells him to leave the monastery for good once he has died, saying "I am sending you. Christ is with you," and also to go immediately and "Be near your brothers."[98] This mission becomes more explicitly like Christ's towards the end of the novel, when it becomes one of absolution: his brother Dmitri's whole face instantly lights up with bliss when Alyosha assures him of his certainty of his innocence and Dmitri sends him to their other brother, who is losing his wits, saying, "Well, go, love Ivan!"[99] In that last encounter, Alyosha understands his commissioning as divine, echoing Christ's words, "My father hath sent me," when he tells Ivan, "The murderer was not you, do you hear, it was not you! God has sent me to tell you that."[100]

Alyosha is perhaps more representative of Christ in his silence than in his words, in the absence of "the least expression of contempt or condemnation of anyone at all."[101] His witness to the truth is indirect, like that of Christ before Pilate, who "answered him to never a word; insomuch that the governor marvelled greatly."[102] It is in his "gift of awakening a special love for himself,"[103] a love that makes possible the dialogue in which the Spirit of truth is present.

---

94. Ibid., 314.
95. Ibid.
96. *The Brothers Karamazov*, 18.
97. *The Brothers Karamazov and the Poetics of Memory*, 314.
98. *The Brothers Karamazov*, 77.
99. Ibid., 597.
100. John 20:21; *The Brothers Karamazov*, 602.
101. Ibid., 19.
102. Matthew 27:14.
103. *The Brothers Karamazov*, 19.

We see it at first in his relationship with his "touchy and easily offended" father who, initially suspicious, soon ends up:

> Hugging and kissing him terribly often, with drunken tears and tipsy sentimentality, true, but apparently having come to love him sincerely and deeply, more than such a man has, of course, ever managed to love anyone else.[104]

It is Alyosha's silence that makes the connection: his father is able to say, "I really feel you're the only one in the world who hasn't condemned me"[105] and "with you alone I have kind moments, otherwise I am an evil man."[106] Alyosha's ability to keep open a relationship is shown again, shortly after he says this, when he comes across a schoolboy who throws stones at him, insults him and bites his finger. When the boy gets no attack in response, he bursts into loud sobs and runs away.[107] Alyosha's restraint has huge consequences: he is able to reconcile him with the group of other boys who have been throwing stones at him and, at the end of the novel on the occasion of the funeral of Ilyushechka (his attacker), he exhorts a group of "about twelve boys":[108]

> Let us never forget how good we once felt here, all together, united by such good and kind feelings as made us, too, for the time that we loved the poor boy, perhaps better than we actually are.[109]

From being their enemy, Ilyushechka has become the one who brings them all together. Alyosha tells them:

> You are all dear to me, gentlemen, from now on I shall keep you all in my heart, and I ask you to keep me in your hearts, too! Well, and who has united us in this good, kind feeling, which we will remember and intend to remember always, all our lives, who, if not Ilyushechka, that good boy, that kind boy, that boy dear to us

104. Ibid.
105. Ibid., 25.
106. Ibid., 174.
107. Ibid., 177–80.
108. Ibid., 768.
109. Ibid., 774.

unto ages of ages! Let us never forget him, and may his memory be eternal and good in our hearts now and unto ages of ages!

The diction is deliberately liturgical and the eternal memory is that true life, eternal and divine, of which I wrote in the very first section of this book. Alyosha announces it to the twelve gathered around him as Christ proclaimed it to his twelve disciples. "Yes, yes!" reply the boys, "with deep feeling in their faces."[110] They tell him, "We love you, we love you" and he reassures them that it is really true "as religion says, that we shall all rise from the dead."[111] The small suffering that Alyosha suffered from Ilyushechka has been united to that of the One who "was afflicted, yet he opened not his mouth" and he shares His joy and satisfaction in seeing "the travail of his soul."[112]

Alyosha is not Christ: at the beginning of the novel he is suffering from adolescent confusion, but at this point he has now found his true identity in Christ. I explored the turning point at which he became "steadfast for the rest of his life" in *The Mystery of Identity*.[113] Here I want to emphasize how this realization of the presence of Christ establishes dialogue among others. The etymology of the word "dialogue" implies that it should: it comes from the Greek words *dia* (δια) meaning "through" and *logos* (λογος) meaning "word," as in "the Word was made flesh,"[114] so it points to mutual understanding through Christ's presence. Alyosha, who radiates Christ's love, never looks down on others. Significantly, he treats the children as equals.[115] Christ, the truth in person, is there in all his relations not as the possession of a private consciousness but in his loving interaction with people, in his relationship with them. This is so without any judgment, either of the morals or faith, of the one with whom he is in dialogue. This lack of judgment is exemplified in his dialogue with his brother Dmitri (with respect to morals) and

110. Ibid., 775.
111. Ibid., 776.
112. Isaiah 53:7, 11.
113. Brooklyn, NY: Angelico Press, 2022, 96–98.
114. John 1:14.
115. *The Brothers Karamazov*, 177.

with his brother Ivan (with respect to faith). Such dialogue is possible because:

> Alyosha was sure that no one in the whole world would ever want to offend him, and not only would not want to but even would not be able to. For him this was an axiom, it was given once and for all, without argument....[116]

That is to say that Alyosha loves everyone with the charity spoken of by Saint Paul, which is "not easily provoked, thinketh no evil; Rejoiceth not in iniquity, but rejoiceth in the truth; Beareth all things, believeth all things, hopeth all things, endureth all things."[117]

Dmitri, like others, responds to this love: "almost in a sort of ecstasy" he says, "I really . . . re-al-ly . . . (understand?) . . . love only you!"[118] He can confide in Alyosha the full range of his (and the human) condition, exclaiming, "Let me be cursed, let me be base and vile, but let me also kiss the hem of that garment in which my God is clothed."[119] The truth emerges not so much through the cognac that he consumes, as through the dialogue into which he enters. We might almost say that Alyosha is following the "synodal way of being silent, praying, listening, and speaking, rooted in the word of God,"[120] this last being Saint Paul's word about not being provoked and so on. He acknowledges a common human (or at least Karamazov) truth in Dmitri's admission of his sensuality even if he isn't so far up in it, saying, "I'm the same as you."[121] Dmitri goes on to make a full and frank confession of his amatory waywardness and financial compromise. His situation is fraught in the extreme and he asks Alyosha to intervene. He agrees, saying, "I believe God will arrange it as he knows best..."[122]

---

116. Ibid., 101.

117. 1 Corinthians 13:5–7.

118. *The Brothers Karamazov*, 104.

119. Ibid., 107.

120. https://www.synod.va/content/dam/synod/assembly/synthesis/english/2023.10.28-ENG-Synthesis-Report.pdf Synthesis Report: A Synodal Church in Mission, October 2023, Part 1—The Face of the Synodal Church, 1. Synodality: Experience and Understanding, Convergences, a).

121. *The Brothers Karamazov*, 109.

122. Ibid., 122.

Alyosha has here something of a sacerdotal role: it is as though what has transpired between the two brothers is the sacrament in which Christ brings healing to sin-torn humanity. Of course, Alyosha is imperfectly representative of Christ (much more so than at the end of the novel when, as mentioned above, he in some sort absolves both his brothers), but the same can be said of every priest formally and canonically hearing confessions in the person of Christ. Yet the priest, irrespective of his worthiness, makes Him present *ex opere operato* (by the work done) in the sacrament of the Eucharist. Can the same not be said of the sacrament of reconciliation? And, if it can, is not the Truth in Person in that sacrament? The truth will be there in the obvious sense if the confession is honest (like Dmitri's), but the higher, divine truth will also be present if (as the Church believes) it is Christ and not the priest himself who forgives the sins. So truth is present in the honest dialogue between God and man, and fully and precisely in the Person who is both God and Man. Like Dmitri and the woman in the gospel,[123] when we touch "the hem of that garment" which He wears, we are healed from the hemorrhage of blood (which is life, and so truth) that comes from the lie "and the father of it."[124] He transubstantiates untrue living into true life.

Dmitri's wild life is less of an obstacle to the dialogue that is the presence of the Spirit of Christ than is the unbelief of Ivan: you can cope with the bathwater if you've got the Baby. Yet Dostoevsky does not flinch from the artistic challenge of showing its presence even here: he understands that if you are only depicting a select group, you are not presenting the truth of life; if you are not sensitive to what is divine in the dialogic encounter of Christ's life in his faithful with all of humanity, you are neglecting His Truth. This sensitivity comes at a cost: the refusal of a commanding and defining narrative means that the voice of unbelief is heard in its fullest force. So much is this the case that Dostoevsky is sometimes mistaken for an advocate of hopeless unbelief. For example, J.M. Coetzee's novel, *The*

---

123. Luke 8:43–48.
124. John 8:44.

Master of Petersburg,[125] which has him as its central character brilliantly recreates his world with its acutely painful suffering, but seems to offer nothing more positive than art's ability to describe it beautifully. Furthermore, Ivan's refusal to accept a world in which children suffer has passed into the culture of the world as though it were a defining and conclusive word, repudiating the possibility of a benevolent Creator once and for all. For example, the atheist actor and author Stephen Fry, when asked what he would respond if he were (contrary to his expectation) confronted by God, said, "I'd say, bone cancer in children? What's that about? How dare you create a world in which there is such misery that is not our fault. It's not right, it's utterly, utterly evil." Asked a follow-up question about whether this would help his entry to heaven, he added, "I wouldn't want to get in on his terms. They are wrong."[126] This echoes Ivan's stand: "If the suffering of children goes to make up the sum of suffering needed to buy truth, then I assert beforehand the whole of truth is not worth such a price." Of ultimate harmony, he says, "They have put too high a price on harmony; we can't afford to pay so much for admission. And therefore I hasten to return my ticket."[127] In rejecting suffering, Ivan is by his own admission rejecting truth; it follows that he is aligning himself with the father of lies, whose banal person appears to him in a hallucination towards the end of the novel. Yet, he has a human shield against any counterattack on his position: children, whose suffering we cannot justify. We simply cannot say that everything is all right, because we are not God. We have to fall silent before his voice. Like Dostoevsky, we listen.

But there are other voices also. Here is the voice of an actual (not fictional) fifteen-year-old child enduring terrible suffering from blood cancer:

> I offer all the suffering I will have to endure to the Lord for the pope and for the Church, in order not to go through purgatory and to go straight to heaven.

125. London: Vintage, Random House, 1999.
126. *The Independent*, Saturday, January 31, 2015.
127. *The Brothers Karamazov*, 245.

These words were spoken in a belief "in redemptive suffering—that is, that suffering and personal sacrifices have meaning . . . when they are united to Christ's Passion on the Cross to accomplish God's will."[128] This is a child who said, "We are all invited to climb up Golgotha and take up our cross."[129] And when the doctor gave him the diagnosis of his illness (acute promyeloctic leukemia), he "remained calm and told his mother (who was 'very struck by his attitude, his . . . positivity and serenity') with a smile: 'The Lord gave me a wake-up call.'" He reassured concerned friends "that he was heading toward peace and happiness that cannot be found in this life." His doctors wrote about him:

> His gaze was full of attention . . . of courage, of love, of strong empathy. Shining through him was a faith in God that he had desired and still wanted to pass on to others. . . .

His father reflected on his serenity and lack of complaint—"not a whimper, not a whine, just kindness to everyone, from the medical and nursing staff to all of us."[130] He said in explanation:

> Many Christians live as if God wants to take something away from them. Most of us fail to understand the wonder of God's proposal for us. Carlo understood it.
> He understood that he was headed toward a wonderful goal, far greater than anything we could experience in earthly life. And this made him happy.[131]

And Saint Carlo Acutis made another child happy: a three-year-old Brazilian boy named Matheus Vianna, suffering from a rare congenital malformation of his pancreas and who "could hardly eat without vomiting and was therefore malnourished." The only possible treatment was a transplant, but this was refused because he was too underweight to bear the surgery.[132] Seven years after Carlo's

---

128. Courtney Mares, *Blessed Carlo Acutis: A Saint in Sneakers* (San Francisco, CA: Ignatius Press, 2023), 103.
129. Ibid., 104.
130. Ibid., 105–6.
131. Ibid., 113.
132. Ibid., 115.

death, Matheus' mother brought him to church in Campo Grande in central Brazil and there (in her words):

> Mattheus saw the line of people standing to venerate Carlo's relic and asked me what they were doing. I told him we could pray to Carlo for anything if we wanted to because he was in heaven. Mattheus was on his grandfather's lap when we approached the relic and, before my dad could touch the relic, Matheus kissed it and said out loud, "Stop vomiting!"

When he got home, "Mattheus ate rice, steak, beans, and French fries" for "the first time in his entire life" and, his mother testified, "he was cured because of Carlo." The doctors found that his pancreas was now completely normal; one of them who did not realize that the surgery needed had never taken place, remarked with surprise that it had "left no scars."[133]

Possibly, just possibly, God cares about the suffering of children. I cannot explain it, I can only listen. As for Ivan, Diane Thompson has a comment so pertinent that it is worth quoting at length:

> Ivan says he wants only to stick by the facts, that is, by his 'collection' of 'little facts' and 'little anecdotes' that he has gleaned from hearsay, newspaper cuttings and 'from wherever they turned up'. Horrible as these 'little facts' are, they do not fall within the orbit of his own experience but are at second or third remove to him. They are substitutes which testify to Ivan's failure ever to join his own personal memories with any native system of collective memory, with his family, his native culture, community or religion, from which he feels excluded and alienated in any case. Ivan suppresses his own personal memories, replacing them by anonymous incidents he reads about which seem to confirm his own reading and experiences in the social, historical context. These, in turn, he projects into an ideology of atheistic socialism and nihilism. Furthermore, however noble and sincere Ivan's indignation over the injustices he reads about, he does not have to involve himself personally in them because they all happened someplace else and, in some cases, long ago. However passionate and genuine his project against the suffering of innocent children, it is not a call

133. Ibid., 116.

to remedy injustices against children now, as are Zosima's exhortations, and as is Mitya's urgent wish to do something 'now' for the 'babe'. Nor does he involve himself in the suffering of children going on before his eyes, as Alyosha does. Restricting his examples to events beyond his own purview, Ivan does not have to take responsibility for his word, he can 'play' with nihilism. The voice of conscience in Ivan is satisfied with substitutes.[134]

In a word, Ivan's approach to truth is *impersonal*. That—the seeking of it in abstractions and ideas rather than in person—is the deep root of his refusal "to buy truth" or, to put it another way, to pay the price for it in person, as Christ did before Pilate.

But Alyosha's dialogue with Ivan *is* personal; it is loving. Although Ivan has been keeping his distance from his brother, finally it is he who makes contact, saying, "You seem to love me for some reason, Alyosha."[135] This establishes a dialogue between them and Alyosha responds to Ivan's youthful wish to live "even if it be against logic" and his love of "the sticky little leaves that come out in the spring" with the assertion that "everyone should love life before everything else in the world."[136] In love and in life they share a common truth that unites them. Alyosha meets him in refusing to agree to the suffering of a child in the "building of the edifice of human destiny with the object of making people happy in the finale."[137] He has no right to forgive its infliction, but he points to Christ, whose acceptance of human suffering by full participation enables Him to forgive. Ivan remains ambivalent: he remains in dialogue with Alyosha, yet hesitates to go beyond youthful love of life to a communion with the Lord of life who is Truth in Person. This is expressed in his telling of the celebrated parable of the Grand Inquisitor who colludes with the father of lies to take away human freedom in the name of satisfying humanity's material needs. In this, Christ appears and, like other enemies of the diabolic master plan, is condemned to be burnt. In response, He "approaches the old man and

134. Thompson, *The Brothers Karamazov and the Poetics of Memory*, 148.
135. *The Brothers Karamazov*, 229.
136. Ibid., 230–31.
137. Ibid., 245.

gently kisses him on his bloodless, ninety-year-old lips."[138] This reversal of the meaning of Judas' gesture of betrayal signifies a personal love. Ivan's inclusion of it in his composition indicates his awareness that there is a challenge to the project of tyrannical and abstract control which sacrifices personal freedom for the sake of material satisfaction so that people, though blind to truth, might "consider themselves happy."[139] Yet he "will not renounce" the necessary basis of this control, the formula "everything is permitted." Alyosha's response is to double down on Ivan's intuition of the challenge and to go over to him in silence and gently kiss him on the lips.[140] In doing so, he recognizes the truth in Ivan's parable; it is there between them in the dialogue, and in the kiss.

This is more than meets the western eye. There is an ancient Russian Orthodox tradition of everybody kissing each other on the lips at the celebration of Easter: this is without distinction of age, rank or clerical or marital status, signifying as it does the communion of the next life of "the resurrection from the dead" where they "neither marry, nor are given in marriage."[141] Such a kiss is also traditionally given at the start of Lent as a sign of mutual pardon, and to those who have died or are about to die, indicating both pardon and the hope of the perfect harmony of resurrection life.[142] These meanings coalesce in the kiss Christ gives the Grand Inquisitor: at ninety years old, the latter is close to death; he has told Christ that He is to be burnt; he responds to the kiss by letting Christ go free, reenacting His resurrection. Alyosha's kiss of Ivan makes Christ and His resurrected life present between them; it acknowledges that this is already there in the seed in Ivan's story and in his soul; it argues neither with the idea that "everything is permitted" nor with Ivan's declared intention, "I just want to drag on until I'm thirty, and then—smash the cup on the floor!"[143] Love born of the intuition of

---

138. Ibid., 262.
139. Ibid., 261.
140. Ibid., 263.
141. Luke 20:35.
142. This is indebted to Marguerite Souchon, *Le Dieu de Dostoïevski* (Paris: Éditions Première Partie, 2021), 123–33.
143. *The Brothers Karamazov*, 263.

faith (and not reason) is its source. Alyosha is silent as Christ is before Pilate and again, in the parable, before the Grand Inquisitor. And the man standing before Pilate and before the Grand Inquisitor is the Truth. This is validated in the infinite life of the resurrection and cannot be overcome by the father of lies suggesting that there are people who have to be excluded from it.

And it is the private property of no one. Alyosha is its agent (especially in bringing the children into amity) but he also receives it from a woman whom others do not regard as respectable. Grushenka thinks, "How a man like him must despise a bad woman like me,"[144] yet her declaration of sisterly love rescues him from depravity born of despondency when he loses his beloved spiritual guide and the hope that the latter's sanctity would be miraculously confirmed. Brought to her house by a low friend, he declares, "I came here looking for a wicked soul—I was drawn to that, because I was low and wicked myself, but I found a true sister, I found a treasure—a loving soul" and tells her, "You restored my soul just now."[145] Christ is in their dialogue, between them; He is in their love and respect for each other.

Frank and Freedom

Truth is present in reciprocal relationship. Man is truly alive when open to the infinite mystery of the divine.

This is echoed in the document produced as a synthesis of the October 2023 synod on the synodal way which declared that "reciprocal relationships are the place and form of an authentic encounter with God."[146] It takes us back to the reflections of the Russian philosopher S.L. Frank towards the beginning of this chapter. He finds "essential reality" in such relationships:

---

144. Ibid., 350.

145. Ibid., 351.

146. https://www.synod.va/content/dam/synod/assembly/synthesis/english/2023.10.28-ENG-Synthesis-Report.pdf Synodal Synthesis Report, October 2023 2. Gathered and Sent by the Trinity, Convergences c).

In the "I-thou" relation the transrational essence of reality—the essentially unknowable in reality—is disclosed with particular certainty as *the unity of separateness and mutual penetration.*[147]

The words in italics are the same as those in the citation from him in the first section of this chapter about how we know a person. The implication is that the Truth in the person of Christ or the person of His Holy Spirit (who guides us "into all truth")[148] is present in reciprocal relationships. This is most strikingly the case when the apostles "were all filled with the Holy Ghost, and began to speak with other tongues, as the Spirit gave them utterance" and "the multitude came together, and were confounded, because that every man heard them speak in his own language."[149] Such is the reciprocity here that the multitude come to form one person, the person of Christ, as they are baptized into His Body, the Church.

Each person has the potential to be open to the infinite mystery of Christ, Truth in person. The person is, in Frank's words, "a kind of infinitude"[150] to whose essence belongs "the aura of unknowableness" which can only be apprehended transrationally "as the coincidence of opposites, as the unity of the subjective *and* the objective, the immanent *and* the transcendent."[151] The essence of reality, he says, as:

"living life" (to use Dostoevsky's marvelous term)—not being the object of thought, not being present before us as an object, but only flowing into us and flowing out of us—coincides with the essentially unknowable. It is the eternal mystery in which and by which we live.[152]

The truth, the essence of reality, is alive in and among human persons and is eternal mystery.

Dostoevsky knew this. In his *Diary of a Writer* he observed, "There are general, eternal and—it would seem—forever unexplor-

147. *The Unknowable,* 143.
148. John 16:13.
149. Acts 2:4, 6.
150. *The Unknowable,* 176.
151. Ibid., 177.
152. Ibid., 76.

able depths of human character and spirit."[153] He explored "the mutabilities and indeterminacies of human character"[154] in his story, *The Eternal Husband*. The catalyst for this was an analysis of characters in Russian literature favored by the contemporary literary critic, Nikolai Strakhov, about (to quote the story itself) the "'predatory' type and the 'submissive' one."[155] The tale is of a man who cuckolds, Velchaninov, and a man who is cuckolded, Pavel Pavlovich, and the facile assumption would be that these correspond to the predatory and submissive types respectively. In fact their characters are far more fluid than this. At the climax of the narrative, the latter attacks the former with a knife. As Velchaninov tries to understand this afterwards, "He was clearly aware of only one thing: that Pavel Pavlovich really had wanted to murder him, but had himself, perhaps, not yet known a quarter of an hour before that he would."[156] The attacker's action is not predetermined by character or by anything else: there really is personal freedom in the moment. This is so because the human person opens to the infinite, that is to say, the freedom of God.

It is there that truth and life are to be found. The essence of life, S.L. Frank argues, is "light"—that is, the light of God's truth that "shineth in darkness"[157]—and comments:

> This transrational relationship is revealed in experience in the fact that (Dostoevsky showed this convincingly) whenever a man attempts to close himself off from transcendent reality and live in and from himself by the force of his subjective will alone, he perishes because he becomes the slave and plaything of transcendent forces, namely the dark forces of destruction.[158]

153. Fyodor Dostoevsky, *The Diary of a Writer*, trans. Boris Brasol (Salt Lake City: Peregrine Smith Books, 1985), 91.

154. Joseph Frank, *Dostoevsky: A Writer in His Time* (Princeton, NJ: Princeton University Press, 2010), 596.

155. Fyodor Dostoevsky, *The Eternal Husband*, trans. Hugh Aplin (Richmond, Surrey, UK: Alma Books Ltd., 2007), vi–vii, 86.

156. Ibid., 158.

157. John 1:5.

158. *The Unknowable*, 171–72.

God's freedom is absolute; man's freedom is to participate in this or to become enslaved to the father of lies in the manner of the would-be revolutionary characters of Dostoevsky's novel, *Demons*. To turn away from life and light (as manifest in the One in whom "was life; and the life was the light of men")[159] is necessarily narrowing, however enticing the scheme for which they are forsaken. As Pavel Florensky observed, "As soon as the intelligentsia steps away from faith in life, it becomes necessary to believe in one's clique."[160] Knowing, in the sense of worshipping only what is predictable according to the laws of reason as applied by fashionable ideology, is darkness; unknowing, in the sense of being open to the infinite revealed to us from heaven, is light, and it is life. Again, Dostoevsky gets it right:

> 'Consciousness of life is superior to life, knowledge of the laws of happiness is superior to happiness'—this is what we must fight against.[161]

The truth of human life and happiness can never be narrowed to laws, because the human person is made not for death but to share the infinite light and life of God. So much is implied even in one of the grimmest scenes in Dostoevsky's novels, where the troubled heroine Nastasya Filippovna, lies dead between Rogozhin, her murderer, and Prince Myshkin, the eponymous idiot, who is about to lose his mind altogether. According to how the dialogue is generally translated, Rogozhin says, "Do you notice the smell or not?"[162] Yet the Russian word rendered by "smell," *dookh*, means "spirit." And shortly afterwards he asks:

> "Footsteps! Do you hear? In the big room…"
> They both began to listen.
> "I hear," the prince whispered firmly.

---

159. John 1:4.

160. Florensky, *At the Crossroads of Science and Mysticism*, 105.

161. "The Dream of a Ridiculous Man," trans. Olga Shartse, in *The Russian Soul: Selections from 'A Writer's Diary'* (Honiton, UK: Notting Hill Editions, 2017), 108.

162. Fyodor Dostoevsky, *The Idiot*, trans. Richard Pevear and Larissa Volokhonsky (London: Everyman's Library, 2002), 608.

"Footsteps?"
"Footsteps."[163]

There is no indication that anyone else can be there; we are explicitly told that it is only "after many hours" that people do come.[164] The implication is that the spirit of Nastasya, whose unabbreviated name "Anastasya" means "Resurrection," lives on.[165] It is subtle: we cannot say we *know* she is alive, rather we are directed towards the unknowable.

The human person cannot be reduced to laws. But what of the earthly creation as a whole? Much discourse about it uses law as a metaphor. Yet there is another, more personal, way of thinking about it. It does after all tell us about God, "for the invisible things of him from the creation of the world are clearly seen, being understood by the things that are made, even his eternal power and Godhead."[166] The next chapter explores personal imaging of this channel of God's truth.

163. Ibid., 610.
164. Ibid., 611.
165. This is indebted to Marguerite Souchon, *Le Dieu de Dostoïevski* (Paris: Éditions Première Partie, 2021), 112–14.
166. Romans 1:20.

E: Earth & Eternity

Mother and Father

The Mother is everything to a little child; with the father she makes sense of the world for it. Nature too is a mother, or at least a sister, sharing with a human person the quality of not being subject to total definition and control.

I mentioned in the introduction how my mother with her personal touch deftly enabled me to overcome being frightened by a vacuum cleaner. In fact mothers do far more to establish their children's relation to the world. It is not an exaggeration to say that to begin with a mother *is* the child's world. This is clearly the case when the child is in the womb, and it is to some extent so for the neonate, depending on the embrace and breast of her or his mother. Indeed, at first there may be no real distinction from the child's point of view between the mother and the world. Mother and Mother Earth are one. And in this, perhaps the child has an insight after the manner of the childlike expectation that a story finishes happily, of which I wrote in Chapter C. Later in this chapter, I will consider some prophetic voices who have in some sense regained the light in the eyes of a child looking at the earth in wonder. These folk integrate such a perspective into an adult awareness of the world's complexity; they journey towards the kingdom of heaven by becoming like little children believing in a happy ending, without being any the less aware than anyone else of the evils in the world. Here I want to consider the natural relation between mother and Mother Nature as it develops in the growing child. The very first development is identifying the mother as other. This in a way corresponds ontogenetically to when God "divided the waters which were under the firmament from the waters which were above the firmament."[1] Here heaven is

1. Genesis 1:7.

divided from land and sea, anticipating the child's realization that mother is not actually part of her or his body, but other. The child begins (literally) to look up to the mother, seeking her gaze, as the religious person looks up to heaven to make contact with the divine. A vital emotional and spiritual connection is established. There follows an extended time of nurture in which the mother fulfils the child's need for feeding. Finally, the child becomes an adult and while not forgetting the maternal care begins to see the mother as in practice more like an equal, a sibling. This is at its starkest in the funeral service where, even if the deceased is the mother of the priest or deacon conducting it, he nevertheless says, "Let us take our sister to her place of rest." So with our relation to the earth, in terms of both personal and collective history: it begins with a trusting looking towards it as the source of our nourishment and ends, if it is healthy, with us seeing the earth as a sister, sharing with us a Creator.

So the truth of the earth is personal, shown to us in a very direct way by our mother. This truth is also personally mediated to us through our mother tongue, normally through words spoken to us by our mother. How vital a mother's making sense of the world for the child by speaking of it is evident from the story of Helen Keller. I wrote in *The Meaning of Blue* about this as reminding us of "how language first disclosed the world to us as children." Helen Keller lost her sight and hearing before she learned to speak. When finally "the mystery of language" was revealed to her through touch, she reported that "each name gave birth to a new thought" and "each object that I touched seemed to quiver with life."[2] To know anything of the truth of creation, we need personal communication of language. This is vital. The thirteenth-century Emperor Frederick the Second ordered an unethical experiment in which a group of children were raised from birth in complete silence. They died before the experiment was completed.[3] Babies never establish a life-giving relation with the world through abstraction: they need the words of a mother or another nurturer.

---

2. *The Meaning of Blue*, 130–31.
3. Piers Paul Read, *A History of the Catholic Church* (Meid Books, 2023), 116.

Such, of course, can be a father. I cited in Chapter B the poignant words from a novel about a man bringing up his son in the most desperate of circumstances. These are spoken to the child who, following his father's death, finds it easier to pray to him than to God: "the breath of God was his breath yet though it pass from man to man through all of time." [4] This is "the breath of life" which, when "the LORD God formed man of the dust of the ground," He "breathed into his nostrils" so that "man became a living soul."[5] It is the breath with which Adam spoke when the Lord brought "every beast of the field, and every fowl of the air "unto Adam to see what he would call them: and whatsoever Adam called every living creature, that was the name thereof."[6] Adam is here speaking the truth about the creation because he is speaking with the breath of God, the source of his life and so the light which reveals the truth. This is passed on from generation to generation so that even in the final desolation God can still speak through a father. Fathers transmit tradition. I remember my own father explaining Archimedes' discovery, marking the level of bath water with a piece of soap, and, on another occasion telling of Captain Oates' heroic sacrifice for the sake of his fellow polar explorers, made with the words, "I am just going outside and may be some time." The truth of creation and its history is personally mediated.

It is significant that in some spiritual traditions, particularly older ones, the mediation is only allowed if it is oral. It is as though the written word is not personal enough. And even when it is written, as in the accounts of the sayings of the Desert Fathers, it is framed as a report of a "word" spoken by a particular sage. This is true of the Bible's accounts of the words of Jesus, as in the saying, "Ye are clean through the word I have spoken unto you."[7] The personal word of the Lord has power to cleanse His followers of men-

4. Cormac McCarthy, *The Road* (London: Pan Macmillan, 2019), 306.
5. Genesis 2:7.
6. Genesis 2:19.
7. John 15:3.

dacity so that they may know the truth and be set free by it.[8] His word is personally transmitted also through succeeding generations, as in the celebrated instance of it being given to John the Evangelist, from him to Saint Polycarp and from Saint Polycarp to Saint Irenaeus. Each is a father and each learns from a father. Even Jesus learns craft and meaning from Saint Joseph. Such is the patristic tradition, which complements by its spiritual reach the motherly teaching that is essential for life. There is of course some interchangeability in what a mother and father do, as is very evident when one of them dies young, but life and truth are given personally or not at all. It follows that our apprehension of the world is personally structured.

This is true in a deeper sense than my mother's ruse to get me to see the vacuum cleaner as a sort of person. The sense of the personal in creation comes not only from parents or other persons, it is there in Mother Nature herself. To talk about nature in this way is rhetorical: even in its time of general use. In C.S. Lewis' words, "She is, for the medievals, only a personification."[9] As such, that belongs to poetry. Yet poetry can speak more truly than the language of a certain kind of science that strives to encompass nature by laws. That this cannot be a complete account is evident from the reality of miracles, which violate such laws. It is also contradicted by the presence of ontological depth in creation, as discussed in Chapter A with reference to the philosophical thought of S.L. Frank and others. Science too comes to an awareness of the impossibility of total definition of created reality in the Heisenberg principle, which implies that the more accurately you know the position of a particle, the less accurately you can know its momentum, and vice versa. Poetry incorporates uncertainty, bodies forth mystery, draws us to depth. In postulating nature as a person, it includes uncertainty. To repeat a citation I made from Frank in the previous chapter in the context of Dostoevsky's understanding of the "unexplorable depths

8. Cf. John 8:32.
9. C.S. Lewis, *The Discarded Image* (Cambridge: Cambridge University Press, 1964), 39.

of human character and spirit,"[10] a person is "a kind of infinitude."[11] Fundamentally, to say that nature is a person is to say that she participates in the openness that belongs to a person: in a word, she is alive.

The delusional enterprise to command and control creation is wittily and elegantly deconstructed by Nassim Nicholas Taleb in his book, *Anti-Fragile*, in which (unafraid to call nature "mother") he argues that robustness in coping with uncertainty is preferable to straining to create certainty. A taste for uncertainty is an indication of life:

> The best way to verify that you are alive is by checking if you like variations. Remember that food would not have a taste if it weren't for hunger; results are meaningless without effort, joy without sadness, convictions without uncertainty, and an ethical life isn't so when stripped of personal risks.[12]

The beat of the healthy human heart is variable; complete loss of variability is a sign that it is dangerously stressed.[13] Variation is necessary for life. Those who "hunger and thirst after righteousness" are filled.[14] The righteousness of Christ before Pilate entails His vulnerability. The joy of life enfolds sorrow: "A woman when she is in travail hath sorrow, because her hour is come: but as soon as she is delivered of the child, she remembereth no more the anguish, for joy that a man is born into the world."[15] Saint Paul applies the principle to nature: "the whole creation groaneth and travaileth in pain together until now."[16] He eschews "convictions without uncertainty" for he knows that "hope that is seen is not hope"[17] and creation is subjected to her travail "in hope."[18] This living quality of

10. Dostoevsky, *The Diary of a Writer*, 91.
11. Frank, *The Unknowable*, 176.
12. Nicholas Nassim Taleb, *Anti-Fragile: Things that Gain from Disorder* (London: Penguin, 2012), 423.
13. McGilchrist, *The Matter With Things*, 1279 and footnote 83. Kindle.
14. Matthew 5:6.
15. John 16:21.
16. Romans 8:22.
17. Romans 8:24.
18. Romans 8:20.

creation is attested to by rheology, the science of the deformation and flow of matter, which assigns a "Deborah number"[19] to materials, including solids (all of which flow under the right circumstances), memorializing the great woman in the Bible, who sang, "The mountains melted from before the LORD."[20]

Biblical Wisdom

The Bible shows us the person of Wisdom, informing the Creator's work and making people wise.

The Bible, however, attributes more than mobility to creation. It shows us a personal aspect of what is made that goes beyond being a mother: it presents Mother Nature herself as in a sense mothered. Such is the implication of these words of Wisdom (in person) in the book of Proverbs:

> I was set up from everlasting, from the beginning, or ever the earth was. When there were no depths, I was brought forth; when there were no fountains abounding with water. Before the mountains were settled, before the hills was I brought forth: While as yet he had not made the earth, nor the fields, nor the highest part of the dust of the world. When he prepared the heavens, I was there: when he set a compass upon the face of the depth: When he established the clouds above: when he strengthened the fountains of the deep: When he gave to the sea his decree, that the waters should not pass his commandment: when he appointed the foundations of the earth: Then I was by him, as one brought up with him: and I was daily his delight, rejoicing always before him.[21]

Wisdom is here conceived (the metaphor implies that even a thought is by its nature personal) as being involved in creation by her presence not as Creator but as the principle of its coherence. There is not some master algorithm, one day to be discovered, that establishes nature as it is, but a living truth best imagined as per-

---

19. *The Matter With Things*, 2791. Kindle.
20. Judges 5:5.
21. Proverbs 8:23–30.

sonal. Wisdom's relation to the Creator is described in the book of Ecclesiasticus:

> There is one wise and greatly to be feared, the Lord sitting upon his throne. He created her, and saw her, and numbered her, and poured her out upon all his works.[22]

Wisdom, "created before all things,"[23] is here presented as the personal manifestation of God's creative thought, not nature but the intelligence that fashions nature, which is shown in the life and beauty of nature. Sophia is *natura naturans* rather than *natura naturata*. She extends her forming influence not only in the wise disposition of nature, but also in the growth in wisdom of human persons. Jesus speaks of her as the mother of those who are wise:

> John came neither eating nor drinking, and they say, He hath a devil. The Son of Man came eating and drinking, and they say, Behold a man gluttonous, and a winebibber, a friend of publicans and sinners. But wisdom is justified of her children.[24]

The children of wisdom, here exemplified by John the Baptist and Jesus, show her to be just, for they know that there is "a time to every purpose under the heaven,"[25] a time to fast and a time to feast and they know when those times are. There is an intelligence in the ordering of nature; those who order their own relations with nature rightly live by this same intelligence who is as it were their mother.

It makes intuitive sense to see this intelligence as in some way a person, since the higher contains the lower, not the other way around. Of course machines can outcompute people, but they do not live and that is related to their inability to receive and recognize living truth. They can assess whether information accords with other information, but are not themselves able to enter into that friendship in which Jesus says, "All things that I have heard of my Father I have made known unto you."[26] However agile they are in

---

22. Ecclesiasticus 1:8–9.
23. Ecclesiasticus 1:4.
24. Matthew 11:18–19.
25. Ecclesiastes 3:1.
26. John 15:15.

processing information, there is no living spirit in them; they record what has been put in them but are themselves dead. The creation is not a machine but living; the intelligence in nature is living thought and thought does not exist in the abstract, as Dostoevsky understood so well. Breath is the primordial symbol of life and wisdom is identified as such in the Bible at the beginning of this account of her reach:

> She is the breath of the power of God, and a pure influence flowing from the glory of the Almighty: therefore can no defiled thing fall into her. For she is the brightness of the everlasting light, the unspotted mirror of the power of God, and the image of his goodness. And being but one, she can do all things: and remaining in herself, she maketh all things new: and in all ages entering into holy souls, she maketh them friends of God, and prophets. For God loveth none but him that dwelleth with wisdom. For she is more beautiful than the sun, and above all the order of stars: being compared with the light, she is found before it. For after this cometh night: but vice shall not prevail against wisdom. Wisdom reacheth from one end to another mightily: and sweetly doth she order all things.[27]

She is both living and unsullied by life: "lively, clear, undefiled."[28] She is closer to God than creation, "set up from everlasting,"[29] and so inviolably virgin. "Flowing from the glory of the Almighty" she is the one through whom "the brightness of the everlasting light" is channeled into creation. This comes about by her "entering into holy souls" and making them "friends of God, and prophets." On the earth there is a clash between light and darkness, good and evil, but she is above that as "the breath of the power of God" and "being compared with the light, she is found before it." She is above that primal division when "God divided the light from the darkness."[30] That is why "vice shall not prevail" against her. Yet, for all her eminence, her brightening and renewing presence is in some sense perceivable in creation.

27. Wisdom of Solomon 7:25–8:1.
28. Ibid., 7:22.
29. Proverbs 8:23.
30. Genesis 1:4.

Prophetic voices speak of it, if only from recollections of early childhood. Such is the voice of Wordsworth, who recalls when "meadow, grove, and stream,/ The earth, and every common sight" seemed "appareled in celestial light,/ The glory and freshness of a dream." He writes, "Nothing can bring back the hour/ Of splendour in the grass, of glory in the flower," yet his very remembrance and its poetic expression in a way makes it present.[31] And in *The Prelude* he writes of an adult experience:

> When at my feet the ground appear'd to brighten,
> And with a step or two seem'd brighter still;
> Nor had I time to ask the cause of this,
> For instantly a Light upon the turf
> Fell like a flash: I looked about, and lo!
> The Moon stood naked in the Heavens, at height
> Immense above my head, and on the shore
> I found myself of a huge sea of mist,
> Which, meek and silent, rested at my feet[32]

The implication that the mist, "meek and silent," is a human presence conveys the living quality of nature, but above all this is established by the light of the moon ("naked" like a person) which for the moment appears as "the brightness of the everlasting light" characteristic of wisdom. There is a silent subtext of the moon as Diana, the chaste goddess, a poetic rendering of Wisdom "the unspotted mirror of the power of God" who reflects the light of the sun, imaging "the glory of the Almighty." This relation to the Divine is explicit in the poet's further pondering:

> A meditation rose in me that night
> Upon the lonely Mountain when the scene
> Had pass'd away, and it appear'd to me
> The perfect image of a mighty Mind,
> Of one that feeds upon infinity,

---

31. William Wordsworth, *Ode on Intimations of Immortality from Recollections of Early Childhood* (https://www.poetryfoundation.org/poems/45536/ode-intima-tions-of-immortality-from-recollections-of-early-childhood).

32. William Wordsworth, *The Prelude* (Oxford: Oxford University Press, 1956), Book XIII, lines 36–45.

That is exalted by an underpresence,
The sense of God…[33]

The mention of "infinity" evokes the celestial realm in which anti-nomies meet, where what is above ("exalted") is one with what is below ("an underpresence") since space, like time, is transcended. There is a presence, as it were, of Wisdom in person.

Jon Fosse expresses awareness of such a presence in his short novel, *A Shining*, published in 2023. It is about a man who goes for a drive out of sheer boredom, abandons his car in a wood after it gets stuck there and wanders, after the manner of Dante, into the dark. He tells his story:

> I stand and look straight ahead into the impenetrable darkness. And I see the darkness change, no, not the darkness itself, but something separates from the darkness and comes towards me. Now I see it clearly. Something's coming towards me, and maybe it's a person. Or what. Yes, it probably has to be a person. But it can't be a person. It's just not possible that I'm seeing a person, not here, not now. But what is it then. I see the outline of something, and it looks like a person. Because it can't very well be anything else, can it. I stand totally still. I stand like I don't dare move. Now it's really as dark as it can get and there in front of me I see the out-line of something that looks like a person. A shining outline, get-ting clearer and clearer. Yes, a white outline there in the dark, right in front of me. Is it far away or is it nearby. I can't say for sure. It's impossible, yes, impossible to say whether it is close or far away. But it's there. A white outline. Shining.[34]

The ambiguity about whether the presence is far or near echoes that in the Wordsworth lines about being exalted by an underpresence, suggesting some kind of radiance from the Divine which is both transcendent and immanent. That the presence "has to be a person" and "can't be a person" is an antinomy pointing to what is beyond, and within, the rationality of this world. It is a poetic rendering of the deep truth of creation, poetry speaking more accurately of its

33. Ibid., lines 66–72.
34. Jon Fosse, *A Shining*, trans. Damion Searls (London: Fitzcarraldo Editions, 2023), 17.

ontological depth than any algorithmic formula could. "The shining whiteness keeps getting closer" and the ambiguity persists: "It can't possibly be a person. But then what is it. Because it looks like a person. It's shaped like a person."[35] The encounter gets more personal:

> Suddenly I felt something like a hand on my shoulder, heavily but in a way lightly. Or an actual hand. No, it wasn't a hand, but it felt like a hand, and so what was it, since, or maybe if, it wasn't a hand. And then something like an arm, yes it had to be an arm, was laid over my shoulders and holding me, lightly, but I could feel it.

The ambiguity intensifies until the man wonders:

> Or had I now become something like a part of the shining presence. But how could something like that be possible. For the shining presence's arm, if that's the right thing to call it, now felt like something inseparable from my body. . . .[36]

Finally, it is dark again until the moon comes out with "white twinkling stars" and "it's beautiful."[37] The lack of clear boundaries between personhood and the presence, between the presence and the one perceiving and even between the presence and the experience of the beauty of nature underscores the inadequacy of an epistemology or habit of encounter that considers creation merely a thing functioning as a machine would. There is truth in creation and it is alive and there is something personal in it.

All of this belongs to Wisdom as the ordering source of the beauty of nature. The "kind of infinitude"[38] that belongs to a person is hers:

> The first man knew her not perfectly: no more shall the last find her out. For her thoughts are more than the sea, and her counsels profounder than the great deep.[39]

And she engages actively with those who are open to her:

35. Ibid., 18.
36. Ibid., 20.
37. Ibid., 22.
38. *The Unknowable*, 176 (quoted above).
39. Ecclesiasticus 24:28–29.

She is easily seen of them that love her, and found of such as seek her. She preventeth them that desire her, in making herself first known unto them. Whoso seeketh her early shall have no great travail: for he shall find her sitting at his doors. To think therefore upon her is perfection of wisdom: and whoso watcheth for her shall quickly be without care. For she goeth about seeking such as are worthy of her, sheweth herself favourably unto them in the ways and meeteth them in every thought.[40]

Wisdom "preventeth them that desire her": that is to say, she comes to them before they come to her. Receptivity to wisdom is a way of engaging with the world very different from the rapacious thirst for control and exploitation that characterizes the mindset that has caused so much damage to the planet in recent centuries. It is concerned with rapport and harmony; it is two-way; it allows her to change "such as seek her" for she "meeteth them in every thought." It is a personal encounter open to the truth which is not something to be possessed but rather a fashioner of these seekers so that, at peace with the world, they become "without care."

Beatrice

Beatrice is for the poet Dante a personification of spiritual wisdom, who guides him to the height of heaven.

If the moon can in the poetic imagination be a bodying forth of the ordering intelligence that shines through creation, then *a fortiori* a human person can be such. In Dante's *Divine Comedy*, the poet is inspired in his ascent from hell to heaven through purgatory by the blessed spirit of Beatrice, whom he saw and loved while she was yet on earth. She is presented as "a light 'twixt truth and intellect,"[41] the radiance in person of the divine intelligence as communicated to the human mind through creation. She addresses him from under a veil "twined of Minerva's leaves,"[42] indicating her embodiment of the

40. Wisdom of Solomon 6:12–16.

41. Dante, *The Divine Comedy: 2 Purgatory*, trans. Dorothy L. Sayers (Harmondsworth, UK: Penguin, 1955), Canto 6, line 45 ("lume fia tra 'l vero e lo 'intelletto").

42. Ibid., Canto 30, line 68 ("cerchiato delle fronde di Minerva").

sagacity of the Greek goddess of wisdom. Challenging Dante to be truthful about his life, she is revealed as "splendour of living light eternal."[43] Dante has come to this, she says, by "That desire of me which bore/ Thy love along with it to seek the Good."[44] According to the Dominican, Kenelm Foster, commentating on *The Divine Comedy*, "All human desires *are* radically one, as stemming from a substance that is one."[45] It follows that under Beatrice's beneficent influence Dante (as a character in the epic) is being made true: that is to say, his love is being purified so that it is a love for the supreme good, Divine Truth, for "to lose sight of truth is to begin to miss the way to God."[46] This parallels the approach to the poem taken by the psychotherapist, Mark Vernon, whose *Dante's Divine Comedy* is significantly subtitled, "A Guide for the Spiritual Journey." He highlights Dante's insistence on "the crucial role of erotic love in relation to spiritual enlightenment"[47] and considers that the hermeneutic key to the work is the journeyer's "perceptual development,"[48] which is to say he becomes more open to divine truth by the purification of his love. Beatrice is "much more than the object of his infatuation," becoming a star guiding him "in his search for constant, eternal love."[49] She is "an incarnation of Sophia,"[50] the personification of wisdom, and her face is "glowing with truth."[51] Love for her awakes in him a desire in him "not primarily for another person" though it powerfully seems like that at first, but "for divine life."[52]

Vernon reflects that "the common human experience called fall-

43. Dante, *The Divine Comedy, 2: Purgatorio*, trans. John D. Sinclair (Oxford: Oxford University Press, 1962), Canto 31, line 139 ("isplendor di viva luce etterna").

44. Dante, *The Divine Comedy: 2 Purgatory*, trans. Dorothy L. Sayers), Canto 31, lines 22–23 ("Per entro i mie' desiri,/ che ti menavano ad amar lo bene").

45. Kenelm Foster, *The Two Dantes* (London: Darton, Longman & Todd, 1977), 37.

46. Ibid., 53.

47. Mark Vernon, *Dante's Divine Comedy: A Guide for the Spiritual Journey* (Brooklyn, NY: Angelico Press, 2021), xiv.

48. Ibid., xv.

49. Ibid., 189.

50. Ibid., 326.

51. Ibid., 390.

52. Ibid., 265.

ing in love," as Dante does with Beatrice, "can lead not just to
another person but to divine life, by learning to discern what's
beautiful more deeply."[53] It can lead too to what at the highest (or
deepest) level is the same, to greater awareness of what is true.
Indeed, its potential outcome is "delightful awareness of what is
beautiful, good, and true." Yet, as Vernon and the whole of the
ascetical and cultural tradition are aware, it can go horribly wrong,
even as far as "an uncontrolled rape of life itself." This is all too evident in the tragedy of abortion ending life to facilitate the indul-
gence of lust. Even in love stories with a happy ending, as
Shakespeare bears witness, the course of true love never did run
smooth. Getting to the sweet spot for the one who loves like Dante
involves "the painful struggle to reform his desires, his perceptions,
his knowledge, and his will so that he can become capable of paradise."[54] The beginning of this, which applies both to love of another
person and to love of God, is the realization that one is not at the
center of the universe. Romeo looking up at Juliet and the religious
devotee bereft of consolation from God both have this borne in on
them. Decentering from the self is the beginning of the move
towards truth. In Dante's work the love of the human person leads
to love of God. This in a sense corresponds to the gospel which says
love of neighbor is "like" love of God. In a spousal context love can
issue in the person of a child who, even if not actually called
"Sophia," is a manifestation of the truth of God; in a religious context love can issue in the persons of spiritual children, since no one
goes to heaven alone. In either case, there is a being made true in
God, which simply amounts to God, not self, being at the center of
life, which He truly is. The illusion of the self being the center is
overcome in service and in prayer.

Commenting on the ability of Virgil, Dante's poet guide to the
afterlife, to know intuitively what is in his mind, Vernon says:

This sharing of minds will become an increasing feature of the
journey to God. It will double in intensity when Dante meets Bea-

53. Ibid., 9.
54. Ibid., 192.

trice. It arises, I think, with the realization that consciousness—meaning thoughts and feelings—is not the private feature of existence it is commonly taken to be. Awareness of what is on another's mind grows with the recognition that the consciousness of two people is, at base, one.

Like Dostoevsky seeing the divine in dialogue, the psychotherapist points to "a unity that sustains everyone."[55] The journey to the truth, poetically transcribed in Dante's ascent from hell through purgatory to paradise, is the development of the awareness of this unity as the light in which everything is seen clearly. The first celestial sphere in Dante's cosmography is that of the moon which, as for Wordsworth climbing the mountain, or the votary of Diana the chaste goddess, or Fosse's character enjoying an epiphany in the snowy woods, images divine illumination by reflecting the light of the sun. Such light shows the deep truth of what there is: "To be in the diamond-pearl light of the moon is to be in the state of mind where the immortal begins to shine through the mortal, the necessary emerges from the contingent, the incorruptible radiates through the mutable."[56]

Beatrice, "intent upon the sun,"[57] is like the moon to Dante. He receives light through her, whom he loves. The poet invents a term for what happens to him, "trasumanar," transhumanization or "passing beyond humanity," which he says cannot be denoted by words.[58] Contemporary pretensions to transhumanism are an inversion of what Dante describes. He is speaking of what happens when someone is made true by the divine light; the transhumanist project is an attempt to go beyond God-given human nature by force of will. The one is contemplative, the other tries to reach independence of the divine; the one looks to God, the other looks away

---

55. Ibid., 206.

56. Ibid., 304.

57. Dante, *The Divine Comedy: 3 Paradise*, trans. Dorothy L. Sayers and Barbara Reynolds (Harmondsworth, UK: Penguin, 1975), Canto 1, line 46 ("rivolta e riguardar nel sole").

58. Dante, *The Divine Comedy: 3 Paradise*, trans. by John D. Sinclair (Oxford: Oxford University Press, 1961), Canto 1, lines 70–71 ("Trasumanar significar per verba/ non si porìa").

from Him; the one allows the will to be conformed to God, the other steels the will of the self. Significantly, Dante describes himself as "changed within" through having his eyes fixed on Beatrice.[59] The change is to participation in the true life and light of God and it comes through the person of the blessed soul whom he loves. He can say simply, "Beatrice gazed on heav'n and I on her."[60] Receiving from her explanations of the ordering of creation, he recognizes the same power at work that first inspired his love: "The sun that warmed my bosom first with love/ Had brought the beauteous face of truth to light."[61] Beatrice is "the sun" for him by reflection, show-ing in her person the warmth and light of God, but this divine sun also shines directly in his heart, inspiring his love and bringing him understanding in his mind. Both senses are included if we interpret it as that which is between them and unites them. Such is God's love: it makes the disparate one, overcoming separation without loss of diversity. Furthermore, it overcomes the disjunction of time: the same sun that warms his young heart with love enlightens his middle-aged mind with understanding. The love, transcending time, contains the understanding that is to be unfolded; indeed, it unites the heart and mind. It is ever new with the fervor of youth and ever ancient with the wisdom of age. In eternity they are one in the person made whole, made true.

Beatrice, and the great throng of the blessed, are made whole and true by the person of Christ. She looks toward him with her face "all aglow with love;/ And in her eyes such joyousness."[62] The sight is too much for Dante and he cries out to Beatrice, who explains why it is so overpowering:

---

59. Ibid., lines 64–69 ("Beatrice tutta nell'etterne rote/ fissa con li occhi stava; ed io in lei/ le luci fissi, di là su remote./ Nel suo aspetto tal dentro mi fei, qual si fè Glauco nel gustar dell'erba/ che'l fè consorte in mar delli altri Dei.").

60. Dante, *The Divine Comedy: 3 Paradise*, trans. by Dorothy L. Sayers and Bar-bara Reynolds, Canto 2, line 22 ("Beatrice in suso, e io in lei guardava").

61. Ibid., Canto 3, lines 1–2 ("Quel sol che pria d'amor mi scaldò 'l petto,/ di bella verità m'avea scoverto").

62. Ibid., Canto 23, lines 22–23 ("Parìemi che 'l suo viso ardesse tutto,/ e li occhi avea di letizia sì pieni").

Outshining myriad lamps, One Sun I knew
  Which kindled all the rest, even as our sun
  Lights the celestial pageantry we view.

And through the living radiance there shone
  The shining Substance, bright, and to such end
  Full in my face, my vision was undone.

O Beatrice! belovèd guide, sweet friend!
  She said: "That which now overmasters thee
  Is might which nothing can evade or fend.

Herein the wisdom and the power see
  That opened between Heaven and earth the road
  Longed for and awaited ardently."[63]

Christ, powerless before Pilate and mocked on the cross for being unable to save Himself, is "the power of God, and the wisdom of God"[64] that nothing can resist. He is the way to heaven, "the true Light that lighteth every man that cometh into the world,"[65] and "the resurrection, and the life."[66] He is the truth in person, the truth that makes persons true.

Although simply the glimpse of this truth is enough to overcome Dante, what he beholds makes him strong enough to look at Beatrice's smile, as she tells him:

"Lift up thine eyes and look on me a while;
  See what I am; thou hast beheld such things
  As make thee mighty to endure my smile."[67]

63. Ibid., Canto 23, lines 28–37 ("vidi sopra migliaia di lucerne/ un sol che tutte quante l'accendea,/ come fa il nostro le viste superne;/ e per la viva luce trasparea/ la lucente sustanza tanto chiara/ nel viso mio, che non la sostenea./ Oh Beatrice dolce guida e cara!/ Ella mi disse: 'Quel che ti sobranza/ è virtù da cui nulla si ripara./ Quivi è la sapïenza e la possanza/ ch'aprì le strade tra 'l cielo e la terra,/ onde fu già sì lunga disïanza.'").

64. 1 Corinthians 1:24.

65. John 1:9.

66. John 11:25.

67. Dante, *The Divine Comedy: 3 Paradise*, trans. Dorothy L. Sayers and Barbara Reynolds, Canto 23, lines 46–48 ("'Apri li occhi e riguarda qual son io:/ tu hai vedute cose, che possente/ se' fatto a sostener lo riso mio.'").

He struggles to say how wonderful that is, but Beatrice points beyond herself to the person in whom the Word of Truth was given flesh, Mary:

> "Why art thou so enamoured of my face
> Thou wilt not turn thee to the garden bright
> Shone on by Christ, and flowering in his rays?

> "There blooms the rose wherein God's Word was dight
> With flesh, and there the lilies blow whose scent
> Wooed man to take the road that runs aright."[68]

Christ, "full of grace and truth,"[69] could only come among us with the consent of a person: Mary, "the Rose of Sharon, and the lily of the valleys."[70] Truth is personal and, even in person, cannot come without being received by a person. And it can be received by any number of persons, as witnesses "the fellowship of the elect who sup/ With Christ the lamb"[71] of which Beatrice says, "Behold how great the white-robed company!"[72] The final destination of the journey on which Beatrice leads Dante is among them; it is the "place" (which is beyond place, of course) where, unable to describe it, he can say, "Yet, as a wheel moves smoothly, free from jars,/ My will and my desire were turned by love,/ The love that moves the sun and the other stars."[73] That love is God and God is eternally true; where can love be, except among persons, so where can truth be except among persons?

---

68. Ibid., Canto 23, lines 70–75 ("Perchè la faccia mia sì t'innamora,/ che tu non ti rivolgi al bel giardino/ che sotto i raggi di Cristo s'infiora?/ Quivi è la rosa in che il verbo divino/ carne si fece; quivi son li gigli/ al cui odor si prese il buon cammino.").

69. John 1:14.

70. Song of Solomon 2:1.

71. Dante, *The Divine Comedy: 3 Paradise*, trans. by Dorothy L. Sayers and Barbara Reynolds, Canto 24, lines 1–2 ("sodalizio eletto alla gran cena/ del benedetto Agnello").

72. Ibid., Canto 30, line 129 ("quanto è 'l convento delle bianche stole!").

73. Ibid., Canto 33, lines 143–45 ("ma già volgeva il mio disio e 'l velle,/ sì come rota ch'ingualmente è mossa,/ l'amor che move il sole e l'altre stelle.").

E: Earth & Eternity

Russian Sophiologists

The poetic witness of theologians to the personal presence of Holy Wisdom shows us that the creation is alive. Beauty speaks of this.

Poetry, which is not confined to the "narrow coffin of logical definition,"[74] sees truth as personally present in creation. Michael Martin, who has written extensively about awareness of such a person, observes, "It is precisely in the attenuation of rigid conceptuality brought about by a poetic intuition that Sophia appears."[75] Alexander Blok, in his poem "Verses about the Beautiful Lady," gives voice to this sense of *Hagia Sophia*, Holy Wisdom, which grew in the late nineteenth and early twentieth century so-called "Silver Age" of Russian cultural and intellectual life:

> The heavenly is not measured by the mind,
> The azure is hidden from minds.
> Only rarely do seraphim bring
> Holy dreams to the chosen of the worlds.
> And I imagined the Russian Venus,
> Entwined in a heavy tunic,
> Passionless in her purity, joyless without measure,
> The features of her face expressing a tranquil dream.
> She has come down to earth not for the first time
> But crowding round her for the first time
> Are her new heroes and champions...[76]

The first line indicates that reason on its own cannot define the transcendent; the "azure" of the second line denotes heavenly and eternal truth (as explained in Chapter A). The "Russian Venus" is a manifestation of Sophia in the poet's country; she is "passionless in her purity" for wisdom "passeth and goeth through all things by reason of her pureness."[77] She comes "down to earth" for she links

74. *The Pillar and Ground of the Truth*, 7.

75. Michael Martin, *The Submerged Reality: Sophiology and the Turn to a Poetic Metaphysics* (Brooklyn, NY: Angelico Press, 2015), 185.

76. Michael Martin, ed., *The Heavenly Country: An Anthology of Primary Sources, Poetry, and Critical Essays on Sophiology* (Brooklyn, NY: Angelico Press, 2016), 240.

77. Wisdom 7:24.

eternity and earth, being both "one only" and "manifold."[78] She has always done this, but now there are new "champions" of her person. Blok himself was a follower of one of the first: Vladimir Solovyov.[79] The latter influenced Pavel Florensky, particularly through Russian Symbolist poets,[80] and Sergei Bulgakov.[81] Dealing with poetic reality, they do not subscribe to a shared defined scheme, though they can all be called sophiologists. As Michael Martin writes, "The sophiologies of Solovyov, Florensky, and Bulgakov, interpenetrating at points, diverging at others, never achieving either consensus or center are emblematic of an intuitive approach to questions of God."[82] There is some accord, however: "the Russian tradition of sophiology teaches" that wisdom is not "a fourth divine person, but rather the very middle between divine transcendence and created immanence."[83]

The earliest of these sophiologists, Solovyov, had an encounter remarkably similar to that of Dante with Beatrice. Boris Jakim, the translator of his semi-fictional memoir *At the Dawn of Mist-Shrouded Youth*, judges that in this meeting "Sophia, the Divine Radiance, found abode in a living woman."[84] The memoir tells of a woman called Julie rescuing him from falling between two railway train carriages:

> I learned this later. When I regained consciousness, I saw only the bright sunlight, a strip of the blue sky, and in that light and in the midst of that sky, the face of a beautiful woman was bending down to me, and she was gazing at me with marvelous familiar eyes and whispering something quiet and gentle to me.

---

78. Wisdom 7:22.

79. *The Heavenly Country*, 168.

80. *The Pillar and Ground of the Truth*, xi.

81. Sergei Bulgakov, *The Bride of the Lamb*, trans. Boris Jakim (Grand Rapids, MI: Eerdmans, 2002), xi–xii.

82. *The Submerged Reality*, 168.

83. Ibid., vii (Adrian Pabst in the Foreword).

84. Vladimir Solovyov, *Sophia, God & A Short Tale About the Antichrist*, Also Including *At the Dawn of Mist-Shrouded Youth*, trans. Boris Jakim (Brooklyn, NY: Angelico Press, 2014), 47.

There is no doubt that this was Julie and that those were her eyes, but how everything else had changed! A rosy light was emanating from her face! How tall and magnificent she was! Something miraculous had happened within me. It was as if my entire being with all its thoughts, feelings, and desires had melted away and become a single infinite sweet, luminous, and passionless sensation; and in this sensation, as in a clear mirror, one miraculous image was fixedly reflected; and I felt and knew that this one image contained all. I loved with a new, all-engulfing, and infinite love; and in this love I felt the whole fullness and meaning of life for the first time.[85]

The "blue sky" is highly significant, for "blueness, as is well-known, symbolizes air, sky, and therefore the presence of Divinity in the world through His creativity, through His powers."[86] Florensky, whose words these are, goes so far as to say, "Sophia is the true Sky."[87] The implication is that the sky is an expression, or instantiation, of Sophia, rather than her simply reflecting the quality of the sky. This makes sense in the light of the verse from Proverbs, "The LORD possessed me in the beginning of his way, before his works of old"[88] and the following passage, cited above, about Wisdom being there when God created the world. In this understanding, the sky is the symbol of what is between God and the world and Sophia is who is truly between God and the world, analogous but not identical to the way in which Christ is the "true bread" and "true vine" and so on, the created realities pointing to what belongs to eternity. This is not to say that Sophia is in any way creator: creation belongs to God the Father who, in the felicitous image of Saint Irenaeus, created the world with his two hands, the Son and the Holy Spirit. It is rather to say that "she is the breath of the power of God, and a pure influence flowing from the glory of the Almighty: therefore can no defiled thing fall into her."[89] She is the personal and in a sense motherly expression of the divine radiance in creation which

85. Ibid., 66–67.
86. *The Pillar and Ground of the Truth*, 390.
87. Ibid., 399.
88. Proverbs 8:22.
89. Wisdom 7:25.

cannot be sullied, so it is significant that the effect of Solovyov's encounter with Julia is his entire being miraculously becoming "a single infinite sweet, luminous, and passionless sensation." Of Sophia, scripture says, "being but one, she can do all things,"[90] so that it is apt that for Solovyov "this one image contained all." This all is essentially "the whole fullness and meaning of life," for the meaning of our lives is the deepest, fullest and truest reality.

In addition to this mediated experience of Sophia, Solovyov has left us a poetic expression of three direct encounters about which he says (to her), "Have you not thrice appeared to my real sight?/ You have not been a figment of the mind."[91] The first took place when he was just nine years old, on the feast of the Ascension in 1862, before the meeting described above.[92] As on the latter occasion, color was highly significant, both outwardly and inwardly: "Azure was all around; azure was in my soul." The azure is the communication of the eternal with the earthly, the personal presence of wisdom. He addresses her thus:

> Suffused with a golden azure, and your hand
> Holding a flower that came from other lands,
> You stood there smiling a smile of radiance.[93]

The azure is golden, for it is tinged with "the glory of the Almighty"; the flower is "from other lands," those that are celestial; the "radiance" of her smile is that of divinity.

His second direct encounter with Sophia was at "the British Museum," synonymous then, as it was for Karl Marx, with its library where, he claims, "mysterious powers led me to choose for reading/ Everything possible concerning her." Here he said to her:

> "O blossoming of divinity! I feel
> Your presence here. But why have you not revealed
> Yourself to my eyes since I was a child?"

Once again he knows the presence of the personal interface between earth and eternity:

90. Wisdom 7:27.
91. Solovyov, *Sophia, God & A Short Tale About the Antichrist*, 103.
92. *The Heavenly Country*, 392.
93. Solovyov, *Sophia, God & A Short Tale About the Antichrist*, 104.

Hardly had I thought these words
When all around was filled with golden azure
And before me she was shining again—
But only her face, it was her face alone.

And he rises joyfully above the narrow rationality of the earth:

That instant was one of happiness much prolonged.
My soul again became blind to things of earth.
And if I spoke, any "sober" ear
Would consider my speech incoherent and stupid.[94]

He seeks a fuller revelation than that of Sophia's face and is told to go to Egypt. This he does for "reason remained quite silent—like an idiot" and steams "across the shimmering deep-blue" (depth as well as height is a symbol of the divine) to Cairo where he is told, "I am there in the desert. Go to meet me." He does and as he wakes from a deep sleep there, "The fragrance of roses wafted from heaven and earth" and once again he meets the looking of azure eyes:

And in the purple of the heavenly glow
You gazed with eyes full of an azure fire.

Her gaze is "like the first shining/ Of universal and creative day." She is, in person, the unfolding of the divine design of creation. It is all included:

What is, what was, and what will be were here Embraced within that one fixed gaze…[95]

"Overseeing all things"[96] she is "one only" although "manifold."[97] She contains everything for the visionary:

I saw it all, and all of it was one,
One image there of beauty feminine…
The immeasurable was confined within that image.
Before me, in me, you alone were there.[98]

94. Ibid., 105–7.
95. Ibid., 107–10.
96. Wisdom 7:23.
97. Wisdom 7:22.
98. Solovyov, *Sophia, God & A Short Tale About the Antichrist*, 110.

The essence of creation is "beauty feminine," to be known in single-ness of heart and singleness of vision. Here, earth touches heaven, and this is what Solovyov shows us. In Michael Martin's words: "His poetic landscape is utterly and absolutely a realm between heaven and earth, at the horizon of Sophia's appearing."[99] Solovyov's influence was wide and enduring. He was a close friend of Dostoevsky and there was even a lecture he gave in Petersburg attended by both Dostoevsky and Tolstoy, though these two never met.[100]

Pavel Florensky is heir to Solovyov's sophiological teaching. He quotes a characterization the latter gave in a speech of Sophia as "the higher and all-embracing form and living soul of nature and the universe, eternally united and uniting itself with Divinity in the temporal process, and connecting Him with all that is" and comments: "In brief Sophia is the memory of God, in the holy depths of which is all that is and outside of which is death and madness."[101] The teaching is about the connection between the eternal and earthy, the realm between heaven and earth. It is confirmed for Florensky in the words of the mystic, Count Speransky: "She is the mother of all that is outside God, for she herself is the first external being."[102] He finds apt expression of it in an icon of the Novgorod Cathedral of Sophia, founded by Prince Vladimir in 1045:

The heavenly spheres, full of stars, surrounding Sophia indicate Sophia's cosmic power, her rule over the whole universe, her cos-mocracy. The turquoise or sky-blue color of this environment symbolizes the air, then the heaven, and then the spiritual heavens, the world on high, in the center of which lives Sophia. For the color sky-blue attunes the soul to contemplation, to detachment from the earthly, to quiet longing for peace and purity. This blue of the heavens, this projection of light on darkness, this boundary between light and darkness is a profound image of heavenly creation, i.e., an image of the boundary between Light rich in being and Darkness-Nothingness, an image of the Intelligent World.[103]

99. *The Heavenly Country*, 394.
100. J. Frank, *Dostoevsky: A Writer in His Time*, 770.
101. *The Pillar and Ground of the Truth*, 282.
102. Ibid., 241.
103. Ibid., 271–72.

Florensky argues that "the unity of creation is not an indifferent unity of chaotic elements but an organic unity of orderedness," and cites the twelfth-century Jewish thinker Maimonides: "the entire universe, that is, the highest sphere with everything it contains, is nothing but an individual whole.... The difference between entities found in it is like the difference between the organs of a human individual." It follows that "it is necessary to view the universe as a single living individual" and each person is a microcosm of this living whole.[104]

The truer the person, the more she or he will be imbued with (to cite again the Bible characterization of Wisdom) "the breath of the power of God" and radiate "the glory of the Almighty," for, in Florensky's words:

> She [Sophia] is the true ornament of a human being, permeating all of his pores, shining out in his gaze, spilling out with his smile, rejoicing in his heart with an ineffable joy, reflected in his every gesture, surrounding a man, at moments of spiritual uplift, by a fragrant cloud and radiant nimbus, raising him above "the world's confusion," so that, remaining in the world, he becomes "not of the world," supramundane.

It follows that "Sophia is Beauty." Indeed, "only Sophia is essential Beauty in all of creation. Everything else is only tinsel and the superficial smartness of clothing." [105] Her beauty is that of which poets speak. The understanding of this as personal saves us from the reductive model of the cosmos that thinks of it (effectively, if not explicitly) as the result of a master algorithm and ourselves as characters in a computer game, ultimately determined by the limits the programmers have set. The algorithmic cosmos is dead; the personal cosmos is alive and instinct with sublimity, outwardly and inwardly. This is not to say there are no limits on life in the latter: there is constraint, the horizontal axis of the cross taking us where we would rather not go, as well the vertical axis which lifts us up, but

104. Ibid., 203.
105. Ibid., 254.

that only makes it more sublime. Indeed, it is so sublime that God Himself is present in it.

God is not an algorithm or any kind of artificial intelligence; He is the Creator. "The idea of creation," wrote Sergei Bulgakov, the Russian theologian who as it were picked up the sophiological torch from Florensky, "is *personal* and presupposes a personal God."[106] Creation is not mechanical. There is a remote analogy to divine creativity in human creativity. The script of a great play, such as Shakespeare's *Macbeth*, does not determine how it is to be performed down the ages; it does not specify the exact movements of the actors or the nuances of their voices; it does not blankly refuse any relevance to forthcoming human history as it unfolds. The analogy of personal procreation is even stronger: parents pass on biological specifics to their children and have enormous influence on them, but you do not have to be one to know that they cannot determine what their children do with their lives.

Bulgakov understood that the beauty of the world is also human beauty. That beauty, personal in nature, corresponds to the human person who can contemplate it (or, better, her) as "the glory of the Almighty." The philosophical implication of this is unfolded by S.L. Frank:

> Beauty is the immediate and most directly convincing proof that there is some mysterious kinship between the inner world and the outer world, between immediate self-being and the ground of the outer, objective world.... We perceive in external reality something akin to our most intimate depth, our inner self-being, and at the moment of esthetic enjoyment we stop feeling alone and find in the surrounding external reality the primordial "homeland" of our soul.[107]

The body may be tiny relative to the whole of creation; the soul is not. This instinctive connection with beauty in nature can also happen with the beauty of human craft, especially that which is sacred. In it deep speaks to deep; person to person. Bulgakov reports an

---

106. Bulgakov, *The Bride of the Lamb*, 37.
107. *The Unknowable*, 192.

experience in which the beauty which is Sophia was mediated to him through a Cathedral dedicated to her:

> This heavenly dome, which portrays heaven bending to embrace the earth, gives expression in finite form to the infinite, to an all-embracing unity, to the stillness of eternity, in the form of a work of art which, though belonging to this world, is a miracle of harmony itself.[108]

Wisdom, in nature and in art, draws us to this unity, this stillness.

The Holy Family

Joseph, Mary and Jesus embody wisdom.

Wisdom leads us whence she came, as once she led the wise men. She leads us to the Holy Family. If there was ever a gathering among which truth was to be found, ever a dialogue in which truth was spoken, ever a family into which truth was born, it is this. Here is a scene born anew every year, here a beauty that remains unsullied by exploitation, here a joy that cannot be destroyed. Hither comes Wisdom, knowing that this is the way; hither Sophia, the contact person between earth and divine truth; hither Beauty, recognizing the Giver of her life in the Child.

She is welcomed by Joseph, the person in charge. There are no words recorded for him. Like Saint Thérèse, and all the saints, he knows that the highest wisdom is to remain unknown, seeking not the glory that comes from people. His wisdom is from above. It is oneiric wisdom: he receives it as he dreams from "the angel of the Lord."[109] Dreams transcend time and so potentially are open to what is eternal. People from throughout my life cohabit the same dream; sometimes, as I mentioned above, they image what is to come; sometimes I glimpse what is holy in them. Florensky reports and analyzes the remarkable phenomenon of a sudden shock in the waking world being the end point of a long narrative leading up to

108. Sergei Bulgakov, *Sophia: The Wisdom of God* (Great Barrington, MA: Lindisfarne Press, 1993), 1.
109. Matthew 1:20; 2:13.

it. He gives the example of a dreamer being awoken by the metal bedstead of his bed, which has somehow broken and heavily struck his neck. In his dream this is the blade of the guillotine falling upon him, the final end of a long and complicated involvement in the events of the French Revolution. "Dream time," Florensky observes, "is *turned inside out.*" The whole history of the dream comes from the moment of its end: "the goal is comprehended as living energy that shapes actuality as its creative form."[110] I often have what I think of as "pluperfect" dreams: dreams in which there is a whole history which has happened to me that I have never experienced, waking or sleeping. The patriarch for whom Saint Joseph is named has oneiric wisdom. He knows from the way his brothers' sheaves in his dream "made obeisance" to his sheaf and the way "the sun and the moon, and the eleven stars made obeisance" to him that his brothers will be his supplicants.[111] And he can interpret dreams: those of the butler and the baker in the prison about how Pharaoh will deal with them, and that of Pharaoh himself about the seven years of plenty and the seven years of famine.[112] Saint Joseph, however, is not simply a dreamer: he has practical wisdom also, in his craft and in his care of the Holy Family whom he takes to a place of safety, first Egypt and then Nazareth.

Wisdom takes her acolytes, the Magi, to Mary, *sedes sapientiae,* her very seat and dwelling place. The Blessed Virgin is overshadowed by the Spirit of Truth; she is identified with that Spirit; she is the bearer of the Truth. Of her, Thomas Merton wrote: "The Blessed Virgin Mary is the one created being who enacts and shows forth in her life all that is hidden in Sophia."[113] She is the perfect personal realization of the ordering intelligence of the creation. Our tainted nature's solitary boast, she opens the earth to eternity. "Her radiant sophianicity" and "her boundless grace" draw all generations to her. She has "a kind of special connection with Heaven, a kind of heav-

110. Pavel Florensky, *Iconostasis,* trans. Donald Sheehan and Olga Andrejev (Crestwood, NY: St Vladimir's Seminary Press, 1996), 41.
111. Genesis 37:6–10.
112. Genesis 40:1–22; 41:14–32.
113. *The Heavenly Country,* 262.

enliness."[114] Through her person, a fallen world is reunited with the Truth that is God. In her person is gathered "the church of the living God, the pillar and ground of the truth."[115]

Wisdom leads the Magi to her Child, wrapped "in swaddling clothes."[116] Barely able to move, unable to speak, here is the folly of vulnerability in person. Yet, "the foolishness of God is wiser than men; and the weakness of God is stronger than men."[117] Here is He to whom all wisdom tends, the Truth in Person. Here is the Fashioner of wisdom. As He is the key which opens heaven, as He is the east from which light comes, so is He the wisdom which lives from Truth. As Advent, the season which looks towards this manifestation, becomes more urgent in its looking, the Church apostrophizes Him as all of these, beginning with wisdom:

> *O Sapientia, quae ex ore Altissimi prodisti, attingens a fine usque ad finem, fortiter suaviterque disponens omnia: veni ad docendum nos viam prudentiae.*

As I said in the introduction, it was on the eve of the day on which this is sung that the concept and form of this book came to me, wanting to be "of the truth,"[118] wanting to hear His voice whose wisdom comes from the silence of the crib, the silence before Pilate, the silence of eternity. To Him the Fathers of the Church have given the words about that wisdom whose power and radiance are His own: "Wisdom reacheth from one end to another mightily: and sweetly doth she order all things."[119] To Him the Church cries out, "O come to teach us the way of truth."[120]

To Him, and to Truth, come the wise with "their treasures," with "gold, and frankincense, and myrrh."[121] Their gold, their most valued treasure, is His for He is their highest good, their King to whom

114. *The Pillar and Ground of the Truth*, 265.
115. 1 Timothy 3:15.
116. Luke 2:7.
117. 1 Corinthians 1:25.
118. John 19:37.
119. Wisdom of Solomon, 8:1.
120. From the English version of the Latin antiphon.
121. Matthew 2:11.

all power is given "in heaven and in earth."[122] Their frankincense, offering to the Most High, is His for He is their Lord and their God. Their myrrh is His, for they know that He has come to share in the sufferings of their earthly life and so give them a meaning that will shine for all eternity. He has, indeed, come to share our death.

Resurrection

Eternal life validates personal truth, glimpsed in beauty and realized in the marriage supper of the lamb.

We saw in Chapter C that truth could only be such in the person of Christ in the light of the resurrection: if violence and death can destroy Him, then truth is not undying and therefore not really such. If the intelligent ordering of the earth, the beauty of the wisdom that was at its creation, succumbs without return to entropy, then the personal is, finally, absent, whatever the appearance has been: the law of nature has trumped the "pure influence flowing from the glory of the Almighty."[123] Similarly, if a beloved person such as Beatrice who means the world to the one who loves her and so in some sense gives coherence to creation, can become totally extinct, then truth cannot be personal for the person does not endure. Yet "in the sight of the unwise"[124] it seems that the person who dies is absent for ever and reason cannot persuade otherwise. A prophetic voice is needed, such as that of Isaiah crying:

> All flesh is grass, and all the goodliness thereof is as the flower of the field: The grass withereth, the flower fadeth: because the spirit of the LORD bloweth upon it: surely the people is grass. The grass withereth, the flower fadeth: but the word of Our God shall stand for ever.[125]

Neither the fading of the beauty of flower and field nor the death of people is denied, yet the Word by whom "all things were made"[126]

122. Matthew 28:18.
123. Wisdom of Solomon, 7:25.
124. Ibid., 3:2.
125. Isaiah 40:6–8.
126. John 1:3.

stands for ever. Their essential, personal nature therefore endures. The antinomy of life and death is transcended in the "Alpha and Omega, the beginning and the ending,"[127] which in the person of the Lord is one and the same. In eternity there is no before and after, so the going forth is the return and its ending the beginning.

Hence there is "a new heaven and a new earth."[128] Hence the "quickening spirit" of "the last Adam" makes persons alive in glory and immortality. Saint Paul explains this resurrection of the human person in terms of nature: a seed dies and so becomes something wonderfully more beautiful.[129] God fashions the creation with time which is, as Plato observed, the moving image of eternity, and nature shows us that the beauty which, in the person of wisdom, fashions the earth is enduring through the perennial rebirth of spring. Yet it is not only in what happens over time that the undying beauty of truth is shown to us. Earth is the far point from eternity: the other traditional elements of fire, air and water each in their own way image the Spirit. Yet in God, in the Word that is God, distance is closeness, and the beauty of earth, "through a glass, darkly,"[130] images the eternal glory of the face of God. Beauty is transcendent, expressing what does not die. S. L. Frank saw this and gave it this expression:

> The immanent essence of beauty consists in the fact that in it we apprehend and experience immediately and explicitly in the most outer aspect of being the absolute value of being, its meaningfulness and inner groundedness.[131]

Value, meaning, is what endures and "what the beautiful expresses is simply *reality itself* in its abstractly inexpressible concreteness, in its essential unknowableness."[132] Beauty is truth, in all its mystery.

The consciousness of the human person also evidences enduring truth, for it transcends what is passing, containing before and after

127. Revelation 1:8.
128. Ibid., 21:1.
129. 1 Corinthians 15:35–57.
130. Ibid., 13:12.
131. *The Unknowable*, 190.
132. Ibid., 191.

in memory and anticipation, sometimes waking, sometimes sleeping. The human person beholding beauty is in some sense seeing truth, which is expressed by it. More profoundly, perhaps, the truth is in the *relationship* between the person and the beauty, shadowing—and finally inheriting by adoption—the relationship of Son to the Father, which relationship is nothing less than the Spirit of Truth, the Holy Spirit and the beholding of the perfect beauty of the face of God. Each person is the seed of this beatitude. Because the human person is capable of this vision of glory, he or she is potentially open to the fullness of truth both in its wholeness and in its undying quality. Our relationships on earth also seem to indicate that the eternal memory that belongs to truth belongs to the person. Bulgakov observes "the usual intuition of parents regarding their children" that they exist "supratemporally":

> They cannot allow there was a time when their children did not exist. This same intuition is, in general, applicable to all whom we love and recognize by love. This intuition bears witness to the depth in which being is rooted in eternity.[133]

Similarly, when one's outlook and interests are aligned with those of a friend, it can seem that this person has always been known, even if by the calendar it has not been for many years. The experience of being in love also speaks of eternity: when the lover says, "Thou art beautiful, O my love,"[134] or, "He is altogether lovely,"[135] he or she is recognizing the eternal truth of which even passing beauty speaks. Furthermore, the yearning to belong to the beloved and for the beloved to belong to oneself forever implies an eternal being. If marriage vows are simply "till death do us part," they can nonetheless instantiate on earth the eternal communion of beatitude.

It is no accident therefore that Scripture repeatedly speaks of this communion, this blessedness, this realization of true and undying being in terms of a wedding feast. "Blessed," it says, "are they which are called unto the marriage supper of the Lamb."[136] The union of

133. Bulgakov, *The Bride of the Lamb*, 104.
134. Song of Solomon, 6:4.
135. Ibid., 5:16.
136. Revelation 19:9.

Christ with the Church which this celebrates is the union of each member with God and the unity of all with all. It is in this all-embracing unity that truth is realized, the Spirit of truth making all one in love. It is anticipated in the "beginning of miracles" Jesus worked "in Cana of Galilee"[137] in which water "was made wine"[138] and in every Mass in the presencing of the Lord on the altar. It is prophesied by Isaiah as transcending death, and so separation:

> And in this mountain shall the LORD of hosts make unto all people a feast of fat things, a feast of wines on the lees, of fat things full of marrow, of wines on the lees well refined. And he will destroy in this mountain the face of the covering cast over all people, and the vail that is spread over all nations. He will swallow up death in victory; and the Lord GOD will wipe away tears from off all faces; and the rebuke of his people shall he take away from off all the earth: for the LORD hath spoken it.[139]

The mountain is a symbol of transcendence of all the contradictions of the earth, the coincidence of opposites in God's eternity, the truth that is above. Even an earthly wedding celebration gives an intimation of this as it brings together, rejoicing in a union, people who would not normally meet. If it is held in a garden where people can walk and talk, that will image paradise, for this word is from the Greek for garden; if people drink, their inebriation will foreshadow being filled with the Spirit; if they dance together, they will anticipate the joyful unity of their heavenly homeland. Their glad rags will speak of their destiny of remaining by being clad in "a wedding garment" that fits them for eternal bliss.[140]

In a sense the eternal nuptials that our earthly wedding celebrations prefigure are not just a celebration of the happy union of all the blessed with their heavenly spouse, they are also a celebration of the wedding of heaven and earth, Spirit and matter, Word and flesh. Florensky writes, "It is love that unites the two worlds" and cites the words of Zosima, the spiritual elder of Alyosha in *The Brothers*

---

137. John 2:11.
138. Ibid., 2:9.
139. Isaiah 25:6–8.
140. Matthew 22:11.

Karamazov: "The great thing is that there is a mystery here, that the fleeting aspects of the earth and eternal Truth have come into contact here."[141] When his elder dies, Alyosha has a dream or vision of his elder at the great wedding banquet of heaven as the gospel about the wedding at Cana is being read out over his coffin. Zosima says, "We are drinking new wine, the wine of a new and great joy." Alyosha goes outside, "filled with rapture," into the night that envelops the earth. Over him hangs boundlessly "the heavenly dome, full of quiet, shining stars." And "the silence of the earth seemed to merge with the silence of the heavens, the mystery of the earth seemed to merge with the mystery of the stars. . . ."[142]

The link between them is love: that is what weaves the wedding garment that allows entry to the feast. Persons are made true by love: true to their friends, true to their brothers and sisters and, concomitantly, true to God. The next chapter looks at the indispensable practicalities of this fashioning.

141. *The Pillar and Ground of the Truth*, 68.
142. *The Brothers Karamazov*, 361–62.

F: Friendship & Fraternity

Weaving a Wedding Garment

Being heaven-ready entails truthful living. Friendship enables this.

As I begin the penultimate chapter, it might be helpful to recapitulate the line of thought I have pursued in this book up to this point. I started with the reflection that abstract reason and algorithms can never properly satisfy our longing for truth. A better place to look is the Bible. This indicates that God imparts truth through persons. Above all, truth comes to us in the person of Christ, "the way, the truth, and the life."[1] It is in communion with Him and in the community this communion forms that we find truth: it is not a private possession, but among us. However, a truth that selectively excludes other voices can only be partial, so we need (as Dostoevsky showed in his art) to be in dialogue. Yet even if we are practically in concord with everyone else on the planet, we are falling short of the truth when we treat this planet as a dead thing to be exploited for the satisfaction of our will. Nature is, as Pope Francis teaches in his encyclical *Laudato Si'*, our sister and some sense of a personal presence in creation helps us to be fully open to the truth that comes to us through it.

Here we come to the crunch point, the fence at which the steed bearing the academic falls, the question we would prefer not to face. Tucked into the consideration in the last chapter of the image of the eschatological banquet celebrating the marriage of the Lamb, the ultimate union with the true and the beautiful, is a mention of the need for a wedding garment. The gospel parable from which this comes says that this command is given concerning the person who does not have one:

1. John 14:6.

> Bind him hand and foot, and take him away, and cast him into outer darkness; there shall be weeping and gnashing of teeth.[2]

Wanting to bring out the joy of the ultimate celebration, I forbore to emphasize this. Yet to say no more about it is to collude with the division that vitiates the common pursuit of truth in our time: the division between what is outside a person and what is within. The general assumption is that if empirically verifiable data confirm what a person finds, that person has found truth. This is true *up to a point.* It can bring us to a practical, provisional, serviceable truth. Yet this is not the truth we long for in our deepest being. To find that, we need to be true in our own persons.

All that has so far been considered in this book as a positive help in the quest for truth can be considered as exterior to our own persons: the Bible, the people it tells us about, Christ and His Church, those with whom we enter into dialogue, the earth herself—these are all out there. Yet knowledge, as the scholastic aphorism says, is according to the knower. If we are not true, how can we see truly? If we cannot see truly, how can we see the truth? The Sermon on the Mount puts it bluntly:

> If thine eye be evil, thy whole body shall be full of darkness. If therefore the light that is in thee be darkness, how great is that darkness![3]

This is that same darkness into which the person not wearing a wedding garment is cast. Already something of it is perceptible in this life. If we share the divine point of view of our lives and the whole of creation—"God saw every thing that he had made, and, behold, it was very good"[4]—and trust in His promise "that all things work together for good to them that love God,"[5] we shall have sunnier lives than if we do not. Bitterness obfuscates. Yet the prevailing assumption is that the exterior is the only criterion and that there is no such thing as a judgment of what is in a person's heart, this latter

2. Matthew 22:13.
3. Matthew 6:23.
4. Genesis 1:31.
5. Romans 8:28.

being private, subject only to self-assessment and just as valid as what is in anybody else's heart. This can seem logical from an atheist point of view because it would be preposterous for people to be poking around in each other's hearts saying what should be there and what should not, even if the gospel injunction "judge not that ye be not judged"[6] is not invoked. It only makes sense if there is a God who knows "what is in a man"; if there is truth with which a person's heart can be more or less aligned; if there is a final judgment.

If this is not the case then there is a separation between what belongs to the public domain and can be commonly verified and what belongs to the private domain and cannot be part of the agreed truth that forms the bonds of society. This is not to say that the latter cannot be cultivated. There are any number of books about how you can foster or even flatter your inner self. It is simply that this whole business of "the inward man" is in a separate category. The common truth, or what passes as such, is concerned with practicalities; the personal truth is private and expected not to impact what is public. This is evident in the general trend of religious publishing: there are books loosely categorized as "spiritual" about one's inner life, but they are not expected to be at the cutting edge of intellectual life. This is reserved for the academic, which can indeed include theology but not as that which has no more authority (in the assessors' own eyes, I mean) than that it is inspired by the Spirit of Truth and can be verified only by being recognized by those inspired by the same Spirit (including those who make up the tradition of such). There are exceptions to this trend: and I gladly and gratefully acknowledge the publisher of the present book as being open to both the mind and the Spirit. Such openness is a reclaiming of the integrity that preceded the split between the cloister and the university.

Given that we want to overcome the privatization of spiritual life, to make that life truthful, we have to relate to other people. Without that relation, we are not so much seeing truthfully as, in Rowan Williams' felicitous phrase, "stuffing the world into the bag of the

6. Matthew 7:1.

ego."[7] Furthermore, the relationship needs to be disinterested in the sense that it does not have anything about it which is *intéressant* as the French say: offering an advantage that is financial or equivalently beneficial. Without that, it simply feeds the delusion that one is God, that everything has meaning only insofar as it contributes some partial advantage to oneself. This is a lie, feeding the most deadly spiritual malady, pride. Only if somebody else matters to us in his or her own right can we begin to overcome this; only by our life being relative to somebody else's life can we begin to be open to the true life which is God's; only in some kind of transcendence of selfish interests can we start to love truly and so know the truth of God who is love.

For this we need to relate to more than people in general. These are interchangeable like so many cans of beans any one of which can be opened for our meal, meaning any particular can is of no concern to us: others are available. People related to in this fashion can be used for our purposes without us escaping the life-denying illusion that our ego is king. A friend, however, is not a can of beans; a friend is a person who is in some way special; a friend is irreplaceable. And so a friend is valuable in his or her own right: above all, a friend's value is not subordinate to some advantage to be gained for oneself, not primarily an opportunity of profit. It is therefore in personal friendship that truth is to be found, over and above that emerging in a more casual relation. This is so for both the giver and receiver of the love of friendship. The giver learns to see without the distortions of plans and purposes; the receiver knows him or her self not as a thing that serves a purpose but as a person of intrinsic worth. This can be reciprocal to a greater or lesser extent, that extent not necessarily depending so much on generosity as on capability: the love of friendship can have a special power when one party is more or less helpless. Indeed, we can say that we are all who we are because our mother, or a particular giver of care, was our friend.

So friendship helps us to weave the wedding garment: openness to the truth, ultimately the truth of God, beholding whom is the perfect joy of the festal banquet of union. It shows us that the truth

7. Rowan Williams, *Passions of the Soul* (London: Bloomsbury, 2024), xvii.

is not to be found in the claiming of private advantage, but rather in giving and receiving the love of recognition, echo of the divine source of our being. Furthermore, we can find the courage to acknowledge or receive the truth about ourselves in a friendship. We can also seek wisdom and true living the more efficaciously when it is a common pursuit with a friend. Before considering more fully (by looking at the writing of someone who has thought very deeply about it) how friendship opens us to truth, it makes sense to acknowledge its particular character and, eschewing abstraction, look at examples that illustrate this.

Three Friendships

The love of a friend can affirm our existence; it can help us face the truth about what is right; it can support us in leading a godly life.

The first of these examples is from a contemporary novel about a friendship between two people, Sam and Sadie, who program computer games: *Tomorrow, and Tomorrow, and Tomorrow*, by Gabrielle Zevin. They meet in a children's hospital where Sam is a patient and Sadie a visitor. They are, in C. S. Lewis's phrase about the classic posture of friendship, "side by side, absorbed by some common interest."[8] The common interest is a Nintendo game. The boy asks the girl, "You want to play the rest of this life?"[9] There is a huge backstory to this utterance, which the novelist reveals to us only gradually so as to build up the importance of the friendship implicitly by way of a tale rather than by telling. It echoes what Sam says to his mother just after they have witnessed a woman throw herself to her death and he, through the kindness of a shopkeeper, is taking refuge in playing a game: "I'm going to play until the end of this life."[10] This is the reason Sam is now in Los Angeles. The immediate revelation however is that "he hasn't said more than two words to anyone in the

8. C. S. Lewis, *The Four Loves* (London: HarperCollins, 2016), 73.
9. Gabrielle Zevin, *Tomorrow, and Tomorrow, and Tomorrow* (London: Penguin Random House, 2022), 19.
10. Ibid., 134.

six weeks since he was injured" in "a horrific car accident" and that "it was a big deal" that he talked to Sadie. She is told that the nurse is wondering if she will come back the next day to talk to Sam again and that it would "probably count" as community service for her Bat Mitzvah.[11] This she does, logging on a timesheet the exact number of hours (609) she has been friends with Sam, despite a warning from her grandmother that this is a moral compromise.[12] When Sam finds out, he doesn't believe Sadie was ever his friend and tells her, with a word of terminal insult, "I never want to see you again."[13]

It is some time later that the reader finds out why this relationship was so highly freighted: in the car accident that caused Sam's injury, his mother (who he thinks is "the most beautiful woman in the world") died and he has since said nothing whatever to anyone, except to tell the driver of the other car as he looked for survivors, "I'm here."[14] The dialogue with Sadie has filled the silence coming from the loss of the vital relationship with his mother: when it appears that her friendship is not true, it cannot bear the weight of this loss. Yet they do meet again when they are college students and in the interaction that follows it is Sadie who is helplessly depressed. Sam visits her repeatedly, offering her little gifts despite her lack of response and the continuing pain from his injury that he experiences walking to her place. She gets better.[15] He does not know, nor does the reader until much later, that she too is suffering from the breaking of a mother-child bond: she has had an abortion following an abusive relationship with a teacher. And she too later turns cold towards Sam when she comes to believe that he sent her to get from this teacher what was needed for the game they were making, knowing that the teacher had been her lover and that this meant he cared more about making the game than about her well-being. "I thought you were my friend," she says. Yet he feels "tenderness and love" when he learns the true reason she had been so dejected, even if he is

11. Ibid., 26.
12. Ibid., 28–30.
13. Ibid., 49.
14. Ibid., 203–7.
15. Ibid., 70–73.

unable to show his own vulnerability (stemming from his injury) at this moment or to say that she is indeed existentially important to him.[16] Later in life, when she and Sam are again not speaking, Sadie herself is challenged to admit to herself that there will never be a person who can mean as much to her as Sam.[17] And they do speak again[18] and even come to tell each other of their mutual love.[19]

The deeply moving account of their ups and downs is framed by the epigraph of the novel, which is this poem by Emily Dickinson:

That Love is all there is,
Is all we know of Love;
It is enough, the freight should be
Proportioned to the groove.

For both of them, love makes them something when they are nothing. Love is the truth of their lives, even when it is compromised or misunderstood. What there is between them means that "no matter how bad the world gets, there will always be players."[20]

Nancy Tucker's novel, *The First Day of Spring*, also tells the story of two people who become friends as children. Alternating chapters narrate childhood and adult life in the first person. The first begins, "I killed a little boy today." These are the words of Chrissie, an eight-year-old child who is chronically neglected: her mother does not even feed her and the greatest gift of her father, who is in prison most of the time, is a solitary marble. The murder is a personal assertion: "*I am here, I am here, I am here.*"[21] It makes her feel that she is "basically God."[22] She knowingly lies to her friend Linda:

'How did he die?' She asked.
'Don't know,' I said. I knew.[23]

16. Ibid., 316–17; 248–52.
17. Ibid., 447.
18. Ibid., 463 ff.
19. Ibid., 477.
20. Ibid., 465.
21. Nancy Tucker, *The First Day of Spring* (London: Penguin Random House, 2021), 1.
22. Ibid., 10.
23. Ibid., 4.

She means to do it again, so she doesn't forget how it feels to be God. She is ticking like a clock till the time comes for another murder. Linda does not even know how to tell the time.

Yet the friendship with Linda is critically important for Chrissie's transition to truth, to adulthood, to knowing that she is not in fact God. That begins with the experience of her second murder. Unlike the first time, she does not think, "This is as good as a person can feel." On the contrary:

> There wasn't any fizzing this time, there was only hate, hate, hate and the sound of Ruthie's feet beating on the floor, slower and slower until they stopped. Ruthie stopped. Everything stopped.[24]

She has only grief. She goes to her friend and takes her to the body. This time her dialogue is truthful:

> 'She's dead.'
> 'How?'
> 'I did it.'
> 'You never.'
> 'I did.'[25]

She also admits to the first murder. Linda will tell her mother and Chrissie no longer wants to hide because it is "lonely being hidden."[26] Knowing that Linda will "have to get a new best friend," she feels she is "being opened up, like a book being cracked at the spine" and she cries: she does not have enough left inside her "to do anything else but cry."

What follows shows the importance of the friendship to which Chrissie has sacrificed her lie. Linda makes to go:

> 'I'm going home now,' she said. 'I'm going to tell my mammy what you did.'
> 'Wait,' I said. I lifted up the skirt of my dress and used it to wipe my face, then reached into the pocket, took out Da's marble, and pushed it towards her. The sunlight made it glint as it rolled across the floor. All the colours in the world.

24. Ibid., 329.
25. Ibid., 353.
26. Ibid., 356.

'Are you giving it me?' she asked, picking it up.
'Yeah,' I said.
'But it's your marble. Your da gave it you. It's your best thing.'
'I want you to have it,' I said.
'Why?' she asked.

Only the reader is told why: "*I want you to remember me. I want you to remember to be my best friend.*"[27] Linda takes the marble with her and Chrissie is left with the body of Ruthie, like Rogozhin with the body of Nastasya Filippovna at the end of Dostoevsky's *The Idiot*.

But Linda does remember. They meet again as adults. Linda still has the marble:

'It was my bit of you, wasn't it? It helped. Helped when I was missing you.'
I felt a tug in the tie that had held us together for the past seventeen years. I stepped forward and I hugged her. She was warm and broad, and she held me so tight I felt we would turn into one woman.[28]

Linda, who has in fact prayed for her, has by her friendship opened her to the truth, indeed to the greatest truth of all: that there is "another story, one with goodies as well as baddies, one where you could turn into a goody even after you had been the baddest baddy."[29]

The friendship between Saint Gregory Nazianzen and Saint Basil, not a fictional one, was explicitly concerned with the pursuit of wisdom and true living. Saint Gregory records:

We were at Athens, progressing in our studies. As time went on, we mutually avowed our affection for each other, and that philosophy was the object of our zeal. Thenceforth we were all in all to each other, sharing the same roof, the same table, the same sentiments, our eyes fixed on one goal, as our mutual affection grew ever warmer and stronger.

Like Chrissie and Linda, they are one: "We seemed to have a single

27. Ibid., 357–59.
28. Ibid., 334–35.
29. Ibid., 371.

195

soul animating two bodies." In their case, the influence towards good is mutual:

> The sole object of us both was virtue and a life led for future hopes, having detached ourselves from this world before departing from it. With this in view, we directed our life and all our actions, following the guidance of the divine precept, and at the same time spurring each other to virtue, and, if it is not too much to say so, being for each other a rule and a scales for the discernment of good and evil.[30]

This corresponds to C. S. Lewis's characterization of friendship in which *"Do you love me?'* means *'Do you see the same truth?'*—Or at least, 'Do you *care about* the same truth?'"[31]

These three examples of friendship show it to be a context for establishing existential, moral and spiritual truth respectively. Sam and Sadie affirm the truth of each other's existence when that seems effectively lost and, if we take the ludic as a metaphor for it, together they find the truth of life. Chrissie begins the long and difficult journey of facing the truth of what she has done through the influence of Linda, despite the latter's lesser mental capacity. Gregory and Basil help each other journey towards sharing the life of God. Love in the lives of all of them is beginning the task of weaving the wedding garment.

Florensky's Philosophy of Friendship

Florensky explored theology in the context of a friendship that opened his heart. Love opens a person to truth. "I" becomes "not-I" also. In his own emptiness, a person finds fullness in his friend. A friend is singled out as special.

Pavel Florensky, whom I introduced at the beginning of this book as having an influence on it second only to that of Dostoevsky, framed his entire exploration of truth, his masterly *The Pillar and Ground of the Truth*, in the context of friendship. Although much of it was

---

30. *The Discourses of Saint Gregory Nazianzen*, Oration 43.
31. *The Four Loves*, 79.

submitted as a thesis for a Master's at the Moscow Theological Academy, it takes the form of twelve letters addressed to his friend and brother in Christ, Sergei Troitsky. This makes for very engaging reading. The text does not make one a student of a professor of theology but a friend with whom the writer is sharing his heart. On the title page is written: *FINIS AMORIS, UT DUO UNUM FIANT –* THE LIMIT OF LOVE: TWO ARE ONE.[32] The "one woman" of Chrissie and Linda and the "single soul" of Gregory and Basil have their echo here. It is a universal aspiration of friendship, given poetic voice by Shakespeare:

> So we grew together,
> Like to a double cherry, seeming parted,
> But yet an union in partition,
> Two lovely berries moulded on one stem;
> So with two seeming bodies, but one heart. . . .[33]

Florensky himself quotes Shakespeare on this subject. Prince Harry responds to the valor of a comrade in arms by saying:

> I did not think thee lord of such a spirit.
> Before I lov'd thee as a brother, John,
> But now I do respect thee as my soul.[34]

His own fraternal bond with Sergei Troitsky was formalized and deepened in a ceremony going back to early Christian times, whose Greek name means "the making of brothers." Here is his own description of it:

> The half-ecclesiastical, half-popular rite of adelphopoiesis is accomplished through an exchange of crosses, a vow of brotherly love and faithfulness before an icon in church and the brothers' alternately holding a burning candle during the Cherubic Hymn.[35]

According to his biographer it was:

---

32. *The Pillar and Ground of the Truth*, 3.

33. *A Midsummer Night's Dream*, Act III, scene ii, lines 208–212.

34. *I Henry IV*, Act 5, scene iv, lines 18–20; *The Pillar and Ground of the Truth*, 319.

35. Ibid., 327.

A state of striving rather than of serene achievement, a kind of voluntary, often painful ascetic pilgrimage, joyfully undertaken in the light and warmth of true love. The relationship was, he felt quite overwhelmingly, his way to Salvation.[36]

Troitsky went to live and teach in Tiflis, Georgia, where Florensky's family lived. The latter meanwhile continued his studies at the Moscow Theological Academy and wrote the letters that constituted his thesis to the one he called, "my meek, my radiant friend," telling him:

> You are not with me, and the whole world seems deserted. I am alone, absolutely alone in the whole world. But my sorrowful loneliness aches sweetly in my heart.[37]

He wrote "of that which was nearest to both their hearts: the problems of belief in the modern world."[38] His friendship with Sergei opened his heart, not only to his friend but to the truth.

That openness endured even when the friendship did not last in the way Pavel expected. Sergei was married to his sister Olga (whom he had got to know in Tiflis) and Pavel felt that the exclusivity of their friendship had been betrayed. "Heart-broken," he did not attend the wedding in Tiflis.[39] Yet, as with Wordsworth and Coleridge—and indeed Saint Gregory and Saint Basil, who later had a difference—the flaws in friendship took nothing away from the efficacy of the catalyst it was in creative endeavor. Further, the very fissure and concomitant suffering can be seen as an occasion for the influx of spiritual light. This is implied in what Florensky wrote in a letter shortly before his martyrdom at the hands of the Soviets:

> The destiny of greatness is suffering, both from the external world and from one's own inner world. This always was, is, and will be so. Why it is so is clear: it is always to be one step behind—society behind its social greatness, and oneself behind one's own personal greatness. This is clear; and the world is constituted in this way:

36. Avril Pyman, *Pavel Florensky: A Quiet Genius* (London: Continuum, 2010), 66.
37. *The Pillar and Ground of the Truth*, 10–11.
38. Pyman, *Pavel Florensky: A Quiet Genius*, 67.
39. Ibid., 68.

one can give to the world only by paying for one's giving in suffering and persecution. The more selfless the giving, the severer the persecution and the harsher the suffering.[40]

Florensky's self-giving towards the end of his life was in imitation of and participation in that of Christ: he "saved the scraps from his own meagre meals and fed them to the starving and dying."[41] This was honored by those who knew him: as his "body was being carried through the camp to the prison gates, hundreds of prisoners risked the rage of their captors to kneel."[42] The openness of heart that began with friendship had developed: in his own marriage, in his devotion to his wife and children, in his ordination to the priesthood, in his ministry and, finally, in his death as a holy martyr.

Sergei Troitsky had a Christian end also. He "was stabbed to death outside his school by a deranged, expelled 17-year-old." In the agony of his death, he cried out:

'Unhappy boy! Why? What for?' and, as his life blood gushed from horrific wounds to throat and stomach: 'I forgive him everything! God be his judge!'[43]

Perhaps in his case also it was friendship that gave him the Christian formation enabling him at the critical moment to imitate his Lord in forgiving the one responsible for his death.

Certainly, in his letters his friend Pavel had fully thought through how friendship can lead one into the light of Christ. Letter Seven, "Sin," explains the barrier to be overcome to enter into that light:

Sin is the fundamental striving of I by which I becomes firm in its isolation and makes of itself the unique point of reality. Sin is what closes off all reality from I, for to see reality is precisely to go out of oneself and to transfer one's I into not-I, into what is other, into what is visible, i.e., it is to love.[44]

Loving is seeing reality: it is seen in the light of Christ, who gives

40. *Iconostasis*, 23.
41. Ibid., 22.
42. Ibid., 23.
43. *Pavel Florensky: A Quiet Genius*, 68.
44. *The Pillar and Ground of the Truth*, 132.

and enables love. Florensky argues that "true Creation or creation in the Truth" is revealed in:

> The personal, sincere love of two, in friendship, when to the loving one is given—in a preliminary way without ascesis—the power to overcome his self-identity, to remove the boundaries of his I, to transcend himself, and to acquire his own I in the I of another, a Friend. Friendship, as the mysterious birth of *Thou*, is the environment in which the revelation of Truth begins.[45]

In other words, truth is personal. It emerges, freed from the partiality of self-centeredness in entering into the world of another person through being able to say "thou," understanding that this encompasses everything. "I" becomes "not-I," becomes the relation between "I and "thou." The self (locked in sin) is lost and forgotten, found and remembered (radiant with light) in the light of the friend.

Martin Buber arrived independently at a similar insight; a more direct philosophical development of Florensky's thought is given by an inheritor of his wisdom, S.L. Frank. He argues that "In every genuine relation of 'thou,' the beloved 'thou' appears to us as *infinitely valuable*" and that because "value and being coincide in the final analysis in the idea of *foundation* or *fundamental being*," it is the case that "love also appears to us as infinitely full of being." This is the same insight Emily Dickinson expresses poetically (in the poem cited above) as "Love is all there is." Frank gives this justification for it:

> After all, love is precisely the apprehension of the genuine reality and, hence, the infinite, inexhaustible depth of being of another soul. But in relation to the infinite, everything that is finite becomes a vanishing quantity, seems to be a kind of "nothing." Therefore it follows from the essence of all true love that I am nothing, count myself as nothing, in relation to the beloved "thou." It follows that my closed, self-contained self-being vanishes from my gaze and is replaced by my being *for* and *in* another soul. But being in another soul, in "thou," nevertheless continues to remain being in the form of "I am," the being of "I," and even appears to me as the genuine being of "I" acquired for the first

---

45. Ibid., 283.

time—precisely as being enriched through the possession of "thou." It is as if that "thou" which I have gained through self-sacrifice gives me my own "I" for the first time, awakens my "I" to truly grounded, positive, and therefore infinitely rich and abundant being.[46]

This "infinitely rich and abundant being" is the life in abundance that Christ offers to His disciples,[47] the sharing in His own life. This life in its fullness comes through "self-sacrifice," yet it is given, in God's wonderful Providence, as Florensky observes in the citation above, "in a preliminary way without ascesis." Love comes as a gift, free to the one who loves and free to the one who is loved. It is a gift through which the gift of Truth (nothing less than the divine, manifest in the Church of the living God) is given. Love "full of grace, manifested only in a purified consciousness" is, in Florensky's words, "the spiritual activity in which and by which knowledge of the Pillar of Truth is given." This activity is neither quick nor easy: it is ascetical, subject to the discipline that growth in the Spirit requires. Yet openness to it begins with the disturbance that love brings:

> Love shakes up a person's whole structure, and after this "earthquake of the soul," he can seek. Love opens for him the doors of the worlds on high, whence drifts the cool of paradise.[48]

Three stages are involved: disturbance, quest and openness to what is above. The path to Truth begins with the upsetting of complacency, continues with the quest that is a continual moving beyond the contours of the ego and is realized at the threshold of heaven.

Florensky's path took him through the self-disclosure of friendship. He believed, in his biographer's words, "that intimate, mutually honest friendship was essential to a fruitful spiritual life."[49] It was his conviction that the love of friendship "takes us out of ourselves, says an authoritative 'Stop!' to the torrent of selfhood"; that it is "the highest point of earth and the bridge to heaven"; that it

---

46. *The Unknowable*, 249.
47. John 10:10.
48. *The Pillar and Ground of the Truth*, 285.
49. *Pavel Florensky: A Quiet Genius*, xvi.

"erases, if only in a preliminary and conditional way, the bounds of selfhood's separateness." It is an intimation of the highest hope, for:

> In a friend, in this other I of the loving one, one finds the source of hope for victory and the symbol of what is to come. And one is thus given preliminary consubstantiality and therefore preliminary knowledge of the Truth.[50]

It is "preliminary" because we cannot conceive this Truth in the terms of the reason that treats of the things of this world; it is a "source of hope" because it "takes us out of ourselves"; it is a foretaste of "consubstantiality" because it is already a kind of participation in God who is love. The knowledge is "preliminary" because it is, in the antinomy that points to it, also not knowing. In the final paragraph of the last of the twelve letters to his friend, Florensky both articulates the impossibility of grasping this Truth he has sought with his friend and gives poetic expression to its appearance:

> To arrive at the Truth, it is necessary to free oneself from one's selfhood, to go out of oneself. But, for us, this is impossible, for we are flesh. But, I repeat, how precisely, in this case, can one grasp hold of the Pillar of the Truth? We do not know and cannot know. We know only that *through the yawning cracks of human rationality, the azure of Eternity is visible.*[51]

Friendship cracks open "human rationality" because it goes beyond the law of identity that says "A=A." As I explored in Chapter A, this taken on its own effectively excludes being and truth, for the absence of connection precludes identification with anything that is other—even belonging to creation is excluded. Friendship leads to truth because "A friend is I that is not-I."[52] In friendship is the antinomy that points beyond mere reason to the life of God in which all opposites coincide. Friendship helps with the practicality of entering this life, for it "gives people self-knowledge" and "reveals where and how one must work on oneself."[53] It takes us towards the truth

---

50. *The Pillar and Ground of the Truth*, 286.
51. Ibid., 348.
52. Ibid., 314–15.
53. Ibid., 315.

of our relationship with God, the truth that we are both nothing in ourselves and capable of receiving fullness of life and glory from Him. In a friendship we count ourselves as nothing in relation to the one we love, as Frank argues in the citation above, but more than that we actually make a gift of our nothingness. "To give from fullness is not difficult,"[54] says Florensky, echoing the words of Jesus about "rich men casting their gifts into the treasury" and the tiny gift of the "poor widow":

> Of a truth I say unto you, that this poor widow hath cast in more than they all: For all these have of their abundance cast in unto the offerings of God: but she of her penury hath cast in all the living that she had.[55]

Penury is the true gift of friendship. Florensky goes on to say, "Give to outsiders from your fullness," and urges us to reserve the gift of poverty for a truly loving friend:

> But give your meagreness, yourself, only to your Friend, secretly, but not before your Friend tells you, "I ask not for yours but for you; I love not yours but you; I cry not about yours but about you."[56]

There is a concomitant commitment to accepting the poverty of the Friend. Citing Saint Gregory Nazianzen's saying, "Friendship should not know any bounds," he understands "this limitlessness of friendship" as "chiefly expressed in the bearing of the *infirmities* of one's friend, without limit, in mutual patience, mutual forgiveness."[57] This mutual acceptance of each other's nothings leads, in an antinomy of the kind that characterizes spiritual life, to fullness of being:

> In friendship, the irreplaceable and incomparable value of each person is revealed in all its beauty. In another I, a person discovers his own actualized potential, made spiritually fruitful by the other I.[58]

---

54. Ibid., 319.
55. Luke 21:1–4.
56. *The Pillar and Ground of the Truth*, 319.
57. Ibid., 310.
58. Ibid., 312.

To be "irreplaceable and incomparable," a friend has to be singled out. In Florensky's telling this is so irrespective of whether the person concerned is outstanding. To choose someone as a friend is to say:

> I wish to view this person, who is ordinary, as extraordinary. I wish to view this person, who is gray and drab, as festive. I wish to view this quite average person as a triumph.[59]

For Florensky, this context of election means that "jealousy is a necessary condition and inevitable side of love." He argues against the notion, born of a conflating of desire and love, that jealousy is necessarily bad:

> The nation with the purest God-consciousness, the chosen Jewish nation, knowing and understanding the love of God more clearly than any other nation, insistently, constantly, and unhesitantly speaks of God's jealousy. The whole Bible is saturated and permeated with God's jealousy and it is impossible to ignore this fact.[60]

God's love for his people is selective: they are a chosen people. Again, there is an antinomy:

> Love is boundless. It is limited neither by place nor by time. It is universal. But this universality of love not only does not exclude but even presupposes isolatedness and separateness.[61]

If love did not separate out a friend, he or she would be replaceable and so would not really matter. The alternative to love with an aspect of jealousy is abstraction, an agenda in the pursuance of which persons can be replaced. God does not love like this. He loves a nation, loves a particular woman: he regards "the low estate of his handmaiden"[62] whom he exalts above all other women and says of her offspring, "This is my beloved Son, in whom I am well pleased"[63] and highly exalting Him gives Him "a name which is above every name."[64] God's love is infinite, so He can single each person out for

59. Ibid., 335.
60. Ibid., 334–35.
61. Ibid., 337.
62. Luke 1:48.
63. Matthew 3:17.
64. Philippians 2:9.

particular love, but it is grounded in the Word made flesh, "this Jesus."[65] An algorithm that calculates what benefit is due to each individual member of society is an altogether false simulacrum of this love. Such abstraction cannot replicate personal and true dilection.

In human as well as divine loving, this entails the one loved being special: "awareness of uniqueness is the condition of love, even in its most imperfect manifestations."[66] Florensky sees "a profound connection between jealousy and the overcoming of the law of identity, this primordial ground of rationality."[67] If love could only say, "I am I," and never, "Thou art I" implying "Thou art mine," it would be trapped in a solipsistic narcissism and openness to truth would be denied it. "Thus," concludes Florensky:

> A striving to attain the Pillar and Ground of the Truth is realized and preserved by jealousy, this force of our spirit that is persecuted and held in contempt by the contemporary consciousness.[68]

John and Jesus

The love of friendship opens the heart to all, so the kingdom of God is proclaimed by disciples in pairs. John is the special friend of Jesus and so channels intimacy with the Lord to all.

The Bible shows us the love of friendship "in living reality,"[69] never as an abstraction. David is foundational for the messianic race, prefiguring in his kingship that of Christ, and foundational for David is his friendship with Jonathan. David is an outsider to the royal household and the king tells his army chief, "Inquire thou whose son the stripling is."[70] Jonathan's love brings him into the royal family:

> The soul of Jonathan was knit with the soul of David, and Jonathan loved him as his own soul. And Saul took him that day, and would let him go no more to his father's house. Then

---

65. Acts 2:32.
66. *The Pillar and Ground of the Truth*, 336.
67. Ibid., 340.
68. Ibid., 343.
69. Ibid., 299.
70. 1 Samuel 17:56.

Jonathan and David made a covenant, because he loved him as his own soul. And Jonathan stripped himself of the robe that was upon him, and gave it to David, and his garments, even to the sword, and to his bow, and to his girdle.[71]

Saul, Jonathan's father, turns against David when he proves a more successful warrior than himself, but Jonathan remains faithful to him. David, for his part, remains respectful towards Saul, the Lord's anointed. Both of them are disinterested: Jonathan is not diverted by family loyalty from friendship and David is not turned into an enemy of Saul, despite the latter's unjust persecution of him. It is as though his heart is expanded by the love of his friend to include his friend's father: indeed, his heart becomes open to the justice of God, manifest in this and later in his own kingship.

When Saul and Jonathan die, he mourns them as one:

Saul and Jonathan were lovely and pleasant in their lives, and in their death they were not divided: they were swifter than eagles, they were stronger than lions.[72]

His love for Jonathan has opened his heart to his king and to his God and he pays the price for it in his grief:

I am distressed for thee, my brother Jonathan: very pleasant hast thou been unto me: thy love to me was wonderful, passing the love of women.[73]

This friendship anticipates and prefigures friendship in the New Testament. Here it is both exclusive and inclusive. As Robert Slesinski observes in his study of Florensky, *The Metaphysics of Love*: "The experience of love given in friendship, i.e., in any one friend, serves as the impulse for our love of all men."[74] The particular love opens the heart, enabling the love of all. Florensky proposes that when the Lord sent his disciples "two and two before his face into every city and place, whither he himself would come,"[75] the pairing was "not a

---

71. 1 Samuel 18:1–4.
72. 2 Samuel 1:23.
73. 2 Samuel 1:26.
74. *Florensky: A Metaphysics of Love*, 219.
75. Luke 10:1.

transitory and accidental collaboration" but "the vital work" of friendship.[76] In this reading, the love of friendship is the seed of the universal love of the kingdom. It is supported by the existence of pairs of promulgators of the gospel with a strong bond, such as Andrew and Peter, sons of Jonah; James and John, sons of Zebedee; Paul and Timothy, his "own son in the faith."[77] The truth of the gospel can be understood as transmitted through personal relations. These are equal, for the very message is that all are infinitely loved by God, and hierarchical, for knowledge is given according to how close people are to the Lord:

> On the outside are external "crowds of people"; then, the secret disciples and adherents, such as Nicodemus, Joseph of Arimathea, Lazarus and his sisters, the women who follow the Lord, and so forth; then, the chosen, the "seventy"; then, the "twelve"; then, the "three," Peter, James, and John; and finally "one," "whom Jesus loved."[78]

We can add to the antinomy represented by Florensky's juxtaposition of the fact of Christian equality with his hierarchical list the even more striking antinomy of the very center and enabler of this truth and life-bearing personal relations, the Lord Jesus, being alone and abandoned: in the garden, on the cross and in His death.

Yet of the men (for the women are more faithful) there is just one "standing by" the cross: John, the beloved disciple. He is in a special and particular way the bearer of the love of friendship animating the followers of Christ. He is not the only one—Jesus is involved in the real risks and costs of human friendship and knows the bitterness of betrayal by his friend Judas—but he includes them all. He becomes family of Jesus when the Lord says to him, "Behold thy Mother!"[79] But the Lord also says, "Whosoever shall do the will of God, the same is my brother, and my sister, and mother."[80] He is the particular friend of Jesus, but the Lord addresses all when he says,

76. *The Pillar and Ground of the Truth*, 306.
77. Ibid., 307; 1 Timothy 1:2.
78. Ibid., 301.
79. John 19:27.
80. Mark 3:35.

"Ye are my friends, if ye do whatever I command you."[81] He commands "That ye love one another, as I have loved you."[82] The flow is in two directions at once: we become His friends by loving one another as He has loved us and we are able to love one another because He is our Friend. As Florensky puts it, "The spiritual life of a person is inseparable from his preliminary communion with others, but the communion is incomprehensible without an already-present spiritual life."[83] There is no before and after in the divine life, and when it breaks into the world as it does in the gospel, it reconciles what is opposite in the metric of temporality.

Furthermore, it reconciles the particular and the universal, the one and the many. John is the particular friend of Jesus, but as I explained in Chapter B, his person contains each follower of the Lord. To all He says:

> I call you not servants; for the servant knoweth not what his lord doeth: but I have called you friends; for all things that I have heard of my Father I have made known unto you.[84]

He has made known "the Word of life," which is nothing less than "that eternal life, which was with the Father."[85] This is that true life, the life of truth, of which I wrote in the introduction, "that which does not succumb to Lethe, the river to drink from which is to forget." It is, ultimately, the life of God the Holy Trinity. It is personal and personally transmitted. It is in the love of John and Jesus and every true friendship is an intimation of it.

Being Siblings

The love of friendship needs to expand to include fraternal relations with all. This is possible in friendship with Christ, who loves everyone. In fraternal community the good is common to all. Beauty and truth are in a shared life.

81. John 15:14.
82. John 15:12.
83. *The Pillar and Ground of the Truth*, 302.
84. John 15:15.
85. 1 John 1:1–2.

However, friendship is not enough. Love of a friend can "degenerate into a peculiar self-love" and having a friend can "become merely the condition of a comfortable life."[86] Even friendship with Jesus is on its own not enough: it needs to bear fruit. He tells us:

> I have chosen you, and ordained you that ye should go out and bring forth fruit, and that your fruit should remain.[87]

Friendship, if it is not to be a conspiracy against the world or a partnership in crime, needs "an outward manifestation and disclosure" of its power to love.[88] Its fruit is love of neighbor as oneself, which remains eternally because "charity never faileth."[89] It enables this love since "in order to treat everyone as oneself it is necessary to *see* oneself at least in one person."[90] This seeing is ontological rather than psychological: that is to say, it is an expansion of one's being rather than a positive emotional response to this person. Such a response is by no means excluded and can ordinarily be the catalyst for this insight, but seeing oneself in a friend does not require it. This is consonant with aspects of a friend's life which cause pain, even if it is acute. We do not wish our head removed if we are suffering from severe toothache nor do we say that a friend is not ourself if there is something wrong in her or his life. In both cases we may want what is wrong extracted but this does not change who we are. We "bear one another's burdens, and so fulfil the law of Christ,"[91] for we see Christ, our Friend and other self, in the hungry, the thirsty, the stranger, the naked, the sick and the imprisoned.[92]

To do this is to share the life of Christ, for Him who is our Friend to be our self. As I wrote in Chapter C, that life is identified in the gospel with light. This is "the true light" which enables us to see our brother or sister as our self. Hence:

86. *The Pillar and Ground of the Truth*, 297.
87. John 15:16.
88. *The Pillar and Ground of the Truth*, 297.
89. 1 Corinthians 13:8.
90. *The Pillar and Ground of the Truth*, 297.
91. Galatians 6:2.
92. Cf. Matthew 25:34–40.

He that saith he is in the light, and hateth his brother, is in darkness even until now. He that loveth his brother abideth in the light, and there is none occasion of stumbling in him. But he that hateth his brother is in darkness, and walketh in darkness, and knoweth not whither he goeth, because that darkness hath blinded his eyes.[93]

Fundamentally, it comes down to sibling relations. In the order of nature, and insofar as this is not corrupted, they tend to truth. The (normally joyful) thing about a sister or brother is that for at least one of you this relation has been there for your whole life. Characteristically (if not necessarily) there is not a hidden past or a concealed aspect of the sibling's character. Time has told, as in other relations time will tell, what is there. Time here images eternity and that eternal truth in which all things are known. The sibling relation images that between children of God which is truthful, because such children know each other and their fraternal relation in the light of the Father's eternal truth.

Such was in the beginning, when "God created the heaven and the earth" and His spirit "moved upon the face of the waters."[94] Yet the fraternal bond was spoilt by the untruth of the serpent. This infection is already implicit at the beginning of the narrative of its violation: "Abel was a keeper of sheep, but Cain was a tiller of the ground." Agricultural activity, such as Cain's, entails ownership. If you are going to raise crops, you need to be able to say, "This is my patch of land, no one else is to come here." If it is common ground, your labor is lost: you need to be sure that the harvest is yours. Yet this is fundamentally untrue. The discussion above about how loving friendship enables us to enter into the truth by the friend becoming my "I" shows why. To say, "This is altogether mine" is equivalent to saying, "I am I" or A=A without qualification, yet such a claim as the latter reduces the "I" to a nugatory existence, for this depends on being more than "I"—it depends on being as such, on creation in which it has being, on the Creator who gives it being. To say it is only itself makes no more sense than saying that a flavor

93. 1 John 2:9–11.
94. Genesis 1:1–2.

is an ice cream. Of course it is difficult for us to think ourselves back into immediately post-lapsarian times because now we take it for granted (as we have to do if we are to get on with the practical business of living) that the categories of "mine" and "yours" denote reality. At the deepest level, however, they do not. This is already implicit in the moral teaching of, for example, Saint Thomas Aquinas that if the alternative is starving to death it is all right to take food from people.[95] It is given a more poetic expression in Thomas Traherne's *Centuries of Meditations*, in which he looks back to the wonder-filled innocence of childhood:

> Eternity was manifest in the Light of the Day, and something infinite behind everything appeared: which talked with my expectation and moved my desire. The city seemed to stand in Eden, or to be built in Heaven. The streets were mine, the temple was mine, the people were mine, their clothes and gold and silver were mine, as much as their sparkling eyes, fair skins and ruddy faces. The skies were mine, and so were the sun and moon and stars, and all the World was mine; and I the only spectator and enjoyer of it. I knew no churlish proprieties, nor bounds, nor divisions: but all proprieties and divisions were mine: all treasures and the possessors of them. So that with much ado I was corrupted, and made to learn the dirty devices of this world. Which now I unlearn, and become, as it were, a little child again that I may enter into the Kingdom of God.[96]

The child knows more truly than the adult, who has to become such again to know the truth. This stage of life ontogenetically replicates primordial human life, which had palpable ontological depth, "something infinite behind everything." The child knows everything as "mine" not in the sense of it not being "yours" but in the sense that there are neither bounds nor divisions. The true reality is precisely that "something infinite" in which everything is one and land is not parceled out into plots.

This makes sense of what to our modern eyes might seem unfair:

---

95. *Summa Theologiae*, Part II of the Second Part, Question 66, Article 7.
96. Thomas Traherne, *Centuries of Meditations*, Third Century, paragraph 3.

And in process of time it came to pass, that Cain brought of the
fruit of the ground an offering unto the LORD. And Abel, he also
brought of the firstlings of his flock and of the fat thereof. And the
LORD had respect unto Abel and to his offering. But unto Cain
and to his offering he had not respect.[97]

Abel, as "a keeper of sheep" would lay no claim to any land as his
own as opposed to its being available to anyone else. He would be
like Traherne as a child, roaming freely and enjoying everything in
God, in whom it and we "live and move and have our being."[98]
Cain, on the other hand, is the archetypal and primordial self-cen-
tered person, resentful because that centering is not recognized: he
is "very wroth" and "his countenance" falls.[99] Just as he considers
his plot of land as "mine" and "not his," so he considers worthy of
respect the lie that what he produces is "mine" and "not his." It is
not: only the truth is worthy of respect, so "unto Cain and to his
offering" the Lord has no respect.

And one lie leads to another and the lies lead to violence, as lies
continue in our own time to lead to violence:

And Cain talked with Abel his brother: and it came to pass, when
they were in the field, that Cain rose up against Abel his brother,
and slew him.[100]

The first lie, the claim of exclusive ownership, leads to a second,
since we may suppose that there was at least the mendacity of con-
cealment in Cain's conversational preamble to their going into the
field. "Not yours" becomes, as it so often does in our contemporary
world, "not you." The concomitant of lack of truth is lack of love,
for which Cain refuses responsibility, saying, "Am I my brother's
keeper?"[101]

Christ's work is to undo the untruth of Cain. He runs into the
same claim of ownership, from the religious authorities of His time.

97. Genesis 4:3–5.
98. Acts 17:28.
99. Genesis 4:5.
100. Genesis 4:8.
101. Genesis 4:9.

This claim is implicit in the question, "Have any of the rulers or Pharisees believed on him?"[102] The truth, they are saying, is theirs, ironically ignoring that they are expressing ignorance of the truth about the Truth in person. Jesus, prefigured by Abel who claims no ownership, does not run a closed shop when it comes to the fight against the father of lies. When John says, "Master, we saw one casting out devils in thy name, and he followeth not us: and we forbad him, because he followeth not us," He responds:

> "Forbid him not: for there is no man which shall do a miracle in my name, that can lightly speak evil of me. For he that is not against us is on our part."[103]

Jesus is totally given: He identifies with the least of His brethren.[104] In His friendship with John He is open to being the Friend of all; in His gift of His mother to John He gives Himself as Brother to all. In teaching us to pray "Our Father" He acknowledges us as siblings "born, not of blood, nor of the will of the flesh, nor of the will of man, but of God."[105] In His instruction to Saint Mary Magdalene, the Apostle to the Apostles, "Go to my brethren, and say unto them, I ascend unto my Father, and your Father; and to my God and your God,"[106] He announces that He is our Brother. We have the same Father, God, and the same mother, Mary. He is victim of the fratricidal violence that slew Abel; He is Victor over the power of evil, restoring in His resurrection the innocence of fraternal relations. In Him we are brothers and sisters who need not make "mine not yours" mean "me not you." From the gift of His Spirit came a community of believers who "had all things in common" and "sold their possessions and goods, and parted them to all men, as every man had need."[107] Saints go on reminding us that "mine" and "yours" is not the deepest truth about creation. Saint John Chrysostom proclaims: "Not to share our wealth with the poor is to rob them and

102. John 7:48.
103. Mark 9:38–40.
104. Cf. Matthew 25:40.
105. John 1:13.
106. John 20:17.
107. Acts 2:44–45.

take away their livelihood. The riches we possess are not our own, but theirs as well." Saint Gregory the Great admonishes: "When we provide the needy with their basic needs, we are giving them what belongs to them, not to us." Pope Saint John Paul the Second states: "God gave the earth to the whole human race for the sustenance of all its members, without excluding or favouring anyone."[108]

This transcending of the division of "mine" and "yours" is still lived in Christian religious communities, in which the goods are common, as the Good (ultimately, God) is there for all. The Bene-dictine Rule, in particular, makes a point of eliminating the untruth of the separation involved in ownership, acknowledging the truth that oneness is deeper than multiplicity. The Abbot is instructed to inspect monks' beds to see that they have no private property and those who want to be monks have to give away their private prop-erty.[109] *Exue omnem proprietatem*, said Louis de Blois, a great Bene-dictine spiritual teacher, "Cast away all ownership."[110] Overcoming ownership is the spiritual path to healing from the fratricidal and to reconciliation to our Father in heaven. Fraternal love is the index of progress on this path. And a double help is offered by religious or monastic life. Because the commitment is lifelong, there is the same advantage of perspective that I commented on above in relation to blood siblings. Prejudice dies over the decades that allow one to see the full picture and understand that a brother cannot be defined by any limitations that he might have. The other help, of course, is shared life in Christ. Unity comes from communion with Him, which takes a sacramental form, as described in Chapter C.

And it has a particular expression in the singing of psalmody together. One psalm in particular, number 133, speaks of it: "Behold how good and how pleasant it is for brethren to dwell together in unity!"[111] Unity is good and pleasant in the sense that back-biting and bitterness are bad and unpleasant, but it is more than that. Like love, truth and beauty, it is a transcendental quality belonging to

108. Pope Francis, *Fratelli Tutti* (London: Catholic Truth Society, 2020), 57–58.
109. Chapters 55 & 58.
110. *Opera* (Paris, 1622), 971 (*Speculum Monachorum*).
111. Psalm 133:1.

God. It is indeed all of these. Unity is love, in a way that uniformity can never be. Each person is accepted as imaging the divine in her or his own way, being in the created order a center, as God is absolutely. That acceptance comes from the awareness of the truth of the being shared by all, which makes possible each life, and which is deeper (or higher) than all, since it comes from the Creator. Ontological depth obviates any need to insist on "mine" rather than "yours" and renders any thought of "me" not "you" pointless self-harm, for an attack on any life is an attack on the life of all. The realization of this truth in unity is beautiful, for beauty is about the whole. That is so for music, theater, and the written word: it is not the notes, the speeches or the paragraphs which are beautiful so much as their aptly ordered coherence. Christian community is beautiful as a person is beautiful, instantiating nothing less than the beauty of Truth in person:

> For as the body is one, and hath many members, and all the members of that one body, being many, are one body: so also in Christ. For by one Spirit are we all baptized into one body.[112]

As with the beauty of a person's body, so the beauty of a community is in the *relation* of the parts. Like truth, as I intimated in Chapter D, it is *among* persons. The beautifully true and the truly beautiful merge. In God love, truth and beauty are one and in community unity is an expression of them all.

Psalm 133 goes on to give us a simile for brethren living together in unity:

> It is like the precious ointment upon the head, that ran down upon the beard, even Aaron's beard: that went down to the skirts of his garments.[113]

The ointment on Aaron's head is his anointing as a priest of God and so the psalm implies that unity brings brethren into the divine presence; his beard has a sacred quality—the book of Leviticus forbids its corners being rounded[114]—and, as cited in Chapter C, the

112. 1 Corinthians 12:12–13.
113. Psalm 133:2.
114. Leviticus 19:27.

book of Wisdom says of Aaron's ephod, "in the long garment was the whole world."[115] In unity God and the world touch. This is more explicit in the final verse of the psalm, which further qualifies the anointing it gives:

> As the dew of Hermon, and as the dew that descended upon the mountains of Zion: for there the LORD commanded the blessing, even life for evermore.[116]

God blesses unity with eternal life because in unity there is the life of all, the life of God which never dies, the life which is our source and our home. "Mine" against "yours" and "me" against "you" is by contrast superficial and separates us from life in separating us from those who share that life.

Universal Fraternity

Openness to the truth means being open to all people, irrespective of their religious belief. Personal presence to others and being true ourselves are needed for this.

Yet, as with the synodality considered in Chapter C which does not bring us to the truth if we exclude dialogue with those who do not share our religious convictions, so fraternity in religious community cannot give us true life if all it accomplishes is transforming "mine" against "yours" and "me" against "you" into "ours" against "yours" and "us" against "you." This is a challenge faced directly by Pope Francis in his encyclical *Fratelli Tutti*. Significantly, one of the contexts of this is the Pope's joint appeal with the Grand Imam Ahmad Al-Tayyeb for "peace, justice and fraternity," invoking "*human fraternity*, that embraces all human beings, unites them and makes them equal."[117] His concluding reference to it echoes the account at the beginning of the encyclical of Saint Francis' meeting with Sultan Malik-el-Kamil, on which he comments, "Francis did not wage a war of words aimed at imposing doctrines; he simply spread the love

---

115. Wisdom 18:24.
116. Psalm 133:3.
117. Pope Francis, *Fratelli Tutti* (London: Catholic Truth Society, 2020), 138–39.

of God"[118] and refers to the scriptural text, "God is love; and he that dwelleth in love dwelleth in God, and God in him."[119] God's love and God's truth are one: to love is to see the truth of the other person, the truth of the depth of her or his being in God and also the truth of the person's God-given particularity. It is to prescind from the Cain-like mindset of what the Pope calls "present-day attempts to eliminate or ignore others."[120] It is to acknowledge "the universal scope" of fraternal love, "its openness to every man and woman."[121]

This depends on personal contact. Digital interaction is no substitute for knowing the truth of the other in person; on the contrary, it can lead to "loss of contact with concrete reality, blocking the development of authentic interpersonal relationships." Pope Francis is trenchant about how digital media, in the absence of the embodied person, take us away from truth and unity:

> They lack the physical gestures, facial expressions, moments of silence, body language and even the smells, the trembling of hands, the blushes and perspiration that speak to us and are a part of human communication. Digital relationships, which do not demand the slow and gradual cultivation of friendships, stable interaction or the building of a consensus that matures over time, have the appearance of sociability. Yet they do not really build community; instead, they tend to disguise and expand the very individualism that finds expression in xenophobia and contempt for the vulnerable. Digital connectivity is not enough to build bridges. It is not capable of uniting humanity.[122]

The difficulty is that selectivity can echo and amplify "me" and "mine" to the point where what is at best a myopic outlook is mistaken for universal truth. The fruit of the tree of the knowledge of good and evil is so thoroughly digested that there is no distinction between what one likes and good or between what one dislikes and evil. The algorithm, taking over from the person, serves the serpent

118. Ibid., 8.
119. 1 John 4:16.
120. *Fratelli Tutti*, 9.
121. Ibid.
122. Ibid., 26.

in his flattering falsity. Real people have to be involved if there is to be truth and unity, for "the process of building fraternity, be it local or universal, can only be undertaken by spirits that are free and open to authentic encounters."[123]

So we come back to the question of the wedding garment. How can we be "free and open"? How can we be open to *every* man and woman? It is a matter of our personal openness to truth. Knowledge is according to the knower: if we are true ourselves, uninfluenced by the father of lies, we shall with sound eyes see the truth of others. The wedding garment is woven in the patterns of our relations with others, and these have been considered in this chapter, but the quality of the fabric depends on the thread with which these patterns are woven. It depends on our likeness and openness to God, who is Truth. The next chapter considers this.

123. Ibid., 28–29.

G: Grace & Glory

Seeing Clearly

We can recover our true nature as the image of God, entering into relationship like that in the Holy Trinity. Openness to God is critical. For this we need pure hearts with freedom from passions that distort our vision. Discernment and struggle are needed to know Divine truth.

The introduction to this book compared its chapters to an ascending scale. We have reached the top note, G. G is for glory, the resplendent truth of God Himself, and G is for grace, His gift by which we come to share that glory. It is a truth of faith that the human person is capable of God, that this sharing is truly possible. Christian tradition has much to say about how it can be reached. It teaches that we are already in the image of God, but that this is more or less occluded by grime. Saint Gregory of Nyssa, for example, says, "If through diligent spiritual practice you cleanse yourself of the filth coating your heart, the divine beauty will illuminate you." He teaches that the divine image can be made new:

> Our inward being, which the Lord calls the heart, once the rust-like pollution with which the evil one has encrusted its beauty is scraped off, will recover its similitude to its archetype and will be filled with goodness.[1]

The Holy Spirit works with us to restore this image, if that is what we want, delicately, gently and patiently: like an expert restorer of an old master painting. The truth of God is already there, but needs to be uncovered. That happens when we look towards God, who is the truth of our being. These words of Saint Paul, quoted in Chapter A, speak of this: "But we all, with open face beholding as in a

---

1. *The Philokalia, Volume Five*, trans. G. E. H. Palmer, Philip Sherrard and Kalistos Ware (London: Faber & Faber, 2024), 110.

glass the glory of the Lord, are changed into the same image from glory to glory, even as by the Spirit of the Lord."[2] The openness is all. Being closed in on oneself precludes the transformation.

Yet this glory is intimated in who we already are: persons. A person is in the image of God, a center of creation, conscious of that of which creation is made, knowing its goodness and thereby summoning it into being even as he or she is called into being. Each of us is "I," subjectively encompassing that knowing and able in some sense to communicate it; each of us is "thou," receiving who we are from another; each of us is she or he, objectively manifesting being. Each reflects God as Holy Trinity, for each person is three and is one. Yet none of us is God, no one has aseity, is able to exist without relating to another. Relation is the truth of our being. True personhood is God's love, "just as the Essence of Divinity is intra-Trinitarian Love. For everything exists truly only insofar as it communes with the God of Love, the Source of being and truth."[3] When we are true, we are beautiful:

> A spirit-bearing person is beautiful, beautiful in a two-fold way. This person is beautiful *objectively*, as the focus of a new, purified contemplation of what is around. In a saint the beautiful, original creature is revealed to us for contemplation. For the saint's contemplation, the original creature is separated from its corruption. Ecclesiality is the beauty of new life in Absolute Beauty, in the Holy Spirit. That is a fact.[4]

"Ecclesiality" in this context is relationship, belonging to the gathering in which I am known as thou, as the Father is known through the Son, and so am revealed by the Spirit of truth as he or she: a person.

The previous chapter examined that context of relationship and how friendship enables the escape from the sterility of self-enclosure and energizes the fraternity that transcends the limitation of a closed circle. Both are needed for the full flourishing of beauty, yet there can be different emphases and they can develop in the oppo-

2. 2 Corinthians 3:18.
3. *The Pillar and Ground of the Truth*, 237.
4. Ibid., 234.

site order. Without any relation at all, though, there is no beauty. This is the deepest meaning of Cyprian of Carthage's phrase, *Salus extra ecclesiam non est*:[5] which can be rendered essentially, if loosely, as "restoration of the person does not happen outside of relation with others." However, the Divine Physician says not only, and not firstly, "Thou shalt love thy neighbour as thyself," but also: "Thou shalt love the Lord thy God with all thy heart, and with all thy soul, and with all thy mind."[6] The two commandments are of course synergistic. The love does not start with us, though: "Herein is love, not that we loved God, but that he loved us, and sent his Son to be the propitiation for our sins."[7] Christ died to make us holy, prayed that we would be made true, beautiful in the truth:

> Sanctify them through thy truth: thy word is truth. As thou hast sent me into the world, even so have I also sent them into the world. And for their sakes I sanctify myself, that they also might be sanctified through the truth.[8]

As Pope Benedict XVI taught, this is fundamentally a prayer that we should be incorporated into Christ, the truth in person. It asks, "Make them one with me, Christ. Bind them to me." It asks that we may be able to say with Saint Paul, "I live; yet not I but Christ liveth in me."[9] It asks that we "acknowledge that the truth makes demands, to stand up, in matters great and small, to the lie which in so many different ways is present in the world; accepting the struggles associated with the truth, because its inmost joy is present within us." [10] The question for us is how to be open to receiving this being made true, how to unclench our fists fastened on their little nothings so as to hold out empty hands to welcome God's restorative grace and the gift of His Christ.

Teaching about this goes back to the early Christian centuries. A pivotal figure in its transmission was Evagrius Ponticus, who was

5. Letter 72.
6. Matthew 22:39, 37.
7. 1 John 4:10.
8. John 17:17–19.
9. Galatians 2:20.
10. *Chrism Mass Homily*, Holy Thursday, 9 April 2009.

himself taught by Saint Gregory Nazianzen and tonsured as reader by Saint Basil, those friends who featured in the previous chapter. His own teaching came to the west through John Cassian, whose writings were influential on and recommended by Saint Benedict, the father of western monasticism. Evagrius could have shone in ecclesiastical circles but instead went into the desert as a monk. The desert is the outward form of that emptiness which is capable of receiving God's gift of His beautifying Spirit. A desert is an empty place where there is nothing and no one; our word "hermit" (which is what Evagrius became) comes from the Greek word for desert, *erimos* (ἔρημος). Going there is a way of becoming a person from whom nothing and no one can take God.

It is a place to weave the wedding garment. Says Evagrius, "The true wedding garment is the dispassion of the deiform soul which has renounced worldly desires."[11] This citation is taken from a collection of spiritual writings influential in the Eastern Church and known as the *Philokalia*, which means "love of the beautiful." This is, essentially, a guide to getting oneself a beautiful wedding garment. The sentence quoted sums up what is involved. The "worldly desires" to be renounced are the illusions that we can ever be satisfied with less than God: the soul is "deiform," made in the image of God. "Dispassion" translates the Greek word *apatheia* (απαθεια), meaning literally "without passion." This does not mean "indifferent" but rather "without partiality," which is to say, open to the abundance and fullness of life given to us by God. It is about freedom, the freedom to love which is the freedom to accept truth and beauty, the freedom to become true and beautiful. John Cassian, in his transmission of the teaching, rendered it as "purity of heart," which he identified as the goal of monks.[12] "Blessed are the pure in heart," says Jesus in the Sermon on the Mount, "for they shall see God."[13] To be pure of heart is to have unclouded vision. "The light

---

11. *The Philokalia*, Vol. One, translated from the Greek and edited by G.E.H. Palmer, Philip Sherrard, Kallistos Ware (London: Faber & Faber, 1979), 52.

12. Ibid., 359, and Cassian, first conference.

13. Matthew 5:8.

of the body is the eye: if therefore thine eye be single, thy whole body shall be full of light,"[14] the light of beautifying and beatifying truth.

This seeing clearly can be compared to taking a photograph with a camera. The picture will be blurred unless we hold the camera still. And so Evagrius asks the one seeking to live this life in the desert:

> Do you desire, then, to embrace this life of solitude, and to seek out the blessing of stillness? If so, abandon the cares of the world, and the principalities and powers that lie behind them; free yourself from attachment to material things, from domination by passions and desires, so that as a stranger to all this you may attain true stillness. For only by raising himself above these things can a man achieve the life of stillness.[15]

The camera can be held still on the Tripod of the Holy Trinity: the Father whose mercy is "from everlasting to everlasting,"[16] the "spiritual Rock" that is Christ the Son,[17] "the Spirit of truth" who guides us "into all truth."[18] The word "stillness" renders the Greek word *hesychia* (ἡσυχια), which the editors of the English translation of the *Philokalia* define as "a state of inner tranquility or mental quietude and concentration which arises in conjunction with, and is deepened by, the practice of pure prayer and the guarding of heart and intellect."[19] It comes when we escape from domination, or being lorded over, by "passions and desires" for what is less than the unbounded bliss that is God, and instead accept as Lord "the Prince of Peace."[20] We rise above them when "we seek those things which are above, where Christ sitteth on the right hand of God."[21] Then, says Saint Paul, "ye are dead, and your life is hid in Christ."[22] That means dead to the things that die, no longer driven this way and that by what passes, and alive to what is eternal and so fully and

---

14. Matthew 6:22.
15. *The Philokalia*, Volume One, 31–32.
16. Psalm 103:17.
17. 1 Corinthians 10:4.
18. John 16:13.
19. *The Philokalia*, Volume One, 365.
20. Isaiah 9:6.
21. Colossians 3:1.
22. Colossians 3:3.

truly alive. It is eating from "the tree of life," which is "in the midst of the garden"; it is undoing of the wrong choice of eating from "the tree of knowledge of good and evil,"[23] which is the mistaking of errant desire for good and unjust aversion for evil; it is returning to God, our true good.

Evagrius envisages this return as a battle against demons, of which there are three principal kinds: "those entrusted with the appetites of gluttony, those who suggest avaricious thoughts, and those who incite us to seek the esteem of men."[24] These correspond to the demonic attack against Jesus in the desert: the temptations to turn stones into bread, to gain by worshipping the devil "all the kingdoms of the world," to become the marvel of men by casting Himself down from "a pinnacle of the temple" and remaining unhurt.[25] As I argued in *The Mystery of Identity*, these are all attempts to divert Him from His true self, which is not limited by food, fabulous riches, or fame.[26] The truth is that His being is unbounded and that by His struggle He wins through to this truth for all of humanity, so that we might know "the length, and depth, and height" of "the love of Christ" and "be filled with all the fulness of God."[27] In Him we know the truth of who we are. Truth is who we are; we become truth, become ourselves in Christ. Winning the struggle in Him, we are not diverted from this truth by the various wrong turnings which, in the account of Evagrius, are included in these three basic temptations. Not giving the body priority over the spirit, we can avoid unchastity; not overly valuing the things of this world or people's esteem, we will not succumb to unjust anger when we are deprived of them; not investing in riches, we will have nothing in which to clothe our pride, and will know the humility of the poor.

To become such a truthful person, we need to know where our desires and passions are truly coming from. For example, Evagrius

23. Genesis 2:9.
24. *The Philokalia*, Volume One, 38.
25. Luke 4:1–13.
26. Angelico Press, 2022, 110–18.
27. Ephesians 3:18–19.

observes that "it often happens that people become excessively worked up for quite trivial reasons." He asks, "Why do you rush into battle so quickly, if you are really above caring about food, possessions and glory?"[28] If we react to something that seems to us defamatory with great anger, then our way towards a more truthful life is in becoming more detached about other people's view of us, so that we can say with Jesus, "I receive not honour from men."[29] One way of doing this is to train ourselves to not defend our reputation against accusations if nothing of practical importance depends on this. If we get red-faced with rage when somebody wants to do something in a different way from that in which we want to do it, then we can become more truthful persons by giving up our self-will. One way of doing this is to become a monk or nun and take a vow of obedience; marriage promises can work in the same way. It is important to note that resisting the actual passion of anger (counting to ten and so on) is only an emergency measure (to deal with the anger that has emerged from our heart). In some cases (such as when it helps deal with the devil's temptations with the contempt they deserve) anger can be wholesome. What is not wholesome is to overvalue what people think of us or to think that because it is our own a point of view has a special veridical status.

It is our values, not our feelings, that are critical. We can have joy in Jesus or joy in an evil predation. We make the joy good or bad by what we treasure: in itself it is innocent. Similarly, the objects of our passions are in themselves innocent. Evagrius explains:

> Just as it is possible to think of water both while thirsty and while not thirsty, so it is possible to think of gold with greed and without greed. The same applies to other things.[30]

There is no fault in the gold, only in the greed. Saint Paul's admonition "love of money is the root of all evil"[31] is sometimes misquoted with the first two words missing, but it is not money which is evil, but the diversion of love to it. And, of course, love in itself is not

28. *The Philokalia*, Volume One, 41.
29. John 5:41.
30. *The Philokalia*, Volume One, 40.
31. 1 Timothy 6:10.

evil: when directed to God and neighbor it is a first-order good. The key word is in the center of the saying: the "root." It is not what is in our mind's eye that matters, but the root in the heart of our passions. If the *heart* is pure, we shall (ultimately) see God and in the meantime not be troubled by the things we see, for "unto the pure all things are pure."[32]

To attain this blessed state, active measures are needed. For example, fasting undermines the over-valuation of bodily pleasures. Evagrius teaches us "to imitate people who are in danger at sea and throw things overboard because of the violence of the winds and the threatening of the waves." The sacks of wheat and the bread they make are good in themselves, but should not be allowed to come before the good of (respectively) our physical or our spiritual life. Yet the measures themselves can be diverted to a life-denying end if:

> We cast things overboard just to be seen doing so by men. For then we shall get the reward we want; but we shall suffer another ship-wreck, worse than the first, blown off our course by the contrary wind of the demon of self-esteem.[33]

"Like some cunning traitor in a city," this "opens the gates to all the demons," the worst of which is pride. The latter requires its own special measures: "intense prayer" and "not doing or saying anything that contributes to the sense of your own importance."[34] All of this, measures against diverted passions and measures against diverted measures, requires effort and it is possible in one's weariness to stop caring about one's spiritual welfare. Here Evagrius reminds us how we are nurtured in our spiritual life by our relations with others. Although we can separate the two great commandments of love of God and of neighbor for the purpose of discussing them, as I have done in (respectively) this and the previous chapter, they do work together. In solitude we breathe in the love of God; in company we breathe out the love of God. "Brethren living in community," according to Evagrius, have a particular advantage in battling the demon of dejection:

32. Titus 1:15.
33. *The Philokalia*, Volume One, 39.
34. Ibid., 46–47.

When people round us fall into misfortune, or are afflicted by illness, or are suffering in prison, or meet sudden death, this demon is driven out; for the soul has only to experience even a little compunction or compassion and the callousness of the demon is dissolved.[35]

Solitude produces a partner virtue to this getting beyond not caring, a moderator of excessive action: gentleness. "There is scarcely any other virtue which the demons fear as much," says Evagrius, and gives a lapidary formulation of the wherefore:

The intellect of the solitary is hard for the demon to catch, for it shelters in the land of gentleness.

To understand this fully it will be helpful to recall the extended citation from René Guénon about "the pure and transcendent intellect," and the discussion that follows it in Chapter A. Here, by way of reminder of the meaning of a key term, is a slightly edited gloss from the English version of *The Philokalia*:

INTELLECT: the highest faculty in man, through which—provided it is purified—he knows God or the inner essences or principles of created things by means of direct apprehension or spiritual perception. Unlike reason, from which it must be carefully distinguished, the intellect does not function by formulating abstract concepts and then arguing on this basis to a conclusion reached through deductive reasoning, but it understands divine truth by means of immediate experience, intuition or simple cognition. The intellect dwells in the depths of the soul; it constitutes the innermost aspect of the heart.[36]

Because the intellect (understood in this sense) is how we know God, its escape from being caught by the evil one is critical. Reason serves premises that are known directly. It follows that whether one's intellect is looking towards God determines whether one serves God or, ultimately, the devil.

Purified, the intellect becomes aware of its true nature:

35. Ibid., 45.
36. Ibid., 362.

When the intellect has shed its fallen state and acquired the state of grace, then during prayer it will see its own nature like a sapphire or the colour of heaven. In Scripture this is called the realm of God that was seen by the elders on Mount Sinai.[37]

Blue is the color of contemplation, openness to the truth, to the divine; it is the color of dispassion in which nothing disturbs peace; it is the color of the celestial, symbolized by the sky, as explored in Chapters A and E. The purified intellect in prayer is diffused with the divine light, as the sky is with the light of the sun. That is why it is blue, like the sky. Evagrius' scripture reference connects it to this Old Testament epiphany in which God's presence is shown in that color:

> Then went up Moses, and Aaron, Nadam, and Abihu, and seventy of the elders of Israel: And they saw the God of Israel: and there was under his feet as it were a paved work of a sapphire stone, and as it were the body of heaven in his clearness.[38]

This realization of the true nature of the intellect is possible for one who is "vigilant in prayer." Evagrius promises such "dispassion of heart." [39] We may suppose he himself came to such vision of the Most High. He died on the feast of the Epiphany, entering the full beholding of the Truth with the Wise Men.

Living Truly

Knowing God, we know the true essence of creation and see it in the perspective of divine light. Understanding our dependence on God's love, we make no claims for our self. Christ is our model.

In beholding the Truth of God, we become true. We cannot possess truth, but we can live truthfully. As I noted in Chapter A, the word "truth" is best used of a person's life in the adverbial form, "truly." To live truly is to be saintly, informed by the Holy Spirit who is "the Spirit of truth" and who, Jesus promises, "will guide you into all

37. Ibid., 49.
38. Exodus 24:9–10.
39. *The Philokalia*, Volume One, 52.

truth."[40] This is a calling for all of us, for God "will have all men to be saved, and to come unto the knowledge of the truth."[41] This is the knowledge of the Truth of God, by the contemplation of which we participate in the divine life, but it is also the knowledge of the truth of things. This is more than is received through sense data and reasoning. It comes from knowing creation through God, in whom it is rooted. To perceive the roots of something is to be aware of its meaning, which is its essential existence. This is the "contemplative insight into many things" which, Evagrius tells us, those who are awakened to "spiritual knowledge" acquire.[42] Saint Maximus the Confessor, ancient elder of the desert, explains how this dawns:

> When the sun rises and casts its light on the world, it reveals both itself and the things it illumines. Similarly, when the Sun of righteousness rises in the pure intellect, He reveals both Himself and the inner principles of all that has been and will be brought into existence by Him.[43]

The One by whom "all things were made"[44] is "the light of the world."[45] This light shines from within, revealing "inner principles." It is how Jesus "knew what was in man."[46] The person in whom this light shines knows things through God rather than the other way around.

Saint John of the Cross explains the dawning of this light in terms of the poetic image of "the awakening of God in the soul." He gives this commentary on a line ("You wake in my heart") in his poem "The Living Flame of Love":

> Here lies the remarkable delight of this awakening: the soul knows creatures through God and not God through creatures. This amounts to knowing the effects through their cause and not the

---

40. John 16:13.
41. 1 Timothy 2:4.
42. *The Philokalia*, Volume One, 47.
43. *The Philokalia*, Volume Two, 64.
44. John 1:3.
45. John 8:12.
46. John 2:25.

cause through its effects. The latter is knowledge *a posteriori*, and the former is essential knowledge.[47]

The light who is Christ illuminates the whole of creation for such a person.

Because this light is spiritual, it makes sense to speak of seeing things in it as well as seeing it in things, for it does not belong to material existence. Hence it was possible for Saint Benedict to see the whole of creation as a very small thing in this light.[48] We might say that he saw the truth of creation, which latter is truly little in the light of God's splendor and glory. Julian of Norwich was given a similar insight by the Lord:

> He showed me a little thing the size of a hazelnut, in the palm of my hand, and it was as round as a ball. I looked at it with my mind's eye and I thought, 'What can this be?' And the answer came, 'It is all that is made.' I marvelled that it could last, for I thought it might have crumbled to nothing, it was so small. And the answer came into my mind, 'It lasts and ever shall because God loves it.' And all things have being through the love of God.[49]

This bears out the words by Florensky quoted above, "everything exists truly only insofar as it communes with the God of Love, the Source of being and truth." The truth is pretty much the opposite of what atheist materialism supposes it to be. The primary reality is God's love; all else depends on it and adds up to no more than a hazelnut.

Saints know this reality, this echo of Paradise where the spiritual enclosed the material. Saint Benedict who, as Pope Saint Gregory the Great said, cannot have written other than as he lived,[50] gave it form in his Rule for monks. This is about living truly, so it is concerned with overcoming the illusion that somehow we exist in our own right, independent of God's love. In the Prologue to the Rule

47. *The Collected Works of St. John of the Cross*, trans. Kieran Kavanaugh O.C.D. and Otilio Rodriguez O.C.D. (Washington, DC: ICS Publications, 1979), 643, 645.
48. Pope Saint Gregory the Great, *Dialogues*, Book Two, Chapter 35.
49. https://julianofnorwich.org/pages/julian-of-norwich-quotes-01.
50. Pope Saint Gregory the Great, *Dialogues*, Book Two, Chapter 36.

the mistaken notion that any goodness we do could come from our-selves rather than God is nailed:

> Those who fear the Lord are not puffed up by their own good observance of rule, but reckoning that the good that is in them could not be wrought by themselves but by God, magnify the Lord working in them and say with the prophet: "Not unto us, O Lord, not unto us, but to Thy Name give glory." Just as also the Apostle Paul attributed nothing to himself concerning his own preaching, but said: "By the grace of God, I am what I am." And again the same Paul said: "He who glories, in the Lord let him glory."[51]

Attributing nothing to oneself is simply truthful. Saint Benedict is clear in the first chapter that he is making arrangements for the sort of monks "who serve under a rule and an abbot"[52] since this is the best way, at least at the outset of the spiritual path, to ensure that no claims are made for oneself. The abbot is not to "be too solicitous about things transitory, things earthly, things perishable, closing his eyes to, or too little weighing the salvation of, the souls committed to his care";[53] if he were, he would be abandoning what is truthful (in the sense of enduring or escaping the waters of Lethe, as explained at the start of this book) for what is, relatively, nugatory. As mentioned in Chapter C, he is to remain open to truth by listen-ing to all, for "it is often to a junior that the Lord reveals what is best."[54] Saint Benedict reminds us of the basic Christian injunction of fidelity to the truth: "Not to utter false witness."[55] The way for his monks to reach the blessed dispassion of which Evagrius wrote is for them to "obey not their own desires and wishes," but follow "the judgment and commands of another."[56] Saint Benedict underlines "the importance of silence,"[57] diminishing the scope of self-asser-tive speech that would take them away from the truth of the silent

---

51. https://www.solesmes.com/sites/default/files/upload/pdf/rule_of_st_bened ict.pdf.
52. Ibid., Chapter One.
53. Ibid., Chapter Two.
54. Ibid., Chapter Three.
55. Ibid., Chapter Four.
56. Ibid., Chapter Five.
57. Ibid., Chapter Six.

presence of God. He guides his disciples to "that heavenly exaltation which is attained through humility in this present life,"[58] step by step. The whole aim of the Rule is the exchange of the false, illusory life centered on the ego for the true, enduring life known in the love of the Lord who said, "Whosoever will save his life shall lose it: but whosoever will lose his life for my sake, the same shall save it."[59]

The model for this stripping of self is Christ, who:

> Made himself of no reputation, and took upon him the form of a servant, and was made in the likeness of men: And being found in fashion as a man, he humbled himself, and became obedient unto death, even the death of the cross.[60]

This is His exaltation. In "signifying what death he should die" by saying, "I, if I be lifted up from the earth, will draw all men unto me,"[61] He is also signifying His being lifted up into heaven. Being raised on the cross is being taken up into glory. He draws people to Himself so they might share that glory, that true life, by giving up the illusion that there is life in reputation, domination and self-advertisement. He is "the way, the truth, and the life,"[62] showing us the path to the truth that endures, the life that is eternal.

Saints Young and Old

Thérèse teaches littleness, confidence and love: the way to true glory. Francis and Dominic overcome lies. Carlo Acutis shows us the highway to heaven: the Eucharist. Anyone can radiate the light of Christ as saints have done. This is true personhood.

Christ drew to Himself Saint Thérèse of Lisieux, who understood that the highest wisdom is to live a life unknown by others, who accepted being stripped like a rose without its petals, who never sought anything except the truth of the love between herself and Jesus. She saw herself as a nothing, a zero placed after the one of

58. Ibid., Chapter Seven.
59. Luke 9:24.
60. Philippians 2:7–8.
61. John 12:32–33.
62. John 14:16.

232

Jesus and so finding the fullness of life. Radiant as she lay on her death bed, she drew attention to trees on which the setting sun was shining and said that without His light, she would be as dark as they would be without the sun. She took no credit for spiritual insights, not claiming them as her own. She was happy to be misunderstood when she refrained from volunteering to respond to a visitor because someone else wanted to do it. She delighted to be considered little: a little paint brush in her contribution to the formation of the novices in contrast to the work of the prioress, a grain of sand in contrast to the mountains representing great saints, a little ball for the Child Jesus to play with and cast aside, a little flower.[63] She considered herself "a poor little nothing, no more than that"[64] and said, "I have to stay little and become more and more so."[65] In her own estimation she was "a *very little soul* who can only offer *very little things* to the good God"[66] and a "poor little piece of useless scrap metal" if she distanced herself from the divine fire.[67] She hastened, she said, "not to the first place, but to the last."[68]

Like an acrobat throwing herself without a safety net into the hands of one who will catch her, like a patient under the necessity of submitting herself to a surgeon operating without an anesthetic, like a fighter pilot wing-tip to wing-tip with a fellow warrior, she had sublime confidence. One of her favorite scripture texts was Job's word about the Lord, "Though he slay me, yet will I trust in him."[69] She believed that we can never have too much confidence in the good God. She was confident that her father's mental illness, and her getting blamed for it on account of her entry into religious life, did not mean that Jesus did not love her; nor did her acute physical suffering from tuberculosis; nor did the dark night of the spirit that

---

63. Thérèse de Lisieux, *Œuvres Complètes* (Paris: Cerf, 1992) 71 & passim.

64. "Un pauvre petit néant, rien de plus." Ibid., 236.

65. "Il faut que je reste petite, que je le devienne de plus en plus." Ibid., 238.

66. "Je suis une *très petite âme* qui ne peut offrir au bon Dieu que de *très petites choses*." Ibid., 276.

67. "Pauvre petit débris de fer inutile, si je m'éloignais du brasier divin." Ibid., 284.

68. "Ce n'est pas à la première place, mais à la dernière que je m'élance." Ibid., 285.

69. Job 13:15.

obscured any sense of heaven for her. On the contrary, she saw all that happened to her as signs of His love for her, of His preparing her for glory by emptying her so that she could be filled with His light and truth and love.

And she loved Him back. She showed her love by her patience with her sisters in religion: the ill-tempered one she had to accompany to the refectory, the one who made an annoying noise while she was trying to pray, the one who interrupted her while she was trying to write the recollections of her life. She showed it by little acts of kindness, such as folding mantles for sisters who had left them lying about, like writing poems for sisters for special occasions, like not waking a sister to deal with a glass of water she was left holding in bed on the last night of her life. She showed it by her heroic commitment to religious life: by going to see the Pope to ask to enter it at a young age, by not showing by any gesture that she was cold in the unheated convent, by denying herself the consolation of associating particularly with her blood sisters in the community.

And the light of glory flooded her. As the huge basilica dedicated to her towers over the crypt where her earthly life is memorialized, as her posthumous fame swamps the extent of her tiny renown in mortal life, as the massive range of miracles exceeds her little labors of sweeping the floor and so on in the convent, so the "exceeding and eternal weight of glory" that is hers outdoes her sufferings, which could never, ever, be called a "light affliction"—except in comparison with that glory.[70] She was right to have confidence in the truth of the love of Jesus for her, for us, for everyone.

The truth of her life in that love is evidenced by her huge presence in the world since her death. There is a false simulacrum of this kind of truth given poetic expression in Shelley's poem about the scattered fragments of stone in the desert, which are all that remains of the ruler who said:

My name is Ozymandias, King of Kings;
Look on my Works, ye Mighty, and despair![71]

---

70. 2 Corinthians 4:17.
71. https://www.poetryfoundation.org/poems/46565/ozymandias.

The true "Lord of lords and King of kings" is "the Lamb" who "shall overcome" by His gentleness.[72] Unlike those who have egotistical empires, He shares His unlimitedness; unlike the father of lies, who "knoweth that he hath but a short time,"[73] and his acolytes, He offers eternity; unlike those who enforce their rule by coming "to steal, and to kill, and to destroy," He comes so that those with whom He shares His kingdom "might have life and have it more abundantly."[74] This loving sharing is seen in all the good that Saint Thérèse has done since she died. There is, for example, a whole book of letters from soldiers in the First World War about how she appeared to and helped them,[75] the huge collection of testimonies of miracles collected for her canonization and the ongoing reports of the help she gives people in our own day. There is no reason to suppose that it will stop.

Those who try to impose themselves on others by lies and violence are doomed to limitation: if evil were not limited, it would have won long ago. Those who live by the Truth who came among us in person have true and everlasting life. It is precisely through them that God's Providence sees that evil does not have the last word. Such was Saint Francis, through whom the Lord rebuilt His Church. Such was Saint Dominic, who founded an order with a special mission to work against lies. Its motto is *Veritas* (Truth) and through their prayer, study and preaching they promulgate the Truth who is Christ. It is remarkable that thousands of men and women are animated by the spirit of Saint Dominic more than eight hundred years after he began his work. His life is true in the deepest sense, that of belonging to what is eternal. That sense is of course connected with the more workaday sense we use of craftsmanship when we say that something is properly aligned, and analogously of human life when it is in line with proper values, for example by calling someone a "true gentleman." Truth in the latter sense leads to

72. Revelation 17:14.
73. Revelation 12:12.
74. John 10:10.
75. *Stronger Than Steel: Soldiers of the Great War Write to Thérèse de Lisieux*, trans. Sr Marie de L'Enfant Jésus (Brooklyn, NY: Angelico Press, 2014).

truth in the former sense: a life truly lived leads to eternal life. No amount of lies and violence can make that untrue, just as Pilate's ordering of the flogging and crucifixion of Christ could not make untrue these words of His:

> I lay down my life, that I might take it again. No man taketh it from me, but I lay it down of myself. I have power to lay it down, and I have power to take it again.[76]

Love, the deepest reality, is stronger than death.

It follows that an early death does not mean a diminished life. God is infinite and to live in His love is to have a life without limits. I feel very privileged to see this unfold in the posthumous life of Carlo Acutis, who was born May 3, 1991, died October 12, 2006 and was beatified on October 10, 2020. Well-established Saints, like Saint Dominic, are like uncles or aunts who have always been around much as they are now; new ones, like Carlo, grow like youngsters full of adventure and promise, and this after their death. They flourish in the growing beneficent influence of their heavenly life on earth. Shortness of mortal life is not an issue. What matters is reflected in what Carlo said shortly before his death: "I am happy to die because I have lived my life without wasting even a minute of it on anything unpleasing to God."[77] What is short is our opportunity for what is infinite; what is sometimes sorrowful is our gateway to what is always joyful; what is imperfect is the seed of what is perfect. The only real unhappiness is to turn away from the way, the truth and the life offered to us, for the sake of what passes. Carlo did not. He looked to Jesus to make him holy as others look to the sun to get a tan and was happy: "happiness," he said, "is looking towards God."[78] He believed that "the Eucharist is the highway to heaven"[79] and it took him there.

Carlo knew the truth spoken of in this hymn written by Saint Thomas Aquinas and translated by the English Jesuit poet Gerard Manley Hopkins:

76. John 10:17–18.
77. https://youth.rcdow.org.uk/voices/carlo-acutis-quotes/.
78. Ibid.
79. Ibid.

Seeing, touching, tasting are in thee deceived;
How says trusty hearing? that shall be believed;
What God's Son has told me, take for truth I do;
Truth himself speaks truly or there's nothing true.[80]

A voice speaks to the heart more directly than "seeing, touching, tasting" and the heart is capable of knowing a truth deeper than that conveyed by more outward senses, which relate to what is passing. Hence "faith cometh by hearing" that which is totally reliable, "the word of God."[81] It comes in response to the Word incarnate, who says, "To this end was I born, and for this cause came I into the world, that I should bear witness unto the truth. Every one that is of the truth heareth my voice."[82] I quoted this in Chapter C; here I want to develop its implications for thinking about the Eucharist. Christ says it before Pilate as He is about to go to His death. It implies that divine truth is not rooted in the power that passes, does not depend on dominance, for "the foolishness of God is wiser than men; and the weakness of God is stronger than men."[83] The hymn celebrates this in its song to the Eucharist:

O thou, our reminder of the Crucified,
Living Bread, the life of us for whom he died,
Lend this life to me, then; feed and feast my mind,
There be thou the sweetness man was meant to find.[84]

The Eucharist takes us beyond what can be seen and passes to what truly endures. It speaks of the antinomy of death and life, of the fragility of our daily life and the greatness of our destiny. It is a feasting of the mind on truth itself, Truth in person; it is the satisfaction of the longing for meaning innate to human nature; it is the delight that is the divinely designated goal of all our questing.

In the Eucharist we see Christ through faith as Saints Peter, James and John saw Him on Mount Tabor when they were "eyewitnesses

---

80. https://hymnary.org/text/godhead_here_in_hiding.
81. Romans 10:17.
82. John 18:37.
83. 1 Corinthians 1:25.
84. https://hymnary.org/text/godhead_here_in_hiding.

of his majesty"[85] and "his face did shine as the sun."[86] In the section "Facing the Truth" in Chapter A, I considered how the human face conveys truth: clearly this is supremely so of the face of Christ as seen on Mount Tabor, but it is so in more ordinary circumstances also. When we challenge someone with, "Say that to my face!" we are in effect questioning the truth of a statement: a face to face encounter is a meeting of two expressions of truth. But more is possible: the truth of Christ can be radiated by any human face, because He wants to share that truth. In his final theological work, *Iconostasis*, Florensky considers how "high spiritual attainment transforms the face into a lightbearing countenance by driving away all darkness."[87] He is making a distinction here between "face" and "countenance." The latter is "a face that has fully realized within itself its likeness to God" so that is "the image of God," meaning:

> Here is depicted the prototype of Him. When we contemplate this holy countenance, we thus behold the divine prototype; for those among us who have transfigured their faces into countenances proclaim—without a word and solely by their appearance to us— the mysteries of the invisible world.[88]

This realization of "an artistic self-portrait" is the result of the ultimate creative endeavor:

> The practice of selfless asceticism, wherein the devoted practitioner, the ascetic, comes—not merely by his words but his entire self together with his words; i.e., not abstractly, not by abstract argumentation—the ascetic comes to *bear witness* and prove the truth of authentic reality.[89]

Jesus says, "Ye are the light of the world," and exhorts His listeners, "Let your light so shine before men, that they may see your good works, and glorify your Father which is in heaven."[90] Florensky applies this latter text to the ascetic bearing witness to "the truth of

85. 2 Peter 1:16.
86. Matthew 17:2.
87. *Iconostasis*, 56.
88. Ibid., 52.
89. Ibid., 56.
90. Matthew 5:14, 16.

authentic reality." Since the Greek word *kalos* (καλός), translated as "good," also means "beautiful," the phrase rendered as "your good works" might better be expressed as "the works of your beauty," that is, "the illumined face whose beauty arises from the dispersal of inward light into the outward appearance."[91] This beauty is truth.

Here, from the final volume of the English translation of the *Philokalia*, is a citation from Symeon of Thessaloniki about two of its authors, Saint Kallistos and Saint Ignatios Xanthopoulos, who radiated this beautiful truth:

> They received the first fruits of the divine light even in this present life, purified as they were through their contemplation and their actions, and they were granted the divine illumination revealed on Mountain [Tabor], just as the Apostles were. This was clearly witnessed by many persons, for their faces were seen to shine like Stephen's, since grace was poured out not only in their hearts but in their visible appearance.[92]

We may not be privileged to meet people whose faces shine like Saint Stephen's, but we can still see something of the truth in people's eyes. It is my experience that those long accustomed to prayer, like elderly nuns, communicate an openness, a sparkling, a radiance in their eyes and those, like Soviet apparatchiks, who have curtailed something of their relation to truth have comparatively dead eyes.

Confirmed in sanctity, beautiful in truth, a human person is the point of contact between God and the world. Such is the fruit of long labor and the gift of great grace; such is the expression of God and the manifestation of the unique. In the words of a Catholic philosopher:

> The person is a deepening mystery, a process of personalization, and not something to be acquired and possessed. Being the central unity of all states a being traverses in order to go towards God, in some manner it is always further on, until the moment when it is fulfilled in the Divine Person who, being the preeminent personality, the very essence of each person, finally bestows on it its true identity. This is a wondrous mystery, since here the maximum of

91. *Iconostasis*, 57.
92. *The Philokalia*, Volume Five (London: Faber & Faber, 2024), 13–14.

identity of all souls with God is also the maximum of distinctiveness for each one of them.[93]

Identity with God is identity for each person, who radiates truth inimitably, who is "the unutterable secret between the relative and the Absolute,"[94] who receives "a white stone, and in the stone a new name written, which no man knoweth saving he that receiveth it."[95]

Angels

Angels are persons. They announce Christ and reflect divine truth. They know the truth of created things directly from God whom they behold and adore. They intervene in our lives.

Persons are uniquely true and truly unique. We can see this in people, but not all persons are people. Angels, the very messengers of God, have a special claim to declare truth. The Archangel Gabriel announces the Truth in person, saying to Mary, "Behold, thou shalt conceive in thy womb, and bring forth a son, and shalt call his name JESUS"[96] and explains:

> The Holy Ghost shall come upon thee, and the power of the Highest shall overshadow thee: therefore also that holy thing which shall be born of thee shall be called the Son of God.[97]

Joseph is also told about this by an angel, who says to him in a dream:

> Fear not to take unto thee Mary thy wife: for that which is conceived of her is of the Holy Ghost. And she shall bring forth a son, and thou shalt call his name JESUS: for he shall save his people from their sins.[98]

Shepherds too, "keeping watch over their flock by night," receive such a message:

---

93. Jean Borella, *Love and Truth: The Path of Christian Charity* (Brooklyn, NY: Angelico Press, 2020), 134–35.
94. Ibid., 134.
95. Revelation 2:17.
96. Luke 1:31.
97. Luke 1:35.
98. Matthew 1:20–21.

And lo, the angel of the Lord came upon them, and the glory of the
Lord shone round about them: and they were sore afraid. And the
angel said unto them, Fear not: for, behold, I bring you good tid-
ings of great joy, which shall be to all people. For unto you is born
this day in the city of David a Saviour, which is Christ the Lord.[99]

Most people do not have the privilege granted to Mary and Joseph
of seeing an angel, but invisibility is an indication of their truth, "for
the things which are seen are temporal; but the things which are not
seen are eternal"[100] and, as I said at the start of this book, "Truth is
that which is eternally remembered." Thomas Aquinas affirms "the
natural immortality of angels," citing their supra-temporal intellectual activity.[101] He also indicates that they have a high degree of
uniqueness: each is its own species, making them more unique than
people.[102] However, like people they are persons, for they have
intelligence[103] and free will[104] and are able to love.[105] Pope Pius XII,
in his encyclical letter *Humani Generis*, declared those who "question whether angels are personal beings" to be in error.[106]

Angels are personal representatives of God, reflecting His truth.
Aquinas explains: "Angelic nature itself is a kind of mirror representing the likeness of God."[107] This looking towards God is
implied in Christ's words:

Take heed that ye despise not one of these little ones; for I say unto
you, That in heaven their angels do always behold the face of my
Father which is in heaven.[108]

This saying can be applied to children, for elsewhere the Lord cites
the words of the psalm, "Out of the mouths of babes and sucklings

99. Luke 2:9–11.
100. 2 Corinthians 4:18.
101. *Summa Theologiae* (Blackfriars, 1968), 27 (1a. 50, 5).
102. *S.T.* 1a. 50, 4.
103. *S.T.* 1a. 54, 5.
104. *S.T.* 1a. 59, 3.
105. *S.T.* 1a. 60, 1.
106. *Humani Generis*, 26–28.
107. *Ipsa natura angelica est quoddam speculum, divinam similitudinem reprae-sentans.* *S.T.* 1a. 56, 3.
108. Matthew 18:10.

thou hast perfected praise."[109] However, it is relevant to all who "become as little children" to "enter into the kingdom of heaven."[110] The unifying factor is openness to reflecting the truth. Young children have a certain docility: they know that they are not themselves the source of truth. Every disciple of Christ is like this, looking not to self but to God for guidance. And God's truth as it needs to be known at a particular time by a particular person is personally mediated by His messenger, that person's guardian angel. Angels can give promptings in the heart or intuitions in the intellect, the faculty through which (as explained above) a person "knows God or the inner essences or principles of created things by means of direct apprehension or spiritual perception."[111]

Angels themselves know through the intellect: their knowledge of creation is from "God who is the cause of creatures and in whom first exist the likenesses of things."[112] Because, compared to other creatures, they are "nearer and more similar to God," in angels all material things pre-exist "more simply and less materially indeed than in the things themselves, albeit more dispersedly and imperfectly than in God."[113] In other words, the truth of things is in the persons of angels, because they are in some way like God in whom is all truth. An angel is "a pure and brilliant mirror" reflecting God's truth and therefore "does not understand by reasoning."[114] Far from "the denial of every principle superior to reason," to cite again René Guénon's characterization of rationalism quoted in Chapter A,[115] they know only by a principle superior to reason. They know directly what human reason finds out indirectly. They soar, as it were, above the university libraries packed with journals full of

---

109. Matthew 21:16.

110. Matthew 18:3.

111. *The Philokalia*, Volume One, 362.

112. *A Deo, qui est creaturarum causa, et in quo primo similitudines rerum existunt. S.T.* 1a. 55, 2.

113. *Deo propinquiores et similiores . . . simplicius quidem et immaterialius quam in ipsis rebus, multiplicius autem et imperfectius quam in Deo. S.T.* 1a. 57, 1.

114. *Speculum purum et clarissimum . . . non intellegit ratiocinando. S.T.* 1a. 58, 4.

115. René Guénon, *The Reign of Quantity and the Signs of the Times* (Ghent, NY: Sophia Perennis, 2001), 94.

learned papers arguing that if one thing is so, another thing follows. They are open to the very source of knowing; they are the angels of Christ, the Truth in person:

> For by him were all things created, that are in heaven, and that are in earth, visible and invisible, whether they be thrones, or dominions, or principalities, or powers: all things were created by him, and for him.[116]

Saint Paul is here referring to higher ranks of angels, who are traditionally understood as being ordered hierarchically. The highest contemplate God most directly, as in the prophet Isaiah's vision in which he saw:

> The Lord sitting upon a throne, high and lifted up, and his train filled the temple. Above it stood the seraphims: each one had six wings; with twain he covered his face, and with twain he covered his feet, and with twain he did fly. And one cried unto another, and said, Holy, holy, holy, is the LORD of hosts: the whole earth is full of his glory.[117]

The covering of the face indicates the sense that the truth of God transcends anything that they are worthy to receive; the covering of the feet their frailty relative to the divine; their wings for flying their readiness to carry out the divine will. In all this they enact the disturbing reality of every encounter with the sovereign truth of God: the prophet Isaiah needs to have his lips touched with "a live coal" before he can be sent to speak on behalf of the Lord;[118] when the apostle Peter witnesses the miraculous power of Jesus, he falls down at His knees saying, "Depart from me; for I am a sinful man."[119] Contemplating absolute truth is searingly humbling. Yet it is the calling of each human person to share the seraphim's worship and join the white-robed and golden-crowned elders who:

> Fall down before him that sat on the throne, and worship him that liveth for ever and ever, and cast their crowns before the throne,

116. Colossians 1:16.
117. Isaiah 6:1–3.
118. Isaiah 6:5–10.
119. Luke 5:8.

saying Thou art worthy, O Lord, to receive glory and honour and power: for thou hast created all things, and for thy pleasure they are and were created.[120]

Our vocation is to:

Come unto mount Sion, and unto the city of the living God, the heavenly Jerusalem, and to an innumerable company of angels, To the general assembly and church of the firstborn, which are written in heaven, and to God the Judge of all, and to the spirits of just men made perfect.[121]

Here is "the church of the living God, the pillar and ground of the truth"[122] in all her glory.

Beholding is adoring; to know God is to love Him. In the words of Saint Ephraim the Syrian:

Truth and Love are wings that cannot be separated,
for Truth cannot fly without Love,
nor can Love soar aloft without Truth.[123]

We can reckon each pair of the wings of the Seraphim in Isaiah's vision to be constituted of truth and love, for angels are persons and so—like humans—as well as being able to know, have free will and are able to love. "Free will," says Aquinas, "belongs to man's dignity. But angels have more dignity than men. Therefore free will, since it is present in men, is much more so in angels."[124] Angels love because, as Augustine says, "love follows from knowledge" and "in angels knowledge is natural and therefore so is love."[125] They even love God more than themselves since "whoever sees Him through

---

120. Revelation 4:10–11.

121. Hebrews 12:22–23.

122. 1 Timothy 3:15.

123. "Twentieth Hymn on Faith," cited in Nicolas Laos, *The Hesychastic Illuminism and the Theory of the Third Light: Metaphysics, Metapolitics and Ethics* (London: White Crane Publishing, 2014), 59.

124. *Libertas arbitrii ad dignitatem hominis pertinet. Sed angeli digniores sunt hominibus. Ergo libertas arbitrii, cum sit in hominibus, multi magis est in angelis. S.T.* 1a. 59, 3.

125. *Dilectio sequitur cognitionem . . . in angelis est cognitio naturalis. Ergo et dilectio naturalis. S.T.* 1a. 60, 1.

His essence cannot possibly fail to love Him" for He is "the common good of all."[126]

As persons knowing and loving God, angels act in pursuance of His purposes in creation. The Archangel Saint Michael, whose name means "who is like God," fights Lucifer who has used his free will to try to establish the lie that he can be equal to God:

> There was war in heaven: Michael and his angels fought against the dragon; and the dragon fought and his angels, And prevailed not: neither was their place found any more in heaven.[127]

He continues his mission of defense on our behalf, "contending with the devil."[128] The Archangel Saint Raphael gives detailed advice to Tobit's son Tobias, telling him to take hold of a fish that has "leaped out of the river" and open it "and take the heart and the liver and the gall." Tobias asks him what use they are, and he responds:

> Touching the heart and the liver, if a devil or an evil spirit trouble any, we must make a smoke thereof before the man or the woman, and the party shall be no more vexed. As for the gall, it is good to anoint a man that hath whiteness in his eyes, and he shall be healed.[129]

And indeed the smoke of the heart and liver drives away the devil, who has been the death of all the previous suitors of Sara, the woman he is through this intervention able to marry, and the gall heals the sight of his father. Yet Tobias "knew not" that Raphael "was an angel."[130] His actions are those of a person, so he assumes he is human. Among the many angelic interventions recorded in the Bible, there are others in which those to whom they come assume that they are simply persons like those they know: for example the appearance of the angel who announces the birth of a son (Samson) to the barren wife of Manoah.[131] Particularly significant for Chris-

---

126. *Quicumque videt eum per essentiam, impossibile est quin diligat ipsum . . . bonum commune omnium. S.T.* 1a. 60, 5.
127. Revelation 12:7–8.
128. Jude 9.
129. Tobit 6:2–8.
130. Tobit 5:4–5.
131. Judges 13:2–24.

tian tradition is that at Mamre, where three angels appear to Abraham:

> And the LORD appeared unto him in the plains of Mamre; and he sat in the tent door in the heat of the day; And he lifted up his eyes and looked, and, lo, three men stood by him: and when he saw them, he ran to meet them from the tent door, and bowed himself toward the ground, And said, My Lord, if now I have found favour in thy sight, pass not away, I pray thee, from thy servant.[132]

Remarkable in this passage is the description of the apparition as simply "the LORD" and Abraham's responding "My Lord." These appellations contain between them the "three" whom Abraham sees, towards whom he runs and before whom he bows. The ancient Christian understanding of the three included in the one is that this is a prefiguring of the mystery of the Holy Trinity: three persons, one God.

Trinity and Truth

The highest truth is the relation among the persons of the Holy Trinity: reality is relationship. We are persons through relationship. The number three structures our awareness of the real. We find our true life in the Holy Trinity.

If, as I have argued throughout this book, truth is personal and God is the supreme and eternal Truth, then the doctrine of the Holy Trinity is the fundamental expression of truth. This does not mean that it can be grasped: God cannot be grasped. It remains a mystery of faith which we know "through a glass, darkly,"[133] for God is infinite and not to be limited by the definitions of our reasonings. The *Catechism of the Catholic Church* is clear:

> The mystery of the Most Holy Trinity is the central mystery of Christian faith and life. It is the mystery of God in himself. It is therefore the source of all the other mysteries of faith, the light

132. Genesis 18:1–3.
133. 1 Corinthians 13:12.

that enlightens them. It is the most fundamental and essential teaching in the "hierarchy of the truths of faith."[134]

Pavel Florensky is equally unambiguous about the path to Truth. In his estimation, the choice is plain: "Either the triune Christian God or the dying in insanity."[135] It is the "supralogical ground" of "the laws of logic."[136] It cannot be reached by discursive reasoning:

> Between the domain of knowledge in concepts, of knowledge about the Truth, of postulative and therefore hypothetical knowledge, and the presupposed, demanded domain of knowledge in intuition, of knowledge of the Truth, of essential knowledge, which contains its own ground and is therefore absolute, there lies an abyss, which cannot be avoided by any detours, across which there is no strength to leap.

Faith is the only bridge across this abyss.[137] The Holy Trinity, in which (according to Nicholas of Cusa) there is "an otherness without otherness, because it is an otherness which is identity,"[138] is not susceptible to the one-thing-or-another thinking we use in our world.

Yet there are indications of the doctrine's consonance with what we know in other contexts. The *Catechism of the Catholic Church* reminds us that the reality of the Divine Persons comes from their relation to each other: "Because it does not divide the divine unity, the real distinction of the persons from one another resides solely in the relationships which relate them to one another."[139] This corresponds to the findings McGilchrist articulates in his pointedly named *The Matter With Things* in the section "What Then is True?":

> Relationships must be primary, since entities *become what they are only through their situation in the context of multiple relations.* All

134. *Catechism of the Catholic Church* (London: Geoffrey Chapman, 1994), paragraph 234, 56.

135. *The Pillar and Ground of the Truth*, 48.

136. Ibid.

137. Ibid., 49.

138. *The Vision of God*, trans. Emma Gurney Salter (Escondido, CA: The Book Tree, 1999), 83.

139. *Catechism of the Catholic Church*, paragraph 255, 60.

entities are essentially interconnected, changing, flowing, ungraspable: their thingness is an emergent property of the field. "It isn't the atoms and molecules that are at the hard core of reality," writes biophysicist Don Mikulecky; "it is the relations between them and the relations between them and things called processes which are at the core of the real world."[140]

The clearly thought through and highly evidenced thesis of the whole book is "relationships are primary, more foundational than the things related."[141] This is echoed by the teaching of the Synod on Synodality relating to being set free from the father of lies: "the salvation to be received and proclaimed is inherently relational."[142] Reality is relationship.

The highest reality is relationship among persons, and the highest persons are those of the Holy Trinity. This follows from what Saint Thomas Aquinas identifies as the dignity of persons, adding, "The dignity of divine nature exceeds all dignity, and for this reason the term 'person' is supremely fitting for God."[143] He is "to the highest degree existing through Himself and able to perceive most perfectly."[144] Aquinas ends his discussion of the use of the word "person" for God by citing Richard of Saint Victor's qualification of what it refers to in this context: "the incommunicable existence of the divine nature."[145] The deepest mystery of reality is the relationship among the persons of the Holy Trinity.

As with the Holy Trinity and as with what are loosely called "things," so with people: they are persons through their relations. We become who we are (under God) through our parents, or our first care-givers; even when they are dead (or perhaps especially then) they establish us as persons. If, in the words of the October 2023 synodality synod cited in Chapter D, "reciprocal relationships

140. *The Matter With Things*, 1543–44. Kindle.

141. Ibid., 15.

142. https://www.synod.va/content/dam/synod/news/2024-10-26_final-document/ENG---Documento-finale.pdf, paragraph 154.

143. *Dignitas divinae naturae excedit omnem dignitatem; et secundum hoc maxime competit Deo nomen 'personae.' S.T.* 1a. 29,3.

144. *Maxime per se ens et perfectissime intelligens.* Ibid.

145. *Divinae naturae incommunicabilis existentia.* Ibid.

are the place and form of an authentic encounter with God,"[146] then it is in those relationships that we find the truth of our personhood, for God is its source. Here is "the transrational essence of reality" that is "the unity of separateness and mutual penetration,"[147] as S. L. Frank puts it. A contemporary writer on the hesychastic tradition goes so far as to say, "The 'person' is ontologically founded on communion."[148] He links this explicitly to the doctrine of the Holy Trinity:

> God does not exist as a pure individual, i.e., as an isolated being; but He exists as a communion of three hypostases. Thus, as John D. Zizioulas has argued, "communion" is an ontological category that describes God's mode of existence. In addition, communion comes from the three hypostases of God, i.e., it is founded on concrete and free persons. By analogy, since, according to the Bible, man is the image of God, "communion" is an ontological category that describes human personhood.[149]

Truth is in persons who are individuals in communion: who are both other and one.

In this, what is human reflects divine reality. Yet the mirroring goes further. Our sense of the real is structured by the number three. I cannot prove this because I cannot stand outside the network of relations to view it: any effort at proof fails in the same way Kurt Gödel showed any attempt to prove a mathematical system from within would fail. Yet, I can suggest it, setting out patterns that can be intuitively seen as reflecting the Holy Trinity. One I have already mentioned, in Chapter D, is the three grammatical persons in language, and the corresponding triunity of father, mother and child in a family. I can speak to you and we can together become aware of what my words articulate. That is a sort of procreation,

---

146. https://www.synod.va/content/dam/synod/assembly/synthesis/english/2023.10.28-ENG-Synthesis-Report.pdf of Synodal Synthesis Report, October 2023 2. Gathered and Sent by the Trinity, Convergenes c).

147. *The Unknowable*, 143.

148. Nicolas Laos, *The Hesychastic Illuminism and the Theory of the Third Light*, 146.

149. Nicolas Laos, *Methexiology* (Eugene, OR: Pickwick Publications, 2016), 95 (citing Zizioulas, *Being as Communion*).

since language in a way brings into being what it articulates. Wordsworth understood this, writing of "the first/ Poetic spirit of our human life" at work in the infant's mind which:

> Even as an agent of the one great mind,
> Creates, creator and receiver both,
> Working but in alliance with the works
> Which it beholds.[150]

There is a parallel to this in the example I gave in Chapter E of Helen Keller, who, when she overcame the barrier to language in her inability to hear or speak, found that each object she touched "seemed to quiver with life."[151] Her teacher of language enabled her to give birth to life. More directly procreatively, a husband saying through his love-making to his wife, "I love you," knowing her in the Biblical sense, enables her to give birth to a child. "I" and "you" procreate "she" or "he." Language, with its parallel three persons, embodies and transmits the truth of the world. Its structure reflects the Holy Trinity and its work echoes that of the creation.

As with language and family, so the individual person reflects the Holy Trinity, for she or he is made in the image of God. Our personal awareness images that of God, the absolute "I." It consists of the knower, the known, and the knowing, as the Holy Trinity is constituted by the Father who is omniscient, the Son who is the Word and the Spirit of Truth.[152] The known is the "not-I" who in friendship becomes "I," thus constituting a true person. There cannot be a person without some kind of awareness. We can equally say that we relate through love, the other wing in Saint Ephraim's hymn, so that our relation with the truth of the other is that of a lover and the other the loved who becomes "I" through the love connecting us. This echoes the dynamic in which Jesus says, "I and my Father are one,"[153] bearing witness that the Father is His "I"

---

150. William Wordsworth, *The Prelude, Version of* 1805 (Oxford: O.U.P., 1956), Book 2, ll. 275–76 and 272–75.

151. *The Meaning of Blue*, 130–31.

152. Cf. Mark Vernon, *Dante's Divine Comedy: A Guide for the Spiritual Journey* (Brooklyn, NY: Angelico Press, 2021), 350.

153. John 10:30.

through the love that is the Holy Spirit. The Holy Trinity is God the Father who is Love, the Son who is His Beloved and the Spirit of Love. This is the understanding of the Holy Trinity that Saint Augustine advances in *De Trinitate*.

Furthermore, the human person as such is triadic, as in Saint Paul's prayer that the "whole spirit and soul and body" of the Thessalonians might be sanctified.[154] Saint John of the Cross teaches that, for the spiritually enlightened person, the Blessed Trinity "inhabits the soul by divinely illumining its intellect with the wisdom of the Son, delighting its will in the Holy Spirit, and absorbing it powerfully and mightily in the delightful embrace of the Father's sweetness."[155] This corresponds to his understanding of the soul as having three faculties: intellect, memory and will, which are purified by the theological virtues of faith, hope and love so that God can dwell in it. These virtues are personally represented in the New Testament by Peter, who is the spokesman for faith by his confession of Jesus as "the Christ, the son of the living God," James who is linked to hope as when Dante writes, "oft thou wert her symbol when of yore/ Upon His three Our Lord shed greater light,"[156] and John, the disciple "whom Jesus loved."[157] Peter, James and John, the privileged three who are close to Jesus and with Him on the Holy Mountain, speak to us respectively of faith in the Father, hope in the Son and the Spirit of love.

"Now abideth faith, hope, charity" writes Saint Paul,[158] indicating that the trinity of theological virtues have eternal—that is, true—value. Klaus Hemmerle, a German bishop of the last century, comments on the continuation of this verse, "the revolutionizing force of the unadorned expression that *love alone remains* can hardly be overestimated." It follows from this that "what becomes central is the displacement of the center of gravity from the self to the other." The implication is that "active participation" in "giving

154. 1 Thessalonians 5:23.
155. *The Collected Works of St. John of the Cross*, 585.
156. Dante, *The Divine Comedy: 3 Paradise*, Canto XXV, lines 32–33 ("tu sai, che tante fiate la figuri,/ quante Iesù ai tre fè più carezza").
157. John 13:23.
158. 1 Corinthians 13:13.

that gives itself" is the ultimate reality.[159] This is the truth of the Holy Trinity. In calling the three Persons One, we are not using the word as it is used in arithmetic. Oneness according to number is not applicable to God: there cannot be one of Him as though there could be others like Him. Nor does "three" imply replication, as it does in the mass production of industrialization and in the parallel status of the subjects of tyranny. Rather it means that there is no isolated aloofness in God, but that He is—to use Meister Eckhart's favored metaphor—boiling over with love. And that is a love we can share in the Son in the power of the Spirit.

Meanwhile, in our life here below, the sign of three is everywhere; it is the trace of truth in our world. Verbal communication has three origins: "I" who speak, "You" who hear what I say, and "language," which is the given through which we communicate. This echoes what happens when the Father speaks all things to the Son and we know them through the Spirit. Time itself is a reverberation of the Holy Trinity. As Bishop Hemmerle says, "Only if we understand the whole of time in and from the past, the future, and the present, can we understand time at all."[160] Space too speaks of the Trinity with its three dimensions, as does matter with its three states as solid, liquid, and gaseous. Philosophy fails when it ignores the fundamental truth of three persons in One God. Such is the thesis of Sergei Bulgakov's masterly work, *The Tragedy of Philosophy*. His criticism of modern philosophy questions its use of its axiomatic basis:

> The "law" of identity, whose inverse counterpart is the law of contradiction, is fundamental; it is thought's self-definition and self-cognizance, which secures thought's continuity and keeps its immanent course free from leaps and hiatuses. Yet this law—or, more accurately, this postulate—of identity, which is applicable to everything which falls within the boundaries of thought, is nevertheless completely inapplicable to the origin of thought.[161]

159. Klaus Hemmerle, *Theses Towards a Trinitarian Ontology*, trans. Stephen Churchyard (Brooklyn, NY: Angelico Press, 2020), 35.

160. Ibid., 41.

161. *The Tragedy of Philosophy*, trans. Stephen Churchyard (Brooklyn, NY: Angelico Press, 2020), 15.

The proposition "I am A," he argues, "always contains a synthesis of *I* and *not-I*." Although "I is revealed in the not-I and through the not-I, which thereby becomes the I," there is a question to which there cannot be a logical answer: "How can the subject be defined by the predicate, the I by not-I?"[162] Philosophy that ignores the Trinitarian structure of language is a monologue, vulnerable to the distortion of making the "I" absolute, after the manner of Lucifer, or of making the predicate absolute in its search for embodiment—another of "the faces of Lucifer" who works as "the prince of this world."[163] It employs "the most fundamental, most primary concept, that of *substance*," in an "incorrect and simplified monistic fashion."[164] Truth is not a dead thing, and our speech testifies to this: "Substance is a *living proposition* consisting of a subject, a predicate, and a copula."[165] Likewise, to make the copula absolute, as in a philosophy exclusively concerned with being, ignores the reality that "being is always concrete and definite" not general.[166] The living truth is articulated in grammatical structure. Subject, object and the link between them echo the Father, the Son and the Holy Spirit; they speak of life and truth.

Through union with Christ we enter this life of the Holy Trinity revealed on the occasion of His baptism:

> And Jesus, when he was baptized, went up straightway out of the water: and, lo, the heavens were opened unto him, and he saw the spirit of God descending like a dove, and lighting upon him: and lo a voice from heaven, saying, This is my beloved Son, in whom I am well pleased.[167]

This is true life because it is open to the transcendent, to "the heavens." It does not depend on "bread alone,"[168] nor on angelic protec-

---

162. Ibid., 15–16.
163. Ibid., 124.
164. Ibid., 236.
165. Ibid.
166. Ibid., 107.
167. Matthew 3:16–17.
168. Matthew 4:4.

tion against death ("they shall bear thee up"),[169] nor on empire ("all the kingdoms of the world"),[170] as proposed by the father of lies, because this life is infinite, contains all truth, contains God. Here is truth because here is the eternal: three persons in one God—unbounded ontological depth, self-giving and relationship united in absolute truth and opened to us. Anything else is by way of a shadow, a sign, a map.

"I" and "thou" alone are not enough, for they can be partners in solipsism, but a third person in their love sets a seal on the objectivity of their knowing. Let Pavel Florensky, whose insight illuminated the inception of this book, speak as it draws to a close:

> The self-provenness and self-groundedness of the Subject of the Truth, I, is the relation to He through Thou. Through Thou the subjective I becomes the objective He, and, in the latter, I has its affirmation, its objectivity as I. He is I revealed. The Truth contemplates Itself through Itself in Itself. . . . Truth is the contemplation of Oneself through Another in a Third: Father, Son and Spirit.[171]

Three is the number of life, the bridge between the one and the many, the joining together of beauty, truth and goodness, the number of the human family, the number of the Lord Jesus, who is "the way, the truth, and the life,"[172] the beginning of whose life was witnessed by the three wise men and who rose from the dead on the third day.[173] It "characterizes all that possesses relative self-sufficiency" and "appears everywhere as a kind of fundamental category of life and thought."[174] It is given to us in the fabric of reality and in the fact of revelation. The teaching of Three Persons in one God, "the subject of all of theology, the theme of the whole liturgy, and commandment of all life,"[175] is above logic—but it is also source of

169. Matthew 4:6.

170. Matthew 4:8.

171. *The Pillar and Ground of the Truth*, 37.

172. John 14:6.

173. Cf. Wolfgang Held, *The Quality of Numbers 1 to 31*, trans. Matthew Barton (Edinburgh, Scotland: Floris Books, 2012), 25–26.

174. *The Pillar and Ground of the Truth*, 421.

175. Ibid., 347.

our ability to reason, the basis on which we can make sense of reality, the giver of meaning. The eternal Father, the "maker of heaven and earth, of all that is, seen and unseen,"[176] is the personal source of the truth of creation; the Son, "the way, the truth, and the life," is the truth in a human person; the person of the Holy Spirit is "the spirit of truth"[177] who will guide us "into all truth."[178] Their life is true life. And it can be our life too.

Glory be to the Father and to the Son and to the Holy Spirit.

176. Nicene Creed, *Catechism of the Catholic Church*, paragraph 197, 47.
177. John 15:26.
178. John 16:13.

Epilogue

A Culture of Truth

Dialogue is the milieu of truth, so here is a response to early readers. Openness to God and to others allows divine truth to shine in our hearts. Life in monasteries and families exemplifies this.

That's it; that's the book I wrote. Stop here if you want. But I think I owe you a little more: I have emphasized how truth emerges in dialogue and is among us, as the Lord said He was, and as Dostoevsky tried to show in his art. This essay in understanding has been blessed by discerning early readers. So to be true to such light as I have been given, I should respond to what those kind readers have offered me by way of feedback. I should be open to mystery, to truth beyond my control, to listening to another. In the words of the novelist Cormac McCarthy, "You cannot credit yourself with a truth that has no resonance."[1] These are the words of the central character in his final novel, who is both receiving therapy for insanity and undercutting commonly held assumptions with the depth of her thinking. One is that anything can be real without relation to anything else. Her logic is, "If space contained but a single entity the entity would not be there. There would be nothing for it to be there to."[2] This echoes what the djinn or hallucinatory figure says to her in the previous, penultimate and parallel novel:

You can't have anything till another thing shows up. That's the problem. If there's just one thing you cant say where it is or what it is. You cant say how big it is or how small or what color it is or how much it weighs. You cant say if it is. Nothing is anything unless there's another thing.[3]

1. *Stella Maris* (London: Picador, 2023), 163.
2. Ibid., 38.
3. *The Passenger* (London: Picador, 2023), 213 [sic].

Here is a parallel to what Pavel Florensky wrote somewhat over a century earlier (which I quoted in the first chapter) about A necessarily also being not-A. It is as though the false path of seeking truth in the separated and in the individual that people walked along, perhaps most of all in those intervening years, has been cordoned off by the two writers. Truth, under God, is never solitary. That is why I am a Catholic and why I need friends.

One friend said the book was best left with the final consideration of the Holy Trinity, that having reached this *ne plus ultra* of truth in person it would be anti-climactic to return to the mundane and mechanized. Yet others have wanted more of a take-home message: some sense of how an average Joe who is not in monastic vows could live a life more truthful in relation to God and other people; some idea of what makes for a culture of truth that fosters personhood; some clarification of where the systemic as such can be beneficial to persons without itself being personal. Peter wanted to stay on the mount of the transfiguration where godhead was manifest, yet he had to come down to earth and deal with what was there. So it seems that this book should do likewise. There he is confronted by evil that resists the exorcism that the disciples of the Lord are attempting and that corresponds to another point that a friend made: a person can be a channel of goodness and truth, but any complete reckoning of this needs to take into account that a person can be a source of evil and lies. What does this imply about truth and personhood and how will it finally end? What follows is an attempt to enter into dialogue with these responses, in the order in which they are outlined in this paragraph.

So, to the person who wants to relate more truthfully to God and to people, I would say it is primarily about awareness. A quiet openness to God comes from cultivating the intellect (in the scholastic sense as discussed in Chapter A, which is the same as the sense given the word in the *Philokalia* as cited in Chapter G). That is a kind of unlearning, for it is a learning not to rely on ratiocination unmoored from the harbour of the heart, but on one's innate sense of what is true. It is turning from the finality of death to the mystery of life. It is making the work of the left hemisphere of the brain with its abstractions and temporary certainties (as described by McGilchrist and considered in Chapter A) secondary to the radical receptivity of the right hemisphere. This is a reversal of the culturally dominant epistemology that prioritizes means (the ability to gain a knowledge that works for manipulating nature) over ends (seeing the meaning of nature). It therefore involves work: the effort of going apart to enjoy leisure, not to rest but to contemplate what cannot be manipulated. Essentially, this is prayer. Practically, it involves setting aside something like an hour a day, a day a week and a week a year for prioritizing this choice of purpose over performance, for seeking the peace that the world cannot give, for opening the heart in the still sanctuary of a church or in the beautiful wilderness of nature.

The dynamic involved is articulated in Saint Paul's letter to the Ephesians:

> I bow my knees unto the Father of our Lord Jesus Christ, Of whom the whole family in heaven and earth is named, That he would grant you, according to the richness of his glory, to be strengthened with might by his Spirit in the inner man; That Christ may dwell in your hearts by faith; that ye, being rooted and grounded in love, May be able to comprehend with all the saints what is the breadth and length, and depth, and height; And to know the love of Christ, which passeth knowledge, that you might be filled with all the fulness of God.[4]

"The inner man" for whose strengthening he prays is that in the human person which corresponds to the paradisal state of Adam (mentioned in Chapter B), when all was inward to him, for it was perceived spiritually in its essence and not through the senses belonging to the outward man. To receive from the Spirit the power of seeing in this way is to be no longer divided from a vast and dwarfing creation, to be no longer separated from the past by remorse or from the future by anxiety, for it is a recovery of the God-gifted unity in which all things cohere and a dwelling in the eternal present in which all is now. It is to receive through faith the love God gives us in Christ. If this is not generally animadverted to

---

4. Ephesians 3:14–19.

perhaps that is because it surrounds us as water does a fish "for in him we live, and move, and have our being."[5] It cannot therefore be apparent to the kind of knowing (identified by McGilchrist as characteristic of the left hemisphere of the brain) which is partial, since it fabricates an approximate abstraction of what is for the purpose of gaining a particular advantage. Where this kind of knowing is concerned, the ocean of love (God is love) in which we swim "passeth knowledge." There is however another kind by which we "know the love of Christ," a sacred unknowing, for we cannot contain what contains us except in the sense of being filled to overflowing "with all the fulness of God." The whole of the cosmos is included in this fullness: such is the significance of the phrase, "the breadth and length, and depth and height." And the cosmos, which we can contain spiritually, is but a symbol of the vastness of God's bliss, His delight in loving, His joy in us.

Knowing in this way enables us to delight in others who thereby become our joy. Each person becomes a window to the divine light. In a mind changed to be aware in this fashion, people are no longer instrumentalized. No longer is a person reduced to what her presence means we have to forgo or can gain: somebody who happens to see the last biscuit and eats it is not a mere biscuit-snatcher; one whose labor increases our income is not a mere economic convenience. Each person is the mystery of God made present, before whom we want our self-directed interests to fall silent so as to catch the strains of the music of the divine. Each stains the white radiance of eternity with a particular color unlike any other, communicating a unique meaning from the fullness of God's truth. Such were the first readers of this my text with whom I am here in dialogue and such are you now, dear reader. Each of you is for me truth and potential truth: the realized presence of God and the capacity for realizing the presence of God more fully; each of you with your particular tone and temperament, your personal history and outlook saying, "Here am I in particular and so here is universal personhood made known with unique delineation." You are not, and none of you are, generic, for truth is not abstract: we know it in the person

5. Acts 17:28.

and in person; we know it in the encounter among persons. A new truth in a new person is born of marital encounter between two persons, but truth is born anew in every authentic meeting of persons. And both are in their way the great wedding of the Lamb and His Bride in the Spirit and bond of truth.

A culture of truth is one in which people are aware like this: aware of God and aware of each other, not with a view to private gain but with a view that takes in the whole (ultimately supremely beautiful) picture, a view which (when all is done here below) becomes the beatific vision, the seeing of God. It is a culture in which everything and everyone shows God to us and is therefore (for spiritual realities can be perceived synesthetically) one of delightful harmony. Blessed Kalistos, a fourteenth century patriarch of Constantinople, gives this direction for allowing such music of verity to resound in your heart:

> If you wish to discover the truth, take as your model the lyre player. For he lowers his head and, his ear concentrated intently on the music, he strikes the strings with the plectrum. And when through his art the strings vibrate together, the lyre gives out the melody, and the player's heart throbs with sweetness.

He takes this as the image of the human person:

> The lyre, my beloved, is the heart. The strings are the senses. The plectrum is the mind. When the mind operates according to its spiritual power, it brings about the remembrance of God. Such remembrance fills the soul with ineffable delight and causes rays of divine light to shine forth in the pure intellect.[6]

The light is the harmony in the soul and comes through prayer. A culture of truth, at its highest, is one in which each person is filled with such light and music. A society enjoying this is like an orchestra where each member is an instrument making harmonious music, working together under the conducting of a leader whose own soul is full of harmony. Each in this orchestra plays an instrument which is the whole of it in miniature, the individual strings or whatever being the different players who together make the full and

6. *The Philokalia*, Volume Five, 140.

sweet sound. Harmony in the individual and in the society echo each other. All express the truth.

I propose, without in any way meaning to exclude others, two exemplifications of such expression: the monastery and the family. Both can sing together, though perhaps the former more obviously since praise of God is, at least at one level, its *raison d'être*. This praise is the expression of the primacy of His truth. And here, extracted from a longer song, is an example of praise:

O ye mountains, bless ye the Lord: praise and exalt him above all for ever.

O ye seas and rivers, bless ye the Lord: praise and exalt him above all for ever.

O ye whales, and all that move in the waters, bless ye the Lord: praise and exalt him above all for ever.

O all ye fowls of the air, bless ye the Lord: praise and exalt him above all for ever.

O all ye beasts and cattle, bless ye the Lord: praise and exalt him above all for ever.

O ye children of men, bless ye the Lord: praise and exalt him above all for ever.

O Israel, bless ye the Lord: praise and exalt him above all for ever.

O ye priests of the Lord, bless ye the Lord: praise and exalt him above all for ever.

O ye servants of the Lord, bless ye the Lord: praise and exalt him above all for ever.

O ye spirits and souls of the righteous, bless ye the Lord: praise and exalt him above all for ever.

O ye holy and humble men of heart, bless ye the Lord: praise and exalt him above all for ever.

O Ananias, Azarias, and Misael, bless ye the Lord: praise and exalt him above all for ever.[7]

To sing this canticle and to mean it in one's heart is to enter into the truth of things. "Bless" in this context means "to worship or adore (God); call or hold holy"[8] the Lord and this is the truth of all creation: it points beyond itself to its Maker. The makers of the Tower

---

7. *The Song of the Three Young Men*, 55–66.
8. www.collinsdictionary.com (4th definition in British English).

of Babel made an idol of their particular part of creation as though it were an absolute and having no longer a common absolute could not understand each other, as I pointed out in Chapter B. Here, in this worship, or honoring, of God, creation no longer honors its self (which is, as Meister Eckhart observed, God's contradiction of nothing) but holds holy (set apart, sacred, transcendent) the One from whom it comes. In other words, it announces its true meaning and purpose through the singers. It witnesses to the holiness of God, the supreme truth, testifying that "the invisible things of him from the creation of the world are clearly seen."[9] This particular sequence of praises can be seen as ascending, from the relatively static (mountains) through the dynamic (seas and rivers) and the animate (whales, fowls, beasts and so on) to human persons who most fully embody the truth of God here acknowledged. And within this last category there is also an ascent from people in general (children of men) through a particular, chosen people (Israel) to those who embody this truth in a special way (servants and priests of the Lord, the righteous and the holy). The culmination of the whole sequence is three particular, named persons: Ananias, Azarias, and Misael. They, in the context of the song, have just shown, by surviving "the burning fiery furnace"[10] into which they were thrown for not worshipping other gods, that God's truth transcends earthly truths such as the laws of nature. Praise, then, is characteristic of a culture of truth.

I have already (in Chapters C and F) discussed how the Rule of Saint Benedict is oriented to truth, so let us turn now from the monastery to the family. I have already said something about the transmission of truth in a family (in Chapter B) and (in Chapters C and D) about how a child can be a channel of truth, but this latter consideration merits further development. A child facilitates truth not just by blurting out what the adults are too socialized to say, but by drawing to herself love, without which truth is but a wing without a companion with whom to fly. This can be especially the case when the child in question lacks advanced ratiocinative skills, such

9. Romans 1:20.
10. Daniel 3:20.

as one with Down syndrome. Through such a person there can be an increase in love, given and received.

It can also be said that those who have Down's Syndrome or other cognitively limiting conditions are furtherers of truth. This is so because truth appears, as I emphasized in Chapter D, in what is between or among people and the dependency of such persons generates community, as has been shown in the work of Jean Vanier and the Arche movement. All of this begins, characteristically, in the family with the willingness to welcome such people into the world. Places, like Iceland, where this rarely happens, are cold indeed and without the warmth of love, truth is ill-nurtured and less apparent in persons. Killing (on account of their weakness in reasoning persons) who with their love and their ability to evoke love are paradigmatic of a culture of truth is to make an idol of reason, the latter day Molech. It stands condemned by Holy Writ:

> Thou shalt not let any of thy seed pass through the fire to Molech, neither shalt thou profane the name of thy God: I am the Lord.[11]

It honors the false god of human reason, profaning Divine truth. Song admonishes: "You who build these altars now/ to sacrifice these children,/ you must not do it anymore."[12] Poetry herself links the very image of one just come into the world with the angels of God to exclaim against the horror of wrongful killing:

> ... pity, like a naked new-born babe,
> Striding the blast, or heaven's cherubin, hors'd
> Upon the sightless couriers of the air,
> Shall blow the horrid deed in every eye,
> That tears shall drown the wind.[13]

Worship and welcome: these are the values that characterize a culture of truth, exemplified respectively by the monastic community and by the family without being exclusive to either. Where God is worshipped and where the stranger (newborn or foreigner) is welcomed, there is the presence of truth that transcends the limitations

11. Leviticus 18:21.
12. Leonard Cohen, *Story of Isaac* (leonardcohenfiles.com/storyisaac.html).
13. Shakespeare, *Macbeth*, Act 1, scene vii, lines 21–25.

of one's own particularity. In the truthful relationship between self and other is the reality that eludes the fragmentation of individuality. As Pope Benedict XVI observes:

> Without truth, charity degenerates into sentimentality. Love becomes an empty shell, to be filled in an arbitrary way. In a culture without truth, this is the fatal risk facing love. It falls prey to contingent subjective emotions and opinions, the word "love" is abused and distorted, to the point where it comes to mean the opposite. Truth frees charity from the constraints of an emotionalism that deprives it of relational and social content, and of fideism that deprives it of human and universal breathing-space.[14]

Truth liberates the person from the isolation of the private and "by enabling men and women to let go of their subjective opinions and impressions, allows them to move beyond cultural and historical limitations and to come together in the assessment of the value and substance of things."[15] It is possible, however, for persons to be trapped in untruth.

Untrue Persons

Systems can correct personal untruth, but should be subject to persons: otherwise inhumanity terrifyingly dominates. Consciousness can never be outsourced to a machine.

Hence it is not enough for society to be simply personal, it is also necessary for persons to be truthful and to this end some kind of systemization of societal relations is necessary. An obvious case in point is that of justice. Judges open to personal favor or influenced by personal fear cannot do their job properly; they need to be truthful persons and this requires such aids as forbidding them to pass judgment in cases where they are related to the defendant. The system though is at the service of the personal: because there are safeguards against corruption, the persons who administer justice are

14. *Caritas in Veritate*, Introduction, paragraph 3 (https://www.vatican.va/content/benedict-xvi/en/encyclicals/documents/hf_ben-xvi_enc_20090629_caritas-in-veritate.html).
15. Ibid., paragraph 4.

more likely to be truthful. The systemic purifies persons so that they become less susceptible to succumbing to untruth.Yet it is critically important that systems are servants rather than masters. Any different arrangement feeds the distortion identified by Iain McGilchrist in his first great book, *The Master and His Emissary*,[16] in which the beholding of truth takes second place to computational efficacy. There was a warning about how far wrong this inversion of priority can go in the unjust legal penalties inflicted between 1999 and 2015 on people working for the Post Office in the United Kingdom because the computer system that reported their accounting was faulty and made the innocent subpostmasters appear guilty of theft and fraud. The systemic and mechanized cannot be the ultimate judge of its own justice. Indeed, it can fall victim not only to errors but also to deliberate manipulation. In one sense the internet is the generator of truth among persons: it has helped me write this book (as, for example, in finding the dates above). Yet it can also lead to the distortion of personal truth through its algorithms exploiting and exacerbating the worst in human nature in order to claim people's attention for commercial advantage. And it can be used in the deliberate promotion of lies in, for example, the quest for geopolitical advantage.

Truth is threatened by untrue persons whom systems can to a certain extent correct. This we might call the traditional threat. Systems that persons cannot correct except with great difficulty could be termed the contemporary threat; certainly, this was the problem with the injustice perpetrated by the Post Office. Such systems approach an absolute that is fatal to truth and, concomitantly, to life. The general practice is to have a person somewhere who can intervene to over-ride the system, though such a one can be difficult to reach when most of the public-facing workers have no more authorization to act than their computers give them. Without this possibility there is a complete denial of free will, with the implicit claim that the machine or its programming can choose what is best. This sort of scientistic hubris is what Dostoevsky fought against with such prescience, showing in his art that people would rather

16. Yale University Press, 2009.

choose something bad for themselves than give up their freedom. If there is no free will, there is no mystery. If there is no mystery, there is no truth, for truth is only really such if it is eternal and eternity is only possible in the context of the infinite, which entails mystery. And life is dependent on truth, for it involves a wholeness that coheres and endures, even as it requires a freedom that escapes predictability and is rooted in mystery.

Yet there have been projects that have sought to encompass creation by reason, that ignore what the Lord answers Job out of the whirlwind:

> Where wast thou when I laid the foundations of the earth? declare, if thou hast understanding. Who hath laid the measures thereof, if thou knowest? or who hath stretched the line upon it? Whereupon are the foundations thereof fastened? or who laid the corner stone thereof? When the morning stars sang together, and all the sons of God shouted for joy?[17]

In view of the advances of science, it may be thought that this is a naïve outlook, but it is in the nature of science that its findings are never finally definitive. There are always redefinitions, even of perspectives that seemed settled, in the light of new findings. The ultimate source of all that is is beyond reason in a way that parallels what I said in Chapter A about Kurt Gödel proving that there is always truth in mathematics which cannot be demonstrated in terms of its own system. There is untruth in the denial of this. The appalling consequences of such denial are given an extraordinarily powerful expression in Benjamín Labatut's novel, *The Maniac*.[18] It has been described as "a dark foundation myth about modern technology"[19] and blends historical narrative about physicists and mathematicians of the twentieth century with fictional art. Its epigraph cites a medieval mystic crying out in a terrible voice to one who puts her foot on her neck, "Long have you caused me pain and woe. You are my soul's faculty of reason." Tellingly, it begins with Albert Einstein's soul mate, the physicist Paul Ehrenfest, shooting his fifteen-

---

17. Job 38:4–7.
18. London: Pushkin Press, 2023.
19. Endorsement by Mark Haddon.

year-old Down's syndrome son in the head before turning the gun on himself. The happy child is the victim of the anguish of his father, who writes to Einstein of "a dark unconscious force … slowly creeping into the scientific worldview" in which "reason is now untethered from all other deeper, more fundamental aspects of our psyche."[20] He is concerned by the direction in which theoretical physics is heading with the replacement of "real, physical intuition" by "brute-force artillery" and "matter, atoms and energy" with "mathematical formulae."[21] He knows of no way to keep his boy "safe from the strange new rationality … beginning to take shape all around them, a profoundly inhuman form of intelligence … completely indifferent to mankind's deepest needs; this deranged reason, this specter haunting the soul of science."[22] He has a particular antipathy for John von Neumann and his "terrifying mathematical guns and unreadably complicated formula apparatus."[23]

Von Neumann is in one sense the eponymous maniac of the novel, yet that sobriquet is shared acronymically with his brain child, a machine they call the "Mathematical Analyzer, Numerical Integrator and Computer. MANIAC for short."[24] The ambiguity of the book's title captures the way the living humanity of its protagonist serves the mechanized rationality of his contriving. One of his co-workers contrasts the two, observing of life, "Its full wealth and complexity cannot be captured by equations, no matter how beautiful or perfectly balanced" and that its chaos is "a mercy, a strange angel that protects us from the mad dreams of reason."[25] But mad dreams there are: the atom bombs dropped on Japan, the Mutually Assured Destruction of the nuclear arms race and the first goal that von Neumann sets for the MANIAC—a thermonuclear calculation that, running non-stop for two months, produces a result indicating that a hydrogen bomb is possible. This leads to a test explosion that produces what appears to be Satan's version of divine light:

20. Benjamín Labatut, *The Maniac* (London: Pushkin Press, 2023), 16.
21. Ibid., 10.
22. Ibid., 22.
23. Ibid., 10.
24. Ibid., 159.
25. Ibid., 145.

During the first instant of the thermonuclear reaction, a brilliant flash of light issued forth from ground zero. . . . Battle-hardened soldiers who had fought and bled in World War II dropped to their knees and prayed. They sensed that something unspeakably wrong was occurring when they saw their bones appear as shadows through their living flesh. Even those inside were almost blinded by streams of light that shone through the smallest cracks and pinholes in secured doors and hatches.[26]

The second goal that von Neumann sets for the MANIAC is to create "a new type of life": self-replicating machines "seeding the universe with their progeny and thriving long after the extinction of the human race."[27] It is as though the devil's light is to be followed by the devil's creatures. He asks the question, "How could machines have a life of their own?"[28] He imagines:

They would spawn and burst into our lives like so many hungry locusts, fighting for their rightful place in the world, carving their own path toward the future while carrying, in some deep corner of their digital souls, a trace whisper of my spirit, a small part of me, the man who had laid down their logical foundations.[29]

Yet machines have only a simulacrum of life: allowing them to take over means killing with logic human freedom, mystery and, ultimately, life. The novel gives an image of this in von Neumann's smashing of his wife's "favorite ceramic elephant,"[30] her love of it (and elephants in general) standing for the mysterious unpredictability of the free human person. She aptly reflects, "How could those lifeless hunks of metal ever compare to us?"[31] Artificially generated randomness cannot replace spirit, nor can the ability to process information ever be consciousness. Creation and uncertainty are concomitant and computers cannot even predict the weather beyond a certain point. Failure is implicit in von Neumann's claim,

26. Ibid., 167.
27. Ibid., 173, 189.
28. Ibid., 247.
29. Ibid., 249.
30. Ibid., 211.
31. Ibid., 210.

"All processes that are stable we shall predict. All processes that are unstable, we shall control."[32] And indeed he loses his zeal after Gödel (whose Incompleteness Theorem I considered in Chapter A) thwarts "his attempts at entangling the entire world in a web of logic."[33] Unmoored rationality takes us away from life, whether in the fireball "hotter than the core of the sun"[34] of the hydrogen bomb or in "the ever-accelerating progress of technology" reaching "a tipping point in the history of the race beyond which human affairs as we know them cannot continue."[35] That way madness lies, for (as I have argued throughout this book) truth is known through the life of the human person. In the novel (I am not speaking of his actual history) von Neumann seems to have an intuition of this, for he comes to feel "almost overwhelming empathy and a deep concern about the general destiny of humanity."[36] And he becomes a Catholic and spends "many hours with a Benedictine monk." His tale is told through the recollections of others and his conversion is recalled by his daughter, who finds this as it were apostasy of her "utmost rationalist" father "most unsettling" and the general changes in him "heart-breaking."[37] Of course as an actual Benedictine monk I have a more positive view of his conversion, which belongs to history as well as to fiction. To me the assessment of him by the economist Paul Samuelson seems apt: "a man so smart he saw through himself."[38] The deepest intelligence is found in self-transcendence. Wisdom is not the creature of cleverness.

The final section of *The Maniac* is concerned with the project of chess master Demis Hassabis of creating "a new mind, a smarter, faster, stranger one than any we had known. AGI: artificial general intelligence. The true son of man."[39] The phrase "son of man" is an allusion to one of the titles Jesus gives Himself in the gospels and

32. Ibid., 213.
33. Ibid., 220.
34. Ibid., 168.
35. Ibid., 250.
36. Ibid., 220.
37. Ibid., 234.
38. www.britannica.com/biography/John-von-Neuman.
39. *The Maniac*, 291.

the implication is that messianic truth comes not from the one who said "I am the way, the truth, and the life,"[40] but from computation set in motion by the contriving of the human brain. The showdown between man and machine is played out between a computer called AlphaGo and a human Go champion.[41] The man has some success: interestingly, a move that wins one game for him is described by a commentator as "divine, a touch from God's hand."[42] Yet—and this is history—the machine wins the match. The novel makes much of how human feeling is greatly invested in the outcome: it is as though the whole race is playing the computer. I can understand this because I did not believe that a computer could beat the world chess champion, Gary Kasparov, and felt affronted when it did. But really this victory is no more significant than a motorbike and its rider winning a marathon. The hermeneutic key is given by the defeated Go champion: "Go is a game that you enjoy, whether you are an amateur or a professional. Enjoyment is the essence of Go. And AlphaGo is very strong, but it cannot know that essence."[43] Enjoyment entails awareness and awareness consciousness. Without consciousness there can be no truth. We might amend Labatut's text—if autocomplete has not already done it for us—and say "Enjoyment is the essence of God." For it is God's knowing something which gives it its reality, its truth and He sees that it is very good. He enjoys it. Such is His bliss. The human person is made in the image of God and shares something of that awareness and so, under the Word made flesh, is the way to truth and the blissful enjoyment of it.

A bright young computer scientist and philosopher, who has read the main text, has observed to me that the digital world is quite capable of being reconfigured so that it enhances human life rather than flattering its baser instincts. This is true. It is all a question of who is in control, the Master or his Emissary. If the latter, then binary is king: there is no unity from which division comes, there is

---

40. John 14:6.
41. Also documented in the film *AlphaGo*.
42. Benjamín Labatut, *The Maniac* (London: Pushkin Press, 2023), 341.
43. Ibid., 345.

only division. God is excluded and so are harmony, peace and joy. If duality is dethroned, then there is that which is beyond opposites, that where they coincide, that to which every antinomy points: the Divine. That dethroning can happen: the King of Kings ever knocks at the door patiently awaiting admission where it is denied. But He cannot be dethroned, and His sovereignty will one day be apparent.

Apocalypse

The Truth will win. Everything covered will be revealed. He who is the way, the truth and the life will come in person.

Meanwhile, although light and love are always offered, there are grim possibilities. As the main character in Cormac McCarthy's final novel says, "When this world which reason has created is carried off at last it will take reason with it. And it will be a long time coming back."[44] Yet, the further the world gets from truth, the nearer Truth gets to it. Reflecting on the destructive power of nuclear weapons and the wars around the globe, it is not difficult to imagine an apocalyptic scenario. But the word "apocalypse" has another meaning, more fundamental than the popular one of utter devastation. The Greek word from which it derives, *apokalypsis* (ἀποκάλυψις) can be translated as "uncovering," from *apo* (ἀπο) meaning "away from" or "off," indicating separation or removal and *kalypsis* (κάλυψις) indicating covering or hiding. To uncover is to reveal and hence the last book of the Bible, called *Apokalypsis Ioannou* (ἀποκάλυψις ἰωάννου) or "the uncovering of John" in the Greek text, is generally known as the Book of Revelation or, from its first verse, as "The Revelation of Jesus Christ."[45] These titles can be understood as pointing to the Lord Jesus revealing to John what will happen, but more fundamentally they relate to the uncovering of the truth by Him at the end of time. The truth is symbolized by "a book written within and on the backside, sealed with seven seals"[46] which is in the right hand of the "Lord God Almighty, which was,

44. *Stella Maris*, 137.
45. Revelation 1:1.
46. Revelation 5:1.

and is, and is to come."[47] It tells of God's final judgment on the world which is in effect His knowledge, since for God to know something is to bring it about. This judgment is concealed by the utmost patience and mercy: it is only at the critical point that the truth of the world's relationship with God is revealed. This point is like that moment in a human relationship when the pretence that there are no difficulties which cannot be dealt with by looking away and asking no questions becomes unbearable and honesty speaks home truths in a stormy encounter. The integrity of the people involved can in this way become a means of the relationship becoming deeper and more truthful. When the whole world is involved in lies and violence, the general culture will reward conformity to lying and penalize fidelity to truth to such an extent that only the Truth in Person, both human and therefore belonging to the world and divine and so independent of it, will be able to bring this moment about. He alone, "the Lion of the tribe of Juda, the Root of David," is worthy "to open the book and to loose the seven seals thereof."[48] Then is manifest the deep truth of the encounter of Jesus with Pilate in "the judgment hall."[49] On the surface Pilate, who is the official of the place, is judging Jesus; in reality He is judging the lies even as He undergoes the tortures which support them. In the breaking of the seals and the afflictions which are thereby unleashed on the world the justice hidden in the time of Pilate is uncovered by the bright light of eternal truth.

And what is hidden in all of time is finally revealed:

> For there is nothing covered, that shall not be revealed; neither hid, that shall not be known. Therefore whatsoever ye have spoken in darkness shall be heard in the light; and that which ye have spoken in the ear in closets shall be proclaimed upon the housetops.[50]

Finally uncovered are not only the truth of the world's relationship with God as time comes to an end but also the truth of all of time, including the truth about our own lives and deeds. The last judg-

47. Revelation 4:8.
48. Revelation 5:5.
49. John 18:33.
50. Luke 12:2–3.

ment reveals what is good and what is bad in them, makes manifest the truth of them. The Truth in person is the Judge. Even He cannot penetrate the mystery of its timing, since:

> Of that day and that hour knoweth no man, no, not the angels which are in heaven, neither the Son, but the Father.[51]

We cannot predict, still less control it. The final truth is, now, hidden in mystery. We cannot judge by an outward and apparent relation to the Lord of history, for He has said:

> Not every one that saith unto me, Lord, Lord, shall enter into the kingdom of heaven; but he that doeth the will of my Father which is in heaven.[52]

Yet we can know that the fulness of life, that which participates in eternal truth, is related to human solidarity, for He will say:

> Come ye blessed of my Father, inherit the kingdom prepared for you from the foundation of the world: For I was an hungered, and ye gave me meat: I was thirsty, and ye gave me drink: I was a stranger, and ye took me in: Naked, and ye clothed me: I was sick, and ye visited me: I was in prison, and ye came unto me.[53]

However hidden, however harassed, however hated, the truth in each human life will triumph in the Person of the One who articulates the truth of all of time, who is "Alpha and Omega, the beginning and the ending," who is and was and is to come, the Almighty.[54] And that will be an embodied, not an abstract truth, for "in Christ shall all be made alive."[55]

I believe in this triumph of Truth and this triumph of a Person. I believe we can share in it. I believe that the light of this "great glory,"[56] even if it can only be seen by the intuition of faith, is strong enough to show us our way through the manifold vicissitudes of our earthly pilgrimage until we come to the truth that is undying,

51. Mark 13:32.
52. Matthew 7:21.
53. Matthew 25:34–36.
54. Revelation 1:8.
55. 1 Corinthians 15:22.
56. Matthew 24:30.

the life that is eternal. The question that might have been asked of my youthful years—"What seek ye?"[57]—has become that addressed to Saint Mary Magdalene, "Whom seekest thou?"[58] The quest for truth has become personal. I leave the penultimate word to Saint Paul: "The truth is in Jesus."[59] The last word, the medium and the message, is He.

57. John 1:38.
58. John 20:15.
59. Ephesians 4:21.

Acknowledgments

I am most grateful to these people who have helped me with the writing of this book, variously alerting me to important source material, checking its text for errors, entering into dialogue about its ideas, or simply encouraging me: Deborah Bell, Julian Bell, Alice Clackson, Sam Davidson, Anne Eason O.S.B., Archibald Elliot, Blake Everitt, Mark Jenkins, Martin McGee O.S.B., Xavier Perrin O.S.B., Felix Porée, Jack Savickas, Benedict Vitai, Andrew Wye. Many thanks to Sir Gabriele Finaldi, Director of the National Gallery in London, for the gift of the cover image. Last, but not least, I am in the debt of my publishers John Riess and James Wetmore not only for accepting my proposal in just two and half hours but also for publishing books (many of them documented in the footnotes) which nourish my intellectual and spiritual life.